W9-BSY-528

OF

S BY

DEX

Ralph Waldo Emerson in 1878

NATURAL HISTORY OF INTELLECT

AND OTHER PAPERS

BY

RALPH WALDO EMERSON

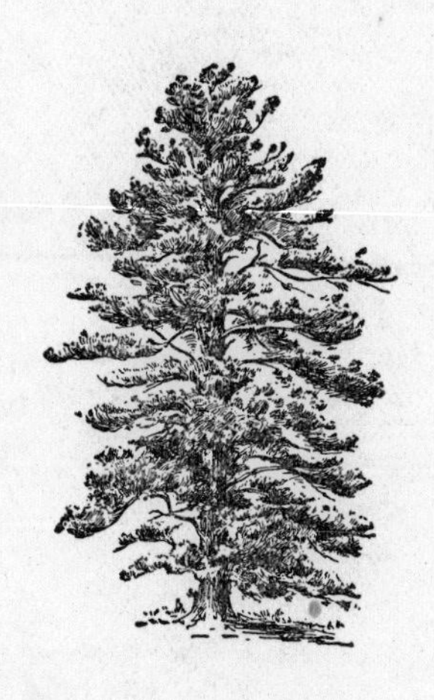

BOSTON AND NEW YORK
HOUGHTON, MIFFLIN AND COMPANY
The Riverside Press, Cambridge

PREFACE

IN this volume, in addition to the papers which it contained in the Riverside Edition, five of Mr. Emerson's lectures appear in print for the first time. They are "Instinct and Inspiration," "The Celebration of Intellect," "Country Life," "Concord Walks," and "Art and Criticism." Some account of the origin, or the circumstances attending the delivery of these lectures, will be found in the Notes. The first of them belonged to the course on Natural History of Intellect and now follows the lecture which bears that name in the Riverside Edition, but is here called "Powers and Laws of Thought." These two, with "Memory," are grouped under the general name of that course. Important passages from another lecture and from other versions of the first here given, are introduced into the Notes to it.

The General Index, which first appeared in the Riverside Edition, has been enlarged and improved by Miss Laura Woolsey Lord, to whom and to many friends who have given valuable help in tracing quotations to their sources, and for information used in the Notes, my thanks are due. I desire to make grateful acknowledgment also to Mr. Waldo Emerson Forbes for assistance given me in my work, and to the heirs of Mr. J. Elliot Cabot and to Mr. George Willis Cooke, Mr. Moncure D. Conway, Mr. Charles J. Woodbury, Mr. John Albee, Dr. Richard Garnett, Dr. William T. Harris, and Mr. F. B. Sanborn, from whose books I have quoted, as well as to Messrs. Houghton, Mifflin & Company for extracts from books of which they own the copyright.

EDWARD WALDO EMERSON.

CONCORD, October 12, 1904.

CONTENTS

LIST OF ILLUSTRATIONS

I

NATURAL HISTORY OF INTELLECT

BACON's perfect law of inquiry after truth was that nothing should be in the globe of matter which was not also in the globe of crystal; that is, nothing should take place as event in life which did not also exist as truth in the mind.

POWER that by obedience grows,
Knowledge that its source not knows,
Wave which severs whom it bears
From the things which he compares.

NATURAL HISTORY OF INTELLECT

I

POWERS AND LAWS OF THOUGHT

I HAVE used such opportunity as I have had, and lately in London and Paris, to attend scientific lectures; and in listening to Richard Owen's masterly enumeration of the parts and laws of the human body, or Michael Faraday's explanation of magnetic powers, or the botanist's descriptions, one could not help admiring the irresponsible security and happiness of the attitude of the naturalist; sure of admiration for his facts, sure of their sufficiency.[1] They ought to interest you; if they do not, the fault lies with you.

Then I thought — could not a similar enumeration be made of the laws and powers of the Intellect, and possess the same claims on the student? Could we have, that is, the exhaustive accuracy of distribution which chemists use in their nomenclature and anatomists in their descriptions, applied to a higher class of facts; to those laws, namely, which are common to chemistry, anatomy, astronomy, geometry, intellect, morals and social life ; — laws of the world ?

Why not? These powers and laws are also facts in a Natural History. They also are objects of science and may be numbered and recorded, like stamens and vertebræ. At the same time they have a deeper interest, as in the order of Nature they lie higher and are nearer to the mysterious seat of power and creation.[1]

For at last, it is only that exceeding and universal part which interests us, when we shall read in a true history what befalls in that kingdom where a thousand years is as one day, and see that what is set down is true through all the sciences ; in the laws of thought as well as of chemistry.[2]

In all sciences the student is discovering that Nature, as he calls it, is always working, in wholes and in every detail, after the laws of the human mind. Every creation, in parts or in particles, is on the method and by the means which our mind approves as soon as it is thoroughly acquainted with the facts ; hence the delight. No matter how far or how high science explores, it adopts the method of the universe as fast as it appears ; and this discloses that the mind as it opens, the mind as it shall be, comprehends and works thus; that is to say, the Intellect builds the universe and is the key to all it contains. It is not then cities or mountains, or animals, or globes that any longer commands us, but only man; not the fact, but so much of man as is in the fact.

In astronomy, vast distance, but we never go into a foreign system. In geology, vast duration, but we are never strangers. Our metaphysics should be able to follow the flying force through all transformations, and name the pair identical through all variety.

I believe in the existence of the material world as the expression of the spiritual or the real, and in the impenetrable mystery which hides (and hides through absolute transparency) the mental nature, I await the insight which our advancing knowledge of material laws shall furnish.[1]

Every object in Nature is a word to signify some fact in the mind. But when that fact is not yet put into English words, when I look at the tree or the river and have not yet definitely made out what they would say to me, they are by no means unimpressive. I wait for them, I enjoy them before they yet speak. I feel as if I stood by an ambassador charged with the message of his king, which he does not deliver because the hour when he should say it is not yet arrived.

Whilst we converse with truths as thoughts, they exist also as plastic forces; as the soul of a man, the soul of a plant, the genius or constitution of any part of Nature, which makes it what it is. The thought which was in the world, part and parcel of the world, has disengaged itself and taken an independent existence.

My belief in the use of a course on philosophy is that the student shall learn to appreciate the miracle of the mind; shall learn its subtle but immense power, or shall begin to learn it; shall come to know that in seeing and in no tradition he must find what truth is; that he shall see in it the source of all traditions, and shall see each one of them as better or worse statement of its revelations; shall come to trust it entirely, as the only true; to cleave to God against the name of God.[1] When he has once known the oracle he will need no priest. And if he finds at first with some alarm how impossible it is to accept many things which the hot or the mild sectarian may insist on his believing, he will be armed by his insight and brave to meet all inconvenience and all resistance it may cost him. He from whose hand it came will guide and direct it.[1]

Yet these questions which really interest men, how few can answer. Here are learned faculties of law and divinity, but would questions like these come into mind when I see them? Here are learned academies and universities, yet they have not propounded these for any prize.

Seek the literary circles, the stars of fame, the men of splendor, of bon-mots, will they afford me satisfaction? I think you could not find a club of men acute and liberal enough in the world. Bring the best wits together, and they are so impatient of each other, so vulgar, there is so much more than their wit, — such follies, gluttonies, partialities, age, care, and sleep, that you shall have no academy.

There is really a grievous amount of unavailableness about men of wit. A plain man finds them so heavy, dull and oppressive, with bad jokes and conceit and stupefying individualism, that he comes to write in his tablets, Avoid the great man as one who is privileged to be an unprofitable companion. For the course of things makes the scholars either egotists or worldly and jocose. In so many hundreds of superior men hardly ten or five or two from whom one can hope for a reasonable word.[1]

Go into the scientific club and harken. Each savant proves in his admirable discourse that he, and he only, knows now or ever did know anything on the subject: "Does the gentleman speak of anatomy? Who peeped into a box at the Custom House and then published a drawing of my rat?" Or is it pretended discoveries of new strata that are before the meeting? This professor hastens to inform us that he knew it all twenty years ago, and is ready to prove that he knew so much then that all further investigation was quite superfluous; — and poor Nature and the sublime law, which is all that our student cares to hear of, are quite omitted in this triumphant vindication.

Was it better when we came to the philosophers, who found everybody wrong; acute and ingenious to lampoon and degrade mankind? And then was there ever prophet burdened with a message to his people who did not cloud our gratitude by a strange confounding in his own mind of private folly with his public wisdom?

But if you like to run away from this besetting sin of sedentary men, you can escape all this insane egotism by running into society, where the manners and estimate of the world have corrected this folly, and effectually suppressed this overweening self-conceit. Here each is to make room for others, and the solidest merits must exist only for the entertainment of all. We are not in the smallest degree helped. Great is the dazzle, but the gain is small. Here they play the game of conversation, as they play billiards, for pastime and credit.

Yes, 't is a great vice in all countries, the sacrifice of scholars to be courtiers and diners-out, to talk for the amusement of those who wish to be amused, though the stars of heaven must be plucked down and packed into rockets to this end. What with egotism on one side and levity on the other, we shall have no Olympus.

But there is still another hindrance, namely, practicality. We must have a special talent, and bring something to pass. Ever since the Norse heaven made the stern terms of admission that a man must do something excellent with his hands or feet, or with his voice, eyes, ears, or with his whole body, the same demand has been made in Norse earth.[1]

Yet what we really want is not a haste to act, but a certain piety toward the source of action and knowledge. In fact we have to say that there is a certain beatitude, — I can call it nothing less, — to which all men are entitled, tasted by them in different degrees, which is a perfection of their nature, and to which their entrance must be in every way forwarded. Practical men, though they could lift the globe, cannot arrive at this. Something very different has to be done, — the availing ourselves of every impulse of genius, an emanation of the heaven it tells of, and the resisting this conspiracy of men and material things against the sanitary and legitimate inspirations of the intellectual nature.[1]

What is life but the angle of vision? A man is measured by the angle at which he looks at objects. What is life but what a man is thinking of all day? This is his fate and his employer. Knowing is the measure of the man. By how much we know, so much we are.[2]

The laws and powers of the Intellect have, however, a stupendous peculiarity, of being at once observers and observed. So that it is difficult to hold them fast, as objects of examination, or hinder them from turning the professor out of his chair. The wonder of the science of Intellect is that the substance with which we deal is of that subtle and active quality that it intoxicates all who approach it. Gloves on the hands, glass guards over the eyes, wire-gauze masks over the face, volatile salts in the nostrils, are no defence against this virus, which comes in as secretly as gravitation into and through all barriers.

Let me have your attention to this dangerous subject, which we will cautiously approach on different sides of this dim and perilous lake, so attractive, so delusive. We have had so many guides and so many failures. And now the world is still uncertain whether the pool has been sounded or not.

My contribution will be simply historical. I write anecdotes of the intellect; a sort of Farmer's Almanac of mental moods. I confine my ambition to true reporting of its play in natural action, though I should get only one new fact in a year.[1]

I cannot myself use that systematic form which is reckoned essential in treating the science of the mind. But if one can say so without arrogance, I might suggest that he who contents himself with dotting a fragmentary curve, recording only what facts he has observed, without attempting to arrange them within one outline, follows a system also, — a system as grand as any other, though he does not interfere with its vast curves by prematurely forcing them into a circle or ellipse, but only draws that arc which he clearly sees, or perhaps at a later observation a remote curve of the same orbit, and waits for a new opportunity, well assured that these observed arcs will consist with each other.

I confess to a little distrust of that completeness of system which metaphysicians are apt to affect. 'T is the gnat grasping the world. All these exhaustive theories appear indeed a false and vain attempt to introvert and analyze the Primal Thought. That is upstream, and what a stream! Can you swim up Niagara Falls?

We have invincible repugnance to introversion, to study of the eyes instead of that which the eyes see; and the belief of men is that the attempt is unnatural and is punished by loss of faculty. I share the belief that the natural direction of the intellectual powers is from within outward, and that just in proportion to the activity of thoughts on the study of outward objects, as architecture, or farming, or natural history, ships, animals, chemistry, — in that proportion the faculties of the mind had a healthy growth; but a study in the opposite direction had a damaging effect on the mind.

Metaphysics is dangerous as a single pursuit. We should feel more confidence in the same results from the mouth of a man of the world. The inward analysis must be corrected by rough experience. Metaphysics must be perpetually reinforced by life; must be the observations of a working man on working men; must be biography, — the record of some law whose working was surprised by the observer in natural action.

I think metaphysics a grammar to which, once read, we seldom return. 'T is a Manila full of pepper, and I want only a teaspoonful in a year. I admire the Dutch, who burned half the harvest to enhance the price of the remainder.

I want not the logic, but the power, if any, which it brings into science and literature; the man who can humanize this logic, these syllogisms, and give me the results. The adepts value only the pure geometry, the aërial bridge ascending from earth to heaven with arches and abutments of pure reason. I am fully contented if you tell me where are the two termini.

My metaphysics are to the end of use. I

wish to know the laws of this wonderful power, that I may domesticate it. I observe with curiosity its risings and its settings, illumination and eclipse; its obstructions and its provocations, that I may learn to live with it wisely, court its aid, catch sight of its splendor, feel its approach, hear and save its oracles and obey them. But this watching of the mind, in season and out of season, to see the mechanics of the thing, is a little of the detective. The analytic process is cold and bereaving and, shall I say it? somewhat mean, as spying. There is something surgical in metaphysics as we treat it. Were not an ode a better form? The poet sees wholes and avoids analysis; the metaphysician, dealing as it were with the mathematics of the mind, puts himself out of the way of the inspiration; loses that which is the miracle and creates the worship.

I think that philosophy is still rude and elementary. It will one day be taught by poets. The poet is in the natural attitude; he is believing; the philosopher, after some struggle, having only reasons for believing.[1]

What I am now to attempt is simply some sketches or studies for such a picture; *Mémoires pour servir* toward a Natural History of Intellect.

First I wish to speak of the excellence of that element, and the great auguries that come from it, notwithstanding the impediments which our sensual civilization puts in the way.

Next I treat of the identity of the thought with Nature; and I add a rude list of some by-laws of the mind.

Thirdly I proceed to the fountains of thought in Instinct and Inspiration, and I also attempt to show the relation of men of thought to the existing religion and civility of the present time.

I. We figure to ourselves Intellect as an ethereal sea, which ebbs and flows, which surges and washes hither and thither, carrying its whole virtue into every creek and inlet which it bathes. To this sea every human house has a water front. But this force, creating nature, visiting whom it will and withdrawing from whom it will, making day where it comes and leaving night when it departs, is no fee or property of man or angel. It is as the light, public and entire to each, and on the same terms.

What but thought deepens life, and makes us better than cow or cat? The grandeur of the impression the stars and heavenly bodies make on us is surely more valuable than our exact perception of a tub or a table on the ground.

To Be is the unsolved, unsolvable wonder. To Be, in its two connections of inward and outward, the mind and Nature. The wonder subsists, and age, though of eternity, could not approach a solution. But the suggestion is always returning, that hidden source publishing at once our being and that it is the source of outward Nature. Who are we, and what is Nature, have one answer in the life that rushes into us.

In my thought I seem to stand on the bank of a river and watch the endless flow of the stream, floating objects of all shapes, colors and natures; nor can I much detain them as they pass, except by running beside them a little way along the bank. But whence they come or whither they go is not told me. Only I have a suspicion that, as geologists say every river makes its own valley, so does this mystic stream. It makes its valley, makes its banks and makes perhaps the observer too. Who has found the boundaries of human intelligence? Who has made a chart of its channel, or approached the fountain of this wonderful Nile?[1]

I am of the oldest religion. Leaving aside the

question which was prior, egg or bird, I believe the mind is the creator of the world, and is ever creating; — that at last Matter is dead Mind; that mind makes the senses it sees with; that the genius of man is a continuation of the power that made him and that has not done making him.

I dare not deal with this element in its pure essence. It is too rare for the wings of words. Yet I see that Intellect is a science of degrees, and that as man is conscious of the law of vegetable and animal nature, so he is aware of an Intellect which overhangs his consciousness like a sky, of degree above degree, of heaven within heaven.

Every just thinker has attempted to indicate these degrees, these steps on the heavenly stair, until he comes to light where language fails him. Above the thought is the higher truth, — truth as yet undomesticated and therefore unformulated.

It is a steep stair down from the essence of Intellect pure to thoughts and intellections. As the sun is conceived to have made our system by hurling out from itself the outer rings of diffuse ether which slowly condensed into earths and moons, by a higher force of the same law the mind detaches minds, and a mind detaches thoughts or intellections. These again all mimic in their sphericity the first mind, and share its power.

Life is incessant parturition. There are viviparous and oviparous minds; minds that produce their thoughts complete men, like armed soldiers, ready and swift to go out to resist and conquer all the armies of error, and others that deposit their dangerous unripe thoughts here and there to lie still for a time and be brooded in other minds, and the shell not be broken until the next age, for them to begin, as new individuals, their career.

The perceptions of a soul, its wondrous progeny, are born by the conversation, the marriage of souls; so nourished, so enlarged. They are detached from their parent, they pass into other minds; ripened and unfolded by many they hasten to incarnate themselves in action, to take body, only to carry forward the will which sent them out. They take to themselves wood and stone and iron; ships and cities and nations and armies of men and ages of duration; the pomps of religion, the armaments of war, the codes and heraldry of states; agriculture, trade, commerce;

— these are the ponderous instrumentalities into which the nimble thoughts pass, and which they animate and alter, and presently, antagonized by other thoughts which they first aroused, or by thoughts which are sons and daughters of these, the thought buries itself in the new thought of larger scope, whilst the old instrumentalities and incarnations are decomposed and recomposed into new.

Our eating, trading, marrying, and learning are mistaken by us for ends and realities, whilst they are properly symbols only; when we have come, by a divine leading, into the inner firmament, we are apprised of the unreality or representative character of what we esteemed final.

So works the poor little blockhead manikin. He must arrange and dignify his shop or farm the best he can. At last he must be able to tell you it, or write it, translate it all clumsily enough into the new sky-language he calls thought.[1] He cannot help it, the irresistible meliorations bear him forward.

II. Whilst we consider this appetite of the mind to arrange its phenomena, there is another fact which makes this useful. There is in Nature a parallel unity which corresponds to the unity in the mind and makes it available. This methodizing mind meets no resistance in its attempts. The scattered blocks, with which it strives to form a symmetrical structure, fit. This design following after finds with joy that like design went before. Not only man puts things in a row, but things belong in a row.

It is certain that however we may conceive of the wonderful little bricks of which the world is builded, we must suppose a similarity and fitting and identity in their frame. It is necessary to suppose that every hose in Nature fits every hydrant; so only is combination, chemistry, vegetation, animation, intellection possible. Without identity at base, chaos must be forever.[1]

And as mind, our mind or mind like ours, reappears to us in our study of Nature, Nature being everywhere formed after a method which we can well understand, and all the parts, to the most remote, allied or explicable,—therefore our own organization is a perpetual key, and a well-ordered mind brings to the study of every new fact or class of facts a certain divination of that which it shall find.

This reduction to a few laws, to one law, is

not a choice of the individual, it is the tyrannical instinct of the mind. There is no solitary flower and no solitary thought. It comes single like a foreign traveller,— but find out its name, and it is related to a powerful and numerous family. Wonderful is their working and relation each to each. We hold them as lanterns to light each other and our present design. Every new thought modifies, interprets old problems. The retrospective value of each new thought is immense, like a torch applied to a long train of gunpowder. To be isolated is to be sick, and in so far, dead. The life of the All must stream through us to make the man and the moment great.[1]

Well, having accepted this law of identity pervading the universe, we next perceive that whilst every creature represents and obeys it, there is diversity, there is more or less of power; that the lowest only means incipient form, and over it is a higher class in which its rudiments are opened, raised to higher powers; that there is development from less to more, from lower to superior function, steadily ascending to man.

If man has organs for breathing, for sight, for locomotion, for taking food, for digesting, for protection by house-building, by attack and defence, for reproduction and love and care of his young, you shall find all the same in the muskrat. There is a perfect correspondence; or 't is only man modified to live in a mud-bank. A fish in like manner is man furnished to live in the sea; a thrush, to fly in the air; and a mollusk is a cheap edition with a suppression of the costlier illustrations, designed for dingy circulation, for shelving in an oyster-bank or among the seaweed.

If we go through the British Museum or the Jardin des Plantes in Paris, or any cabinet where is some representation of all the kingdoms of Nature, we are surprised with occult sympathies; we feel as if looking at our bone and flesh through coloring and distorting glasses. Is it not a little startling to see with what genius some people take to hunting, with what genius some people fish, — what knowledge they still have of the creature they hunt? The robber, as the police reports say, must have been intimately acquainted with the premises. How lately the hunter was the poor creature's organic enemy; a presumption *inflamed*, as the lawyers say, by observing how many faces in the street still remind us of visages in the forest, — the escape from the quadruped type not yet perfectly accomplished.[1]

From whatever side we look at Nature we seem to be exploring the figure of a disguised man. How obvious is the momentum, in our mental history! The momentum, which increases by exact laws in falling bodies, increases by the same rate in the intellectual action. Every scholar knows that he applies himself coldly and slowly at first to his task, but, with the progress of the work, the mind itself becomes heated, and sees far and wide as it approaches the end, so that it is the common remark of the student, Could I only have begun with the same fire which I had on the last day, I should have done something.

The affinity of particles accurately translates the affinity of thoughts, and what a modern experimenter calls "the contagious influence of chemical action" is so true of mind that I have only to read the law that its application may be evident: "A body in the act of combination or decomposition enables another body, with which it may be in contact, to enter into the same state." And if one remembers how contagious are the moral states of men, how much we are braced by the presence and actions of any Spartan soul, it does not need vigor of our own kind, but the spectacle of vigor of any kind, any prodigious power of performance wonderfully arms and recruits us. There are those who disputing will make you dispute, and the nervous and hysterical and animalized will produce a like series of symptoms in you, though no other persons ever evoke the like phenomena, and though you are conscious that they do not properly belong to you, but are a sort of extension of the diseases of this particular person into you.

The idea of vegetation is irresistible in considering mental activity. Man seems a higher plant. What happens here in mankind is matched by what happens out there in the history of grass and wheat.[1] This curious resemblance repeats, in the mental function, the germination, growth, state of melioration, crossings, blight, parasites, and in short all the accidents of the plant. Under every leaf is the bud of a new leaf, and not less under every thought is a newer thought. The plant absorbs much nourishment from the ground in order to repair its own waste by exhalation, and keep itself good. Increase its food and it becomes fertile.

The mind is first only receptive. Surcharge it with thoughts in which it delights and it becomes active. The moment a man begins not to be convinced, that moment he begins to convince.

In the orchard many trees send out a moderate shoot in the first summer heat, and stop. They look all summer as if they would presently burst into bud again, but they do not. The fine tree continues to grow. The same thing happens in the man. Every man has material enough in his experience to exhaust the sagacity of Newton in working it out. We have more than we use. I never hear a good speech at caucus or at cattle-show but it helps me, not so much by adding to my knowledge as by apprising me of admirable uses to which what I know can be turned. The commonest remark, if the man could only extend it a little, would make him a genius ; but the thought is prematurely checked, and grows no more. All great masters are chiefly distinguished by the power of adding a second, a third, and perhaps a fourth step in a continuous line. Many a man had taken the first step. With every additional step you enchance immensely the value of your first.

The botanist discovered long ago that Nature

loves mixtures, and that nothing grows well on the crab-stock, but the blood of two trees being mixed a new and excellent fruit is produced. And not less in human history aboriginal races are incapable of improvement; the dull, melancholy Pelasgi arrive at no civility until the Phœnicians and Ionians come in. The Briton, the Pict, is nothing until the Roman, the Saxon, the Norman, arrives.[1]

It is observed that our mental processes go forward even when they seem suspended. Scholars say that if they return to the study of a new language after some intermission, the intelligence of it is more and not less. A subject of thought to which we return from month to month, from year to year, has always some ripeness of which we can give no account. We say the book grew in the author's mind.

In unfit company the finest powers are paralyzed. No ambition, no opposition, no friendly attention and fostering kindness, no wine, music or exhilarating aids, neither warm fireside nor fresh air, walking or riding, avail at all to resist the palsy of mis-association. Genius is mute, is dull; there is no genius. Ask of your flowers to open when you have let in on them a freezing wind.

The mechanical laws might as easily be shown pervading the kingdom of mind as the vegetative. A man has been in Spain. The facts and thoughts which the traveller has found in that country gradually settle themselves into a determinate heap of one size and form and not another. That is what he knows and has to say of Spain; he cannot say it truly until a sufficient time for the arrangement of the particles has elapsed.

These views of the source of thought and the mode of its communication lead us to a whole system of ethics, strict as any department of human duty, and open to us the tendencies and duties of men of thought in the present time.

Wisdom is like electricity. There is no permanent wise man, but men capable of wisdom, who, being put into certain company or other favorable conditions, become wise, as glasses rubbed acquire power for a time.

An individual body is the momentary arrest or fixation of certain atoms, which, after performing compulsory duty to this enchanted statue, are released again to flow in the currents of the world. An individual mind in like manner is a fixation or momentary eddy in which certain services and powers are taken up and minister in petty niches and localities, and then, being released, return to the unbounded soul of the world.

In this eternal resurrection and rehabilitation of transitory persons, who and what are they? 'T is only the source that we can see; — the eternal mind, careless of its channels, omnipotent in itself, and continually ejaculating its torrent into every artery and vein and veinlet of humanity. Wherever there is health, that is, consent to the cause and constitution of the universe, there is perception and power.[1]

Each man is a new power in Nature. He holds the keys of the world in his hands. No quality in Nature's vast magazines he cannot touch, no truth he cannot see. Silent, passive, even sulkily, Nature offers every morning her wealth to man. She is immensely rich; he is welcome to her entire goods, but she speaks no word, will not so much as beckon or cough; only this, she is careful to leave all her doors ajar, — towers, hall, storeroom and cellar. If he takes her hint and uses her goods she speaks no word; if he blunders and starves she says nothing. To the idle blockhead Nature is poor, sterile, inhospitable. To the gardener her loam is all strawberries, pears, pineapples. To the miller her rivers whirl the wheel and weave carpets and broadcloth. To the sculptor her stone is soft; to the painter her plumbago and marl are pencils and chromes. To the poet all sounds and words are melodies and rhythms. In her hundred-gated Thebes every chamber is a new door.[1]

But he enters the world by one key. Herein is the wealth of each. His equipment, though new, is complete; his prudence is his own; his courage, his charity, are his own. He has his own defences and his own fangs; his perception and his own mode of reply to sophistries. Whilst he draws on his own he cannot be overshadowed or supplanted.

There are two mischievous superstitions, I know not which does the most harm, one, that "I am wiser than you," and the other that "You are wiser than I." The truth is that every man is furnished, if he will heed it, with wisdom necessary to steer his own boat, — if he will not look away from his own to see how his neighbor steers his.

Every man is a new method and distributes things anew. If he could attain full size he would take up, first or last, atom by atom, all the world into a new form. And our deep conviction of the riches proper to every mind does not allow us to admit of much looking over into one another's virtues. Let me whisper a secret; nobody ever forgives any admiration in you of them, any overestimate of what they do or have. I acquiesce to be that I am, but I wish no one to be civil to me.

Strong men understand this very well. Power fraternizes with power, and wishes you not to be like him but like yourself. Echo the leaders and they will fast enough see that you have nothing for them. They came to you for something they had not.

There is always a loss of truth and power when a man leaves working for himself to work for another. Absolutely speaking, I can only work for myself. All my good is magnetic, and I educate not by lessons but by going about my business. When, moved by love, a man teaches his child or joins with his neighbor in any act of common benefit, or spends himself for his friend, or rushes at immense personal sacrifice on some public, self-immolating act, it is not done for others, but to fulfil a high necessity of his proper character. The benefit to others is contingent and not contemplated by the doer.[1]

The one thing not to be forgiven to intellectual persons is that they believe in the ideas of others. From this deference comes the imbecility and fatigue of their society, for of course they cannot affirm these from the deep life; they say what they would have you believe, but what they do not quite know. Profound sincerity is the only basis of talent as of character. The temptation is to patronize Providence, to fall into the accepted ways of talking and acting of the good sort of people.

Each has a certain aptitude for knowing or doing somewhat which, when it appears, is so adapted and aimed on that, that it seems a sort of obtuseness to everything else. Well, this aptitude, if he would obey it, would prove a telescope to bring under his clear vision what was blur to everybody else. 'T is a wonderful instrument, an organic sympathy with the whole frame of things. There is no property or relation in that immense arsenal of forces which the earth is, but some man is at last found who affects this, delights to unfold and work it, as if he were the born publisher and demonstrator of it.

As a dog has a sense that you have not, to find the track of his master or of a fox, and as each tree can secrete from the soil the elements that form a peach, a lemon, or a cocoa-nut, according to its kind, so individual men have secret senses, each some incommunicable sagacity. And men are primary or secondary as their opinions and actions are organic or not.

I know well what a sieve every ear is. Teach me never so much and I hear or retain only that which I wish to hear, what comports with my experience and my desire. Many eyes go through the meadow, but few see the flowers. A hunter finds plenty of game on the ground you have sauntered over with idle gun. White huckleberries are so rare that in miles of pasture you shall not find a dozen. But a girl who understands it will find you a pint in a quarter of an hour.

Though the world is full of food we can take only the crumbs fit for us. The air rings with sounds, but only a few vibrations can reach our tympanum. Perhaps creatures live with us which we never see, because their motion is too swift for our vision. The sun may shine, or a galaxy of suns; you will get no more light than your eye will hold. What can Plato or Newton teach, if you are deaf or incapable? A mind does not receive truth as a chest receives jewels that are put into it, but as the stomach takes up food into the system. It is no longer food, but flesh, and is assimilated. The appetite and the power of digestion measure our right to knowledge. He has it who can use it. As soon as our accumulation overruns our invention or power to use, the evils of intellectual gluttony begin, — congestion of the brain, apoplexy and strangulation.

III. In reckoning the sources of our mental power it were fatal to omit that one which pours all the others into its mould; — that unknown country in which all the rivers of our knowledge have their fountains, and which, by its qualities and structure, determines both the nature of the waters and the direction in which they flow.

The healthy mind lies parallel to the currents of Nature and sees things in place, or makes discoveries. Newton did not exercise more ingenuity but less than another to see the world. Right thought comes spontaneously, comes like the morning wind; comes daily, like our daily bread, to humble service; comes duly to those who look for it. It does not need to pump your brains and force thought to think rightly. Oh no, the ingenious person is warped by his ingenuity and mis-sees.

Instinct is our name for the potential wit. Each man has a feeling that what is done anywhere is done by the same wit as his. All men are his representatives, and he is glad to see that his wit can work at this or that problem as it ought to be done, and better than he could do it. We feel as if one man wrote all the books, painted, built, in dark ages; and we are sure that it can do more than ever was done. It was the same mind that built the world. That is Instinct.[1]

Ask what the Instinct declares, and we have little to say. He is no newsmonger, no disputant, no talker. 'T is a taper, a spark in the great night. Yet a spark at which all the illuminations of human arts and sciences were kindled. This is that glimpse of inextinguishable light by which men are guided; though it does not show objects, yet it shows the way. This is that sense by which men feel when they are wronged, though they do not see how. This is that source of thought and feeling which acts on masses of men, on all men at certain times with resistless power. Ever at intervals leaps a word or fact to light which is no man's invention, but the common instinct, making the revolutions that never go back.

This is Instinct, and Inspiration is only this power excited, breaking its silence; the spark bursting into flame. Instinct is a shapeless giant in the cave, massive, without hands or fingers or articulating lips or teeth or tongue; Behemoth, disdaining speech, disdaining particulars, lurking, surly, invincible, disdaining thoughts, always whole, never distributed, aboriginal, old as Nature, and saying, like poor Topsy, "never was born; growed." Indifferent to the dignity of its function, it plays the god in animal nature as in human or as in the angelic, and spends its omniscience on the lowest wants. The old Hindoo Gautama says, "Like the approach of the iron to the loadstone is the approach of the new-born child to the breast." There is somewhat awful in that first approach.

The Instinct begins at this low point, at the surface of the earth, and works for the necessities of the human being; then ascends step by step to suggestions which are when expressed the intellectual and moral laws.[1]

The mythology cleaves close to Nature; and what else was it they represented in Pan, god of shepherds, who was not yet completely finished in godlike form, blocked rather, and wanting the extremities; had emblematic horns and feet? Pan, that is, All. His habit was to dwell in mountains, lying on the ground, tooting like a cricket in the sun, refusing to speak, clinging to his behemoth ways. He could intoxicate by the strain of his shepherd's pipe,— silent yet to most, for his pipes make the music of the spheres, which, because it sounds eternally, is not heard at all by the dull, but only by the mind. He wears a coat of leopard spots or stars. He could terrify by earth-born fears called *panics*. Yet was he in the secret of Nature and could look both before and after. He was only seen under disguises, and was not represented by any outward image; a terror sometimes, at others a placid omnipotence.[1]

Such homage did the Greek — delighting in accurate form, not fond of the extravagant and unbounded — pay to the unscrutable force we call Instinct, or Nature when it first becomes intelligent.

The action of the Instinct is for the most part negative, regulative, rather than initiative or impulsive. But it has a range as wide as human nature, running over all the ground of morals, of intellect and of sense. In its lower function, when it deals with the apparent world, it is common sense. It requires the performance of all that is needful to the animal life and health. Then it requires a proportion between a man's acts and his condition, requires all that is called humanity; that symmetry and connection which is imperative in all healthily constituted men, and the want of which the rare and brilliant sallies of irregular genius cannot excuse.

If we could retain our early innocence, we might trust our feet uncommanded to take the right path to our friend in the woods. But we have interfered too often; the feet have lost, by our distrust, their proper virtue, and we take the wrong path and miss him. 'T is the barbarian instinct within us which culture deadens.

We find ourselves expressed in Nature, but we cannot translate it into words. But Perception is the armed eye. A civilization has tamed and ripened this savage wit, and he is a Greek. His Aye and No have become nouns and verbs and adverbs. Perception differs from Instinct by adding the Will. Simple percipiency is the virtue of space, not of man.

The senses minister to a mind they do not know. At a moment in our history the mind's eye opens and we become aware of spiritual facts, of rights, of duties, of thoughts, — a thousand faces of one essence. We call the essence Truth; the particular aspects of it we call thoughts. These facts, this essence, are not new; they are old and eternal, but our seeing of them is new. Having seen them we are no longer brute lumps whirled by Fate, but we pass into the council-chamber and government of Nature. In so far as we see them we share their life and sovereignty.

The point of interest is here, that these gates, once opened, never swing back. The observers may come at their leisure, and do at last satisfy themselves of the fact. The thought, the doctrine, the right hitherto not affirmed is published in set propositions, in conversation of scholars and philosophers, of men of the world, and at last in the very choruses of songs. The young hear it, and as they have never fought it, never known it otherwise, they accept it, vote for it at the polls, embody it in the laws. And the perception thus satisfied reacts on the senses, to clarify them, so that it becomes more indisputable.

This is the first property of the Intellect I am to point out; the mind detaches. A man is intellectual in proportion as he can make an object of every sensation, perception and intuition; so long as he has no engagement in any thought or feeling which can hinder him from looking at it as somewhat foreign.

A man of talent has only to name any form or fact with which we are most familiar, and the strong light which he throws on it enhances it to all eyes. People wonder they never saw it before. The detachment consists in seeing it under a new order, not under a personal but under a universal light. To us it had economic, but to the universe it has poetic relations, and it is as good as sun and star now. Indeed, this is the measure of all intellectual power among men, the power to complete this detachment, the power of genius to hurl a new individual into the world.[1]

An intellectual man has the power to go out of himself and see himself as an object; therefore his defects and delusions interest him as much as his successes. He not only wishes to succeed in life, but he wishes in thought to know the history and destiny of a man; whilst the cloud of egotists drifting about are only interested in a success to their egotism.

The senses report the new fact or change; the mind discovers some essential copula binding this fact or change to a class of facts or changes, and enjoys the discovery as if coming to its own again. A perception is always a generalization. It lifts the object, whether in material or moral nature, into a type. The animal, the low degrees of intellect, know only individuals. The philosopher knows only laws. That is, he considers a purely mental fact, part of the soul itself. We say with Kenelm Digby, "All things that she knoweth are herself, and she is all that she knoweth." Insight assimilates the thing seen. Is it only another way of affirming and illustrating this to say that it sees nothing alone, but sees each particular object in just connections, — sees all in God? In all healthy souls is an inborn necessity of presupposing for each particular fact a prior Being which compels it to a harmony with all other natures. The game of Intellect is the perception that whatever befalls or can be stated is a universal proposition; and contrariwise, that every general statement is poetical again by being particularized or impersonated.

A single thought has no limit to its value; a thought, properly speaking, — that is a truth held not from any man's saying so, or any accidental benefit or recommendation it has in our trade or circumstance, but because we have perceived it is a fact in the nature of things, and in all times and places will and must be the same thing,—is of inestimable value. Every new impression on the mind is not to be derided, but is to be accounted for, and, until accounted for, registered as an indisputable addition to our catalogue of natural facts.

The first fact is the fate in every mental perception,—that my seeing this or that, and that I see it so or so, is as much a fact in the natural history of the world as is the freezing of water at thirty-two degrees of Fahrenheit. My percipiency affirms the presence and perfection of law, as much as all the martyrs. A perception, it is of a necessity older than the sun and moon, and the Father of the Gods. It is there with all its destinies. It is its nature to rush to expression, to rush to embody itself. It is impatient to put on its sandals and be gone on its errand, which is to lead to a larger perception, and so to new action. For thought exists to be expressed. That which cannot externize itself is not thought.[1]

Do not trifle with your perceptions, or hold them cheap. They are your door to the seven heavens, and if you pass it by you will miss your way. Say, what impresses me ought to impress me. I am bewildered by the immense variety of attractions and cannot take a step; but this one thread, fine as gossamer, is yet real; and I hear a whisper, which I dare trust, that it is the thread on which the earth and the heaven of heavens are strung.

The universe is traversed by paths or bridges or stepping-stones across the gulfs of space in every direction. To every soul that is created is its path, invisible to all but itself. Each soul, therefore, walking in its own path walks firmly; and to the astonishment of all other souls, who see not its path, it goes as softly and playfully on its way as if, instead of being a line, narrow as the edge of a sword, over terrific pits right and left, it were a wide prairie.

Genius is a delicate sensibility to the laws of the world, adding the power to express them again in some new form. The highest measure of poetic power is such insight and faculty to fuse the circumstances of to-day as shall make transparent the whole web of circumstance and opinion in which the man finds himself, so that he releases himself from the traditions in which he grew, — no longer looks back to Hebrew or Greek or English use or tradition in religion, laws or life, but sees so truly the omnipresence of eternal cause that he can convert the daily and hourly event of New York, of Boston, into universal symbols. I owe to genius always the same debt, of lifting the curtain from the common and showing me that gods are sitting disguised in every company.

The conduct of Intellect must respect nothing so much as preserving the sensibility. My measure for all subjects of science as of events is their impression on the soul. That mind is best which is most impressionable.[1] There are times when the cawing of a crow, a weed, a snow-flake, a boy's willow whistle, or a farmer planting in his field is more suggestive to the mind than the Yosemite gorge or the Vatican would be in another hour. In like mood an old verse, or certain words, gleam with rare significance.

But sensibility does not exhaust our idea of it. That is only half. Genius is not a lazy angel contemplating itself and things. It is insatiable for expression. Thought must take the stupendous step of passing into realization. A master can formulate his thought. Our thoughts at first possess us. Later, if we have good heads, we come to possess them. We believe that certain persons add to the common vision a certain degree of control over these states of mind; that the true scholar is one who has the power to stand beside his thoughts or to hold off his thoughts at arm's length and give them perspective.

It is not to be concealed that the gods have guarded this privilege with costly penalty. This slight discontinuity which perception effects between the mind and the object paralyzes the will. If you cut or break in two a block or stone and press the two parts closely together, you can indeed bring the particles very near, but never again so near that they shall attract each other so that you can take up the block as one. That indescribably small interval is as good as a thousand miles, and has forever severed the practical unity. Such is the immense deduction from power by discontinuity.[1]

The intellect that sees the interval partakes of it, and the fact of intellectual perception severs once for all the man from the things with which he converses. Affection blends, intellect disjoins subject and object. For weal or woe we clear ourselves from the thing we contemplate. We grieve but are not the grief; we love but are not love. If we converse with low things, with crimes, with mischances, we are not compromised. And if with high things, with heroic actions, with virtues, the interval becomes a gulf and we cannot enter into the highest good. Artist natures do not weep. Goethe, the surpassing intellect of modern times, apprehends the spiritual but is not spiritual.[1]

There is indeed this vice about men of thought, that you cannot quite trust them; not as much as other men of the same natural probity, without intellect; because they have a hankering to play Providence and make a distinction in favor of themselves from the rules they apply to the human race.[2]

The primary rule for the conduct of Intellect is to have control of the thoughts without losing their natural attitudes and action. They are the oracle; we are not to poke and drill and force, but to follow them.[3] Yet the spirits of the prophets are subject to the prophets. You must formulate your thought or 't is all sky and no stars. There are men of great apprehension, discursive minds, who easily entertain ideas, but are not exact, severe with themselves, cannot connect or arrange their thoughts so as effectively to report them. A blending of these two — the intellectual perception of truth and the moral sentiment of right — is wisdom. All thought is practical. Wishing is one thing; will another. Wishing is castle-building; the dreaming about things agreeable to the senses, but to which we have no right. Will is the advance to that which rightly belongs to us, to which the inward magnet ever points, and which we dare to make ours. The revelation of thought takes us out of servitude into freedom. So does the sense of right.

Will is the measure of power. To a great genius there must be a great will. If the thought is not a lamp to the will, does not proceed to an act, the wise are imbecile. He alone is strong and happy who has a will. The rest are herds. He uses; they are used. He is of the Maker; they are of the Made.[1]

Will is always miraculous, being the presence of God to men. When it appears in a man he is a hero, and all metaphysics are at fault. Heaven is the exercise of the faculties, the added sense of power.

All men know the truth, but what of that? It is rare to find one who knows how to speak it. A man tries to speak it and his voice is like the hiss of a snake, or rude and chiding. The truth is not spoken but injured. The same thing happens in power to do the right. His rectitude is ridiculous. His organs do not play him true.

There is a meter which determines the constructive power of man,—this, namely, the question whether the mind possesses the control of its thoughts, or they of it. The new sect stands for certain thoughts. We go to individual members for an exposition of them. Vain expectation. They are possessed by the ideas but do not possess them. One meets contemplative men who dwell in a certain feeling and delight which are intellectual but wholly above their expression. They cannot formulate. They impress those who know them by their loyalty to the truth they worship but cannot impart. Sometimes the patience and love are rewarded by the chamber of power being at last opened; but sometimes they pass away dumb, to find it where all obstruction is removed.

By and by comes a facility; some one that can move the mountain and build of it a causeway through the Dismal Swamp, as easily as he carries the hair on his head. Talent is habitual facility of execution. We like people who can do things. The various talents are organic, or each related to that part of nature it is to explore and utilize.

Somewhat is to come to the light, and one was created to fetch it, — a vessel of honor or of dishonor. 'T is of instant use in the economy of the Cosmos, and the more armed and biassed for the work the better.

Each of these talents is born to be unfolded and set at work for the use and delight of men, and, in the last results, the man with the talent is the need of mankind; the whole ponderous machinery of the state has really for its aim just to place this skill of each.

But idea and execution are not often intrusted to the same head. There is some incompatibility of good speculation and practice, for example, the failure of monasteries and Brook Farms. To hammer out phalanxes must be done by smiths; as soon as the scholar attempts it, he is half a charlatan.

The grasp is the main thing. Most men's minds do not grasp anything. All slips through their fingers, like the paltry brass grooves that in most country houses are used to raise or drop the curtain, but are made to sell, and will not hold any curtain but cobwebs. I have heard that idiot children are known from their birth by the circumstance that their hands do not close round anything. Webster naturally and always grasps, and therefore retains something from every company and circumstance.

As a talent Dante's imagination is the nearest to hands and feet that we have seen. He clasps the thought as if it were a tree or a stone, and describes as mathematically. I once found Page the painter modelling his figures in clay, Ruth and Naomi, before he painted them on canvas. Dante, one would say, did the same thing before he wrote the verses.

I have spoken of Intellect constructive.[1] But it is in degrees. How it moves when its pace is accelerated! The pace of Nature is so slow. Why not from strength to strength, from miracle to miracle, and not as now with this retardation — as if Nature had sprained her foot — and plenteous stopping at little stations?

The difference is obvious enough in Talent between the speed of one man's action above another's. In debate, in legislature, not less in action; in war or in affairs, alike daring and effective. But I speak of it in quite another sense, namely, in the habitual speed of combination of thought.

The same functions which are perfect in our quadrupeds are seen slower performed in palæontology. Many races it cost them to achieve the completion that is now in the life of one. Life had not yet so fierce a glow.[1]

Shakspeare astonishes by his equality in every play, act, scene or line. One would say he must have been a thousand years old when he wrote his first line, so thoroughly is his thought familiar to him, and has such scope and so solidly worded, as if it were already a proverb and not hereafter to become one. Well, that millennium in effect is really only a little acceleration in his process of thought.

But each power is commonly at the expense of some other. When pace is increased it will happen that the control is in a degree lost. Reason does not keep her firm seat. The Delphian prophetess, when the spirit possesses her, is herself a victim. The excess of individualism, when it is not corrected or subordinated to the Supreme Reason, makes that vice which we stigmatize as monotones, men of one idea, or, as the French say, *enfant perdu d'une conviction isolée*, which give such a comic tinge to all society. Every man has his theory, true, but ridiculously overstated. We are forced to treat a great part of mankind as if they were a little deranged. We detect their mania and humor it, so that conversation soon becomes a tiresome effort.

You laugh at the monotones, at the men of one idea, but if we look nearly at heroes we may find the same poverty; and perhaps it is not poverty, but power. The secret of power, intellectual or physical, is concentration, and all concentration involves of necessity a certain narrowness. It is a law of Nature that he who looks at one thing must turn his eyes from every other thing in the universe. The horse goes better with blinders, and the man for dedication to his task. If you ask what compensation is made for the inevitable narrowness, why, this, that in learning one thing well you learn all things.[1]

Immense is the patience of Nature. You say thought is a penurious rill. Well, we can wait. Nature is immortal, and can wait. Nature having for capital this rill, drop by drop, as it trickles from the rock of ages, — this rill and her patience, — she husbands and hives, she forms reservoirs, were it only a phial or a hair-tube that will hold as it were a drop of attar. Not having enough to support all the powers of a race, she thins all her stock and raises a few individuals, or only a pair. Not sufficing to feed all the faculties synchronously, she feeds one faculty and starves all the rest. I am familiar with cases, we meet them daily, wherein the vital force being insufficient for the constitution, everything is neglected that can be spared; some one power fed, all the rest pine. 'T is like a withered hand or leg on a Hercules. It makes inconvenience in society, for we presume symmetry, and because they know one thing, we defer to them in another, and find them really contemptible. We can't make a half bow and say, I honor and despise you. But Nature can; she whistles with all her winds, and does as she pleases.[1]

It is much to write sentences; it is more to add method and write out the spirit of your life symmetrically. But to arrange general reflections in their natural order, so that I shall have one homogeneous piece, — a Lycidas, an Allegro, a Hamlet, a Midsummer Night's Dream, — this continuity is for the great. The wonderful men are wonderful hereby. Such concentration of experiences is in every great work, which, though successive in the mind of the master, were primarily combined in his piece.

But what we want is consecutiveness. 'T is

with us a flash of light, then a long darkness, then a flash again. Ah! could we turn these fugitive sparkles into an astronomy of Copernican worlds.[1]

I must think this keen sympathy, this thrill of awe with which we watch the performance of genius, a sign of our own readiness to exert the like power. I must think we are entitled to powers far transcending any that we possess; that we have in the race the sketch of a man which no individual comes up to.

Every sincere man is right, or, to make him right, only needs a little larger dose of his own personality. Excellent in his own way by means of not apprehending the gift of another. When he speaks out of another's mind, we detect it. He can't make any paint stick but his own. No man passes for that with another which he passes for with himself. The respect and the censure of his brother are alike injurious and irrelevant. We see ourselves; we lack organs to see others, and only squint at them.

Don't fear to push these individualities to their farthest divergence. Characters and talents are complemental and suppletory. The world stands by balanced antagonisms. The more the peculiarities are pressed, the better the result. The air would rot without lightning; and without the violence of direction that men have, without bigots, without men of fixed idea, no excitement, no efficiency.

The novelist should not make any character act absurdly, but only absurdly as seen by others. For it is so in life. Nonsense will not keep its unreason if you come into the humorist's point of view, but unhappily we find it is fast becoming sense, and we must flee again into the distance if we would laugh.

What strength belongs to every plant and animal in Nature. The tree or the brook has no duplicity, no pretentiousness, no show. It is, with all its might and main, what it is, and makes one and the same impression and effect at all times. All the thoughts of a turtle are turtles, and of a rabbit, rabbits. But a man is broken and dissipated by the giddiness of his will; he does not throw himself into his judgments; his genius leads him one way, but 't is likely his trade or politics in quite another. He rows with one hand and with the other backs water, and does not give to any manner of life the strength of his constitution. Hence the perpetual loss of power and waste of human life.

The natural remedy against this miscellany of knowledge and aim, this desultory universality of ours, this immense ground-juniper falling abroad and not gathered up into any columnar tree, is to substitute realism for sentimentalism; a certain recognition of the simple and terrible laws which, seen or unseen, pervade and govern.

You will say this is quite axiomatic and a little too true. I do not find it an agreed point. Literary men for the most part have a settled despair as to the realization of ideas in their own time. There is in all students a distrust of truth, a timidity about affirming it; a wish to patronize Providence.

We disown our debt to moral evil. To science there is no poison; to botany no weed; to chemistry no dirt. The curses of malignity and despair are important criticism, which must be heeded until he can explain and rightly silence them.

"*Croyez moi, l'erreur aussi a son mérite*," said Voltaire. We see those who surmount by dint of egotism or infatuation obstacles from which the prudent recoil. The right partisan is a heady man, who, because he does not see many things, sees some one thing with heat and exaggeration; and if he falls among other narrow men, or objects which have a brief importance, prefers it to the universe, and seems inspired and a godsend to those who wish to magnify the matter and carry a point. 'T is the difference between progress by railroad and by walking across the broken country. Immense speed, but only in one direction.

There are two theories of life; one for the demonstration of our talent, the other for the education of the man. One is activity, the busybody, the following of that practical talent which we have, in the belief that what is so natural, easy and pleasant to us and desirable to others will surely lead us out safely; in this direction lie usefulness, comfort, society, low power of all sorts. The other is trust, religion, consent to be nothing for eternity, entranced waiting, the worship of ideas. This is solitary, grand, secular. They are in perpetual balance and strife. One is talent, the other genius. One is skill, the other character.[1]

We are continually tempted to sacrifice genius to talent, the hope and promise of insight to the lust of a freer demonstration of those gifts we have; and we buy this freedom to glitter by the loss of general health.

It is the levity of this country to forgive everything to talent. If a man show cleverness, rhetorical skill, bold front in the forum or senate, people clap their hands without asking more. We have a juvenile love of smartness, of showy speech. We like faculty that can rapidly be coined into money, and society seems to be in conspiracy to utilize every gift prematurely, and pull down genius to lucrative talent. Every kind of meanness and mischief is forgiven to intellect. All is condoned if I can write a good song or novel.

Wide is the gulf between genius and talent. The men we know, poets, wits, writers, deal with their thoughts as jewellers with jewels, which they sell but must not wear. Like the carpenter, who gives up the key of the fine house he has built, and never enters it again.

There is a conflict between a man's private dexterity or talent and his access to the free air and light which wisdom is; between wisdom and the habit and necessity of repeating itself which belongs to every mind. Peter is the mould into which everything is poured like warm wax, and be it astronomy or railroads or French revolution or theology or botany, it comes out Peter. But there are quick limits to our interest in the personality of people. They are as much alike as their barns and pantries, and are as soon musty and dreary. They entertain us for a time, but at the second or third encounter we have nothing more to learn.[1]

The daily history of the Intellect is this alternating of expansions and concentrations. The expansions are the invitations from heaven to try a larger sweep, a higher pitch than we have yet climbed, and to leave all our past for this enlarged scope. Present power, on the other hand, requires concentration on the moment and the thing to be done.

The condition of sanity is to respect the order of the intellectual world; to keep down talent in its place, to enthrone the instinct. There must be perpetual rallying and self-recovery. Each talent is ambitious and self-asserting; it works for show and for the shop, and the greater it grows the more is the mischief and the misleading, so that presently all is wrong.

No wonder the children love masks and costumes, and play horse, play soldier, play school, play bear, and delight in theatricals. The children have only the instinct of the universe, in which becoming somewhat else is the perpetual game of Nature, and death the penalty of standing still. 'T is not less in thought. I cannot conceive any good in a thought which confines and stagnates. The universe exists only in transit, or we behold it shooting the gulf from the past to the future. We are passing into new heavens in fact by the movement of our solar system, and in thought by our better knowledge.[1] Transition is the attitude of power. A fact is only a fulcrum of the spirit. It is the terminus of a past thought, but only a means now to new sallies of the imagination and new progress of wisdom. The habit of saliency, of not pausing but proceeding, is a sort of importation and domestication of the divine effort into a man. Routine, the rut, is the path of indolence, of cows, of sluggish animal life ; as near gravitation as it can go. But wit sees the short way, puts together what belongs together, custom or no custom ; in that is organization.

Inspiration is the continuation of the divine effort that built the man. The same course continues itself in the mind which we have witnessed in Nature, namely the carrying-on and completion of the metamorphosis from grub to worm, from worm to fly. In human thought this process is often arrested for years and ages. The history of mankind is the history of arrested growth. This premature stop, I know not how, befalls most of us in early youth; as if the growth of high powers, the access to rare truths, closed at two or three years in the child, while all the pagan faculties went ripening on to sixty.

So long as you are capable of advance, so long you have not abdicated the hope and future of a divine soul. That wonderful oracle will reply when it is consulted, and there is no history or tradition, no rule of life or art or science, on which it is not a competent and the only competent judge.

Man was made for conflict, not for rest. In action is his power; not in his goals but in his transitions man is great. Instantly he is dwarfed by self-indulgence. The truest state of mind rested in becomes false.

The spiritual power of man is twofold, mind and heart, Intellect and morals; one respecting truth, the other the will. One is the man, the other the woman in spiritual nature. One is power, the other is love. These elements always coexist in every normal individual, but one predominates. And as each is easily exalted in our thoughts till it serves to fill the universe and become the synonym of God, the soul in which one predominates is ever watchful and jealous when such immense claims are made for one as seem injurious to the other. Ideal and practical, like ecliptic and equator, are never parallel. Each has its vices, its proper dangers, obvious enough when the opposite element is deficient.

Intellect is skeptical, runs down into talent, selfish working for private ends, conceited, ostentatious and malignant. On the other side the clear-headed thinker complains of souls led hither and thither by affections which, alone, are blind guides and thriftless workmen, and in the confusion asks the polarity of intellect. But all great minds and all great hearts have mutually allowed the absolute necessity of the twain.[1]

If the first rule is to obey your genius, in the second place the good mind is known by the choice of what is positive, of what is advancing. We must embrace the affirmative. But the affirmative of affirmatives is love. *Quantus amor tantus animus.* Strength enters as the moral element enters. Lovers of men are as safe as the sun. Good will makes insight. Sensibility is the secret readiness to believe in all kinds of power, and the contempt of any experience we have not is the opposite pole. The measure of mental health is the disposition to find good everywhere, good and order, analogy, health and benefit,—the love of truth, tendency to be in the right, no fighter for victory, no cockerel.[1]

We have all of us by nature a certain divination and parturient vaticination in our minds of some higher good and perfection than either power or knowledge. Knowledge is plainly to be preferred before power, as being that which guides and directs its blind force and impetus; but Aristotle declares that the origin of reason is not reason, but something better.

The height of culture, the highest behavior, consists in the identification of the Ego with the universe; so that when a man says I hope, I find, I think, he might properly say, The human race thinks or finds or hopes. And meantime he shall be able continually to keep sight of his biographical Ego,— I have a desk, I have an office, I am hungry, I had an ague,— as rhetoric or offset to his grand spiritual Ego, without impertinence, or ever confounding them.[2]

I may well say this is divine, the continuation of the divine effort. Alas! it seems not to be ours, to be quite independent of us. Often there is so little affinity between the man and his works that we think the wind must have writ them. Also its communication from one to another follows its own law and refuses our intrusion. It is in one, it belongs to all; yet how to impart it?

We need all our resources to live in the world which is to be used and decorated by us. Socrates kept all his virtues as well as his faculties well in hand. He was sincerely humble, but he utilized his humanity chiefly as a better eye-glass to penetrate the vapors that baffled the vision of other men.

The superiority of the man is in the simplicity of his thought, that he has no obstruction, but looks straight at the pure fact, with no color of option. Profound sincerity is the only basis of talent as of character. The virtue of the Intellect is its own, its courage is of its own kind, and at last it will be justified, though for the moment it seem hostile to what it most reveres.

We wish to sum up the conflicting impressions by saying that all point at last to a unity which inspires all. Our poetry, our religion are its skirts and penumbræ. Yet the charm of life is the hints we derive from this. They overcome us like perfumes from a far-off shore of sweetness, and their meaning is that no tongue shall syllable it without leave; that only itself can name it; that by casting ourselves on it and being its voice it rushes each moment to positive commands, creating men and methods, and ties the will of a child to the love of the First Cause.[1]

II

INSTINCT AND INSPIRATION

IN reckoning the sources of our mental power, it were fatal to omit that one which pours all the others into mould — that unknown country in which all the rivers of our knowledge have their fountains, which by its qualities and structure determines both the nature of the waters, and the direction in which they flow. We have a certain blind wisdom, a brain of the brain, a seminal brain, which has not yet put forth organs, which rests in oversight and presence, but which seems to sheathe a certain omniscience; and which, in the despair of language, is commonly called Instinct.

This is that which never pretends: nothing seems less, nothing is more. Ask what the Instinct declares, and we have little to say; he is no newsmonger, no disputant, no talker. Consciousness is but a taper in the great night; but the taper at which all the illumination of human arts and sciences was kindled. And in each man's experience, from this spark torrents of light have once and again streamed and revealed the dusky landscape of his life. 'T is very certain that a man's whole possibility is contained in that habitual first look which he casts on all objects. Here alone is the field of metaphysical discovery, yes, and of every religion and civil order that has been or shall be. All that we know is flakes and grains detached from this mountain. None of the metaphysicians have prospered in describing this power, which constitutes sanity; and is the corrector of private excesses and mistakes; public in all its regards, and of a balance which is never lost, not even in the insane.

All men are, in respect to this source of truth, on a certain footing of equality, equal in original science, though against appearance; and 't is incredible to them. There is a singular credulity which no experience will cure us of, that another man has seen or may see somewhat more than we, of the primary facts; as, for example, of the continuity of the individual, and, eye for eye, object for object, their experience is invariably identical in a million individuals. I know, of course, all the grounds on which any man affirms the immortality of the Soul. Fed from one spring, the water-tank is equally full in all the gardens: the difference is in the distribution by pipes and pumps (difference in the aqueduct), and fine application of it. Its property is absolute science and an implicit reliance is due to it.[1]

All true wisdom of thought and of action comes of deference to this instinct, patience with its delays.

To make a practical use of this instinct in every part of life constitutes true wisdom, and we must form the habit of preferring in all cases this guidance, which is given as it is used. To indicate a few examples of our recurrence to instinct instead of to the understanding: we can only judge safely of a discipline, of a book, of a man, or other influence, by the frame of mind it induces, as whether that be large and serene, or dispiriting and degrading. Then we get a certain habit of the mind as the measure; as Haydon found Voltaire's tales left him melancholy. The eye and ear have a logic which transcends the skill of the tongue. The ear is not to be cheated. A continuous effect cannot be produced by discontinuous thought, and when the eye cannot detect the juncture of the skilful mosaic, the spirit is apprised of disunion, simply by the failure to affect the spirit. Objection and loud denial not less prove the reality and conquests of an idea than the friends and advocates it finds. One often sees in the embittered acuteness of critics snuffing heresy from afar, their own unbelief, that they pour forth on the innocent promulgator of new doctrine their anger at that which they vainly resist in their own bosom. Again, if you go to a gallery of pictures, or other works of fine art, the eye is dazzled and embarrassed by many excellences. The marble imposes on us; the exquisite details, we cannot tell if they be good or not: but long after we have quitted the place, the objects begin to take a new order; the inferior recede or are forgotten and the truly noble forms reappear to the imagination.

The Instinct begins at this low point at the surface of the earth, and works for the necessities of the human being; then ascends, step by step, to suggestions, which are, when expressed, the intellectual and moral laws.[1]

And what is Inspiration? It is this Instinct, whose normal state is passive, at last put in action. We attributed power and science and good will to the Instinct, but we found it dumb and inexorable. If it would but impart itself! To coax and woo the strong Instinct to bestir itself, and work its miracle, is the end of all wise endeavor. It is resistless, and knows the way, is the inventor of all arts, and is melodious, and at all points a god. Could we prick the sides of this slumberous giant; could we break the silence of this oldest angel, who was with God when the worlds were made! The whole art of man has been an art of excitation, to provoke, to extort speech from the drowsy genius. We ought to know the way to our nectar. We ought to know the way to insight and prophecy as surely as the plant knows its way to the light; the cow and sheep to the running brook; or the feaster to his wine. We believe (the drop of blood has latent power and organs) that the rudest mind has a Delphi and Dodona — predictions of Nature and history — in itself, though now dim and hard to read. All depends on some instigation, some impulse. Where is the yeast that will leaven this lump? Where the wine that will warm and open these silent lips? Where the fire that will light this combustible pile? That force or flame is alone to be considered; 't is indifferent on what it is fed.

Here are we with all our world of facts and experience, the spontaneous impressions of Nature and men, and original oracles, — all ready to be uttered, if only we could be set aglow. How much material lies in every man![1] Who knows not the insufficiency of our forces, the solstice of genius? The star climbs for a time the heaven, but never reaches the zenith; it culminates low, and goes backward whence it came.[2]

The human faculty only warrants inceptions. Even those we call great men build substructures, and, like Cologne Cathedral, these are never finished. Lord Bacon begins; Behmen begins; Goethe, Fourier, Schelling, Coleridge, they all begin: we, credulous bystanders, believe, of course, that they can finish as they begun. If you press them, they fly to a new topic, and here, again, open a magnificent promise, which serves the turn of interesting us once more, and silencing reproaches, but they never complete their work. Inspiration is vital and continuous. It is also a public or universal light, and not particular.[3] But genius is as weary of his personality as others are, and he has the royal expedient to thrust Nature between him and you, and perpetually to divert attention from himself, by the stream of thoughts, laws and images.

In the healthy mind, the thought is not a

barren thesis, but expands, varies, recruits itself with relations to all Nature, paints itself in wonderful symbols, appears in new men, in institutions, in social arrangements, in wood, in stone, in art, in books. The mark and sign of it is newness. The divine energy never rests or repeats itself, but casts its old garb, and reappears, another creature; the old energy in a new form, with all the vigor of the earth; the Ancient of Days in the dew of the morning.

Novelty in the means by which we arrive at the old universal ends is the test of the presence of the highest power, alike in intellectual and in moral action. How incomparable beyond all price seems to us a new poem — say Spenser — or true work of literary genius! In five hundred years we shall not have a second. We brood on the words or works of our companion, and ask in vain the sources of his information. He exhibits an exotic culture, as if he had his education in another planet. The poet is incredible, inexplicable.

The poet works to an end above his will, and by means, too, which are out of his will. Every part of the poem is therefore a true surprise to the reader, like the parts of the plant, and legitimate as they. The muse may be defined,

Supervoluntary ends effected by supervoluntary means. No practical rules for the poem, no working-plan was ever drawn up. It is miraculous at all points. The poetic state given, a little more or a good deal more or less performance seems indifferent. It is as impossible for labor to produce a sonnet of Milton, or a song of Burns, as Shakspeare's Hamlet, or the Iliad. There is much loss, as we say on the railway, in the stops, but the running time need be but little increased, to add great results. One master could so easily be conceived as writing all the books of the world. They are all alike. For it is a power to convert all Nature to his use. It is a tap-root that sucks all the juices of the earth.[1]

It is this employment of new means — of means not mechanical, but spontaneously appearing for the new need, and as good as the end — that denotes the inspired man. This is equally obvious in all the fine arts; and in action as well as in fine arts. We must try our philanthropists so. The reformer comes with many plans of melioration, and the basis on which he wishes to build his new world, a great deal of money. But what is gained? Certain young men or maidens are thus to be screened from the evil influences of trade by force of money. Perhaps that is a benefit, but those who give the money must be just so much more shrewd, and worldly, and hostile, in order to save so much money. I see not how any virtue is thus gained to society. It is a mere transference. But he will instruct and aid us who shows us how the young may be taught without degrading the old; how the daily sunshine and sap may be made to feed wheat instead of moss and Canada thistle; and really the capital discovery of modern agriculture is that it costs no more to keep a good tree than a bad one.

But *how*, cries my reformer, is this to be done? *How* could I do it, who have wife and family to keep? The question is most reasonable, — yet proves that you are not the man to do the feat. The mark of the spirit is to know its way, to invent means. It has been in the universe before, of old and from everlasting, and knows its way up and down. Power is the authentic mark of spirit. . . .

What a revelation of power is music! Yet, when we consider who and what the professors of that art usually are, does it not seem as if music falls accidentally and superficially on its artists? Is it otherwise with poetry? . . . Here is a famous Ode, which is the first performance of the

British mind and lies in all memories as the high-water mark in the flood of thought in this age. What does the writer know of that? Converse with him, learn his opinions and hopes. He has long ago passed out of it, and perhaps his only concern with it is some copyright of an edition in which certain pages, so and so entitled, are contained. When a young man asked old Goethe about Faust, he replied, "What can I know of this? I ought rather to ask you, who are young, and can enter much better into that feeling." Indeed, I believe it is true in the experience of all men, — for all are inspirable, and sometimes inspired, — that, for the memorable moments of life, we were in them, and not they in us. ". . . How they entered into me, let them say if they can; for I have gone over all the avenues of my flesh, and cannot find by which they entered," said Saint Augustine. And the ancient Proclus seems to signify his sense of the same fact, by saying, "The parts in us are more the property of wholes, and of things above us, than they are our property."

Yes, this wonderful source of knowledge remains a mystery; and its arts and methods of working remain a mystery: it is untamable; the ship of heaven guides itself, and will not accept a wooden rudder. It must be owned that what we call Inspiration is coy and capricious; we must lose many days to gain one; and in order to win infallible verdicts from the inner mind, we must indulge and humor it in every way, and not too exactly task and harness it. Also its communication from one to another follows its own law, and refuses our intrusion. It is one, it belongs to all: yet how to impart it? This makes the perpetual problem of education. How shall I educate my children? Shall I indulge, or shall I control them? Philosophy replies, Nature is stronger than your will, and were you never so vigilant, you may rely on it, your nature and genius will certainly give your vigilance the slip though it had *delirium tremens*, and will educate the children by the inevitable infusions of its quality. You will do as you can. Why then cumber yourself about it, and make believe be better than you are? Our teaching is indeed hazardous and rare. Our only security is in our rectitude, whose influences must be salutary. That virtue which was never taught us, we cannot teach others. They must be taught by the same schoolmaster. And in spite of our imbecility and terrors, in spite of Boston and London, and universal decay of religion, etc.,

etc., the moral sense reappears forever with the same angelic newness that has been from of old the fountain of poetry and beauty and strength. Nature is forever over education; our famous orchardist once more: Van Mons of Belgium, after all his experiments at crossing and refining his fruit, arrived at last at the most complete trust in the native power. "My part is to sow, and sow, and re-sow, and in short do nothing but sow."

It is not in our will. That is the quality of it, that it commands, and is not commanded. And rarely, and suddenly, and without desert, we are let into the serene upper air. Is it that we are such mountains of conceit that Heaven cannot enough mortify and snub us, — I know not; but there seems a settled determination to break our spirit. We shall not think of ourselves too highly. We cannot even see what or where our stars of destiny are.[1] . . . The inexorable Laws, the Ideas, the private Fate, the Instinct, the Intellect, Memory, Imagination, Fancy, Number, Inspiration, Nature, Duty; — 't is very certain that these things have been hid as under towels and blankets, most part of our days, and, at certain privileged moments, they emerge unaccountably into light. I know not why, but our thoughts have a life of their own, independent of our will. We call genius, in all our popular and proverbial language, divine; to signify its independence of our will. Intellect is universal not individual.[1] . . . I think this pathetic, — not to have any wisdom at our own terms, not to have any power of organizing victory. The only comfort I can lay to my own sorrow is that we have a higher than a personal interest, which, in the ruin of the personal, is secured. I see that all beauty of discourse or of manners lies in launching on the thought, and forgetting ourselves; and though the beatitude of the Intellect seems to lie out of our volition, and to be unattainable as the sky, yet we can take sight beforehand of a state of being wherein the will shall penetrate and control what it cannot now reach. The old law of science, *Imperat parendo*, *we command by obeying*, is forever true; and by faithful serving, we shall complete our noviciate to this subtle art. Yes, and one day, though far off, you will attain the control of these states; you will enter them at will; you will do what now the muses only sing. That is the nobility and high prize of the world.

And this reminds me to add one more trait

of the inspired state, namely, incessant advance, — the forward foot. For it is the curious property of truth to be uncontainable and ever enlarging. Truth indeed! We talk as if we had it, or sometimes said it, or knew anything about it, — that terrific re-agent. 'T is a gun with a recoil which will knock down the most nimble artillerists, and therefore is never fired. The ideal is as far ahead of the videttes of the van as it is of the rear. And before the good we aim at, all history is symptomatic, and only a good omen.

And the practical rules of literature ought to follow from these views, namely, that all writing is by the grace of God;[1] that none but a writer should write; that he should write affirmatively, not polemically, or should write nothing that will not help somebody, — as I knew of a good man who held conversations, and wrote on the wall, "that every person might speak to the subject, but no allusion should be made to the opinions of other speakers;" — that we must affirm and affirm, but neither you nor I know the value of what we say; that we must be openers of doors and not a blind alley; that we must hope and strive, for despair is no muse, and vigor always liberates.

The whole ethics of thought is of this kind, flowing out of reverence of the source, and is a sort of religious office. If there is inspiration let there be only that. You shall not violate its conditions, but we will by all means invite it. It is a sort of rule in Art that you shall not speak of any work of art except in its presence; then you will continue to learn something, and will make no blunder. It is not less the rule of this kingdom that you shall not speak of the mount except on the mount;[1] that there are certain problems one would not willingly open, except when the irresistible oracles broke silence. He needs all his health and the flower of his faculties for that. All men are inspirable. Whilst they say only the beautiful and sacred words of necessity, there is no weakness, and no repentance. But the moment they attempt to say these things by memory, charlatanism begins. I am sorry that we do not receive the higher gifts justly and greatly. The reception should be equal. The thoughts which wander through our mind, we do not absorb and make flesh of, but we report them as thoughts; we retail them as news, to our lovers and to all Athenians. At a dreadful loss we play this game; for the secret Power will not impart himself to us for tea-table talk; he frowns on moths and puppets, passes by us, and seeks a solitary and religious heart.

All intellectual virtue consists in a reliance on Ideas. It must be carried with a certain magnificence. We must live by our strength, not by our weakness. It is the exhortation of Zoroaster, "Let the depth, the immortal depth of your soul lead you." It was the saying of Pythagoras, "Remember to be sober, and to be disposed to believe; for these are the nerves of wisdom."

Why should we be the dupes of our senses, the victims of our own works, and always inferior to ourselves. We do not yet trust the unknown powers of thought. The whole world is nothing but an exhibition of the powers of this principle, which distributes men. Whence came all these tools, inventions, books, laws, parties, kingdoms? Out of the invisible world, through a few brains. Nineteen twentieths of their substance do trees draw from the air. Plant the pitch-pine in a sand-bank, where is no food, and it thrives, and presently makes a grove, and covers the sand with a soil by shedding its leaves. Not less are the arts and institutions of men created out of thought. The powers that make the capitalist are metaphysical, the force of method and the force of will makes trade, and builds towns. "All conquests that history tells of will be found to resolve themselves into the superior mental powers of the conquerors," and the real credentials by which man takes precedence of man, and lays his hand on those advantages which confirm and consolidate rank, are intellectual and moral. The men are all drugged with this liquor of thought, and thereby secured to their several works. It is easy to see that the races of men rise out of the ground preoccupied with a thought which rules them, divided beforehand into parties ready armed and angry to fight for they know not what. They all share, to the rankest Philistines, the same belief. The haberdashers and brokers and attorneys are idealists and only differ in the amount and clearness of their perception. Whether Whiggery, or Chartism, or Church, or a dream of Wealth, fashioned all these resolute bankers, merchants, lawyers, landlords, who administer the world of to-day, as leaves and wood are made of air, an idea fashioned them, and one related to yours. A stronger idea will subordinate them. Yours, if you see it to be nearer and truer. A man of more comprehensive view can always see with good humor the seeming opposition of a powerful talent which has less comprehension. 'T is a strong paddy, who, with his burly elbows, is making place and way for him. Trust entirely the thought. Lean upon it, it will bear up thee and thine, and society, and systems, like a scrap of down.

The world is intellectual; and the man is. Every man comes into Nature impressed with his own polarity or bias, in obeying which his power, opportunity and happiness reside. . . . He is strong by his genius, gets all his knowledge only through that aperture. Society is unanimous against his project. He never hears it as he knows it. Nevertheless he is right; right against the world. All excellence is only an inflamed personality. If he is wrong, increase his determination to his aim, and he is right again. What is the use of trying to be somewhat else? He has a facility, which costs him nothing, to do somewhat admirable to all men. He is strong by his genius, and happy also by the same. The secret of power is delight in one's work. He takes delight in working, not in having wrought. His workbench he finds everywhere, and his workbench is home, education, power and patron. Whilst he serves his genius, he works when he stands, when he sits, when he eats and when he sleeps. The dream which lately floated before the eyes of the French nation — that every man shall do that which of all things he prefers, and shall have three francs a day for doing that — is the real law of the world; and all good labor, by which society is really served, will be found to be of that kind.

All we ask of any man is to be contented with his own work. An enthusiastic workman dignifies his art and arrives at results. Him we account the fortunate man whose determination to his aim is sufficiently strong to leave him no doubt. I am aware that Nature does not always pronounce early on this point. Many men are very slow in finding their vocation. It does not at once appear what they were made for. Nature has not made up her mind in regard to her young friend, and when this happens, we feel life to be some failure. Life is not quite desirable to themselves. It uniformly suggests in the conversation of men the presumption of continued life, of which the present is only one term. We must suppose life to such is a kind of hibernation, and 't is to be hoped they will be very fat and energetic in the spring. They ripen too slowly than that the determination should appear in this brief life. As with our Catawbas and Isabellas at the eastward, the season is not quite long enough for them.

This determination of Genius in each is so strong that, if it were not guarded with powerful checks, it would have made society impossible. As it is, men are best and most by themselves: and always work in society with great loss of power. They are not timed each to the other: they cannot keep step, and life requires too much compromise. Men go through the world each musing on a great fable dramatically pictured and rehearsed before him. If you speak to the man, he turns his eyes from his own scene, and, slower or faster, endeavors to comprehend what you say. When you have done speaking, he returns to his private music. Men generally attempt, early in life, to make their brothers, afterwards their wives, acquainted with what is going forward in their private theatre; but they soon desist from the attempt, in finding that they also have some farce, or, perhaps, some ear- and heart-rending tragedy forward on their secret boards, on which they are intent; and all parties acquiesce, at last, each in a private box, with the whole play performed before himself *solus*.

The source of thought evolves its own rules, its own virtues, its own religion. Its whole equipment is new, and it can only fight with its own weapons. Is there only one courage, one gratitude, one benevolence? No, but as many as there are men. Every constitution has its own health and diseases. A new constitution, a new fever, say the physicians. I think the reason why men fail in their conflicts is because they wear other armor than their own. Each must have all, but by no means need he have it in your form. Each must be rich, but not only in money or lands, he may have instead the riches of riches, — creative supplying power.[1]

. . Within this magical power derived from fidelity to his nature, he adds also the mechanical force of perseverance. He shall keep the law which shall keep him. . . . In persistency, he knows the strength of Nature, and the immortality of man to lie. A man must do the work with that faculty he has now. But that faculty is the accumulation of past days. That you have done long ago helps you now. No rival can rival backward. What you have learned and done, is safe and fruitful. Work and learn in evil days, in barren days, in days of depression and calamity. "There is but one only liberator in this life from the demons that invade us, and that is, Endeavor, — earnest, entire, perennial endeavor."

Follow this leading, nor ask too curiously whither. To follow it is thy part. And what if it lead, as men say, to an excess, to partiality, to individualism? Follow it still. His art shall suffice this artist, his flame this lover, his inspiration this poet. The artist must be sacrificed. Take it sadly home to thy heart, — the artist must pay for his learning and doing with his life. The old Herschel must choose between the night and the day, and draw on his nightcap when the sun rises, and defend his eyes for nocturnal use. Michael Angelo must paint Sistine ceilings till he can no longer read, except by holding the book over his head. Nature deals with all her children so. See the poor flies, lately so wanton, now fixed to the wall or the tree, exhausted and presently blown away. Men likewise, they put their lives into their deed.[1] . . .

There is a probity of the Intellect, which demands, if possible, virtues more costly than any

Bible has consecrated. It consists in an absolute devotion to truth, founded in a faith in truth. . . . The virtue of the Intellect is its own, as its courage is of its own kind: and at last, it will be justified, though for the time it seem hostile to that which it most reveres. . . . I will speak the truth in my heart, or think the truth against what is called God.[1] . . .

One polarity is impressed on the universe and on its particles. As the whole has its law, so each individual has his genius. Obedience to its genius (to speak a little scholastically) is the particular of faith; perception that the tendency of the whole is to the benefit of the individual is the universal of faith. Do not truck for your private immortality. If immortality, in the sense in which you seek it, is best, you shall be immortal. If it is up to the dignity of that order of things you know, it is secure. The sky, the sea, the plants, the rocks, astronomy, chemistry, keep their word. Morals and the genius of humanity will also. In short, the whole moral of modern science is the transference of that trust which is felt in Nature's admired arrangements, to the sphere of freedom and of rational life.[2] . . .

These studies seem to me to derive an importance from their bearing on the universal question of modern times, the question of Religion. It seems to me, as if men stood craving a more stringent creed than any of the pale and enervating systems to which they have had recourse. The Buddhist who finds gods masked in all his friends and enemies, and reads the issue of the conflict beforehand in the rank of the actors, is calm. The old Greek was respectable and we are not yet able to forget his dramas, — who found the genius of tragedy in the conflict between Destiny and the strong *should*, and not like the moderns, in the weak *would*.[1] . . .

Our books are full of generous biographies of Saints, who knew not that they were such; of men and of women who lived for the benefit and healing of nature. But one fact I read in them all, — that there is a religion which survives immutably all persons and fashions, and is worshipped and pronounced with emphasis again and again by some holy person; — and men, with their weak incapacity for principles, and their passion for persons, have run mad for the pronouncer, and forgot the religion. But there is surely enough for the heart and the imagination in the religion itself.[2]

The joy of knowledge, the late discovery that the veil which hid all things from him is really transparent, transparent everywhere to pure eyes, and the heart of trust which every perception fortifies, — renew life for him. He finds that events spring from the same root as persons; the universe understands itself, and all the parts play with a sure harmony.

III

MEMORY

MEMORY is a primary and fundamental faculty, without which none other can work; the cement, the bitumen, the matrix in which the other faculties are embedded; or it is the thread on which the beads of man are strung, making the personal identity which is necessary to moral action. Without it all life and thought were an unrelated succession. As gravity holds matter from flying off into space, so memory gives stability to knowledge; it is the cohesion which keeps things from falling into a lump, or flowing in waves.

We like longevity, we like signs of riches and extent of nature in an individual. And most of all we like a great memory. The lowest life remembers. The sparrow, the ant, the worm, have the same memory as we. If you bar their path, or offer them somewhat disagreeable to their senses, they make one or two trials, and then once for all avoid it.

Every machine must be perfect of its sort. It is essential to a locomotive that it can reverse its movement, and run backward and forward with equal celerity. The builder of the mind found it not less needful that it should have retroaction, and command its past act and deed. Perception, though it were immense and could pierce through the universe, was not sufficient.

Memory performs the impossible for man by the strength of his divine arms; holds together past and present, beholding both, existing in both, abides in the flowing, and gives continuity and dignity to human life. It holds us to our family, to our friends. Hereby a home is possible; hereby only a new fact has value.

Opportunities of investment are useful only to those who have capital. Any piece of knowledge I acquire to-day, a fact that falls under my eyes, a book I read, a piece of news I hear, has a value at this moment exactly proportioned to my skill to deal with it. To-morrow, when I know more, I recall that piece of knowledge and use it better.

The Past has a new value every moment to the active mind, through the incessant purification and better method of its memory. Once it joined its facts by color and form and sensuous relations. Some fact that had a childish significance to your childhood and was a type in the nursery, when riper intelligence recalls it means more and serves you better as an illustration; and perhaps in your age has new meaning. What was an isolated, unrelated belief or conjecture, our later experience instructs us how to place in just connection with other views which confirm and expand it. The old whim or perception was an augury of a broader insight, at which we arrive later with securer conviction. This is the companion, this the tutor, the poet, the library, with which you travel. It does not lie, cannot be corrupted, reports to you not what you wish, but what really befell. You say, "I can never think of some act of neglect, of selfishness, or of passion without pain." Well, that is as it should be. That is the police of the Universe: the angels are set to punish you, so long as you are capable of such crime. But in the history of character the day comes when you are incapable of such crime. Then you suffer no more, you look on it as heaven looks on it, with wonder at the deed, and with applause at the pain it has cost you.[1]

Memory is not a pocket, but a living instructor, with a prophetic sense of the values which he guards; a guardian angel set there within you to record your life, and by recording to animate you to uplift it. It is a scripture written day by day from the birth of the man; all its records full of meanings which open as he lives on, explaining each other, explaining the world to him and expanding their sense as he advances, until it shall become the whole law of Nature and life.

As every creature is furnished with teeth to seize and eat, and with stomach to digest its food, so the memory is furnished with a perfect apparatus. There is no book like the memory, none with such a good index, and that of every kind, alphabetic, systematic, arranged by names of persons, by colors, tastes, smells, shapes, likeness, unlikeness, by all sorts of mysterious hooks and eyes to catch and hold, and contrivances for giving a hint.

The memory collects and re-collects. We figure it as if the mind were a kind of looking-glass, which being carried through the street of time receives on its clear plate every image that passes; only with this difference, that our plate is iodized so that every image sinks into it, and is held there. But in addition to this property it has one more, this, namely, that of all the million images that are imprinted, the very one we want reappears in the centre of the plate in the moment when we want it.

We can tell much about it, but you must not ask us what it is. On seeing a face I am aware that I have seen it before, or that I have not seen it before. On hearing a fact told I am aware that I knew it already. You say the first words of the old song, and I finish the line and stanza. But where I have them, or what becomes of them when I am not thinking of them for months and years, that they should lie so still, as if they did not exist, and yet so nigh that they come on the instant when they are called for, never any man was so sharp-sighted, or could turn himself inside out quick enough to find.

'T is because of the believed incompatibility of the affirmative and advancing attitude of the mind with tenacious acts of recollection that people are often reproached with living in their memory. Late in life we live by memory, and in our solstices or periods of stagnation; as the starved camel in the desert lives on his humps. Memory was called by the schoolmen *vespertina cognitio*, evening knowledge, in distinction from the command of the future which we have by the knowledge of causes, and which they called *matutina cognitio*, or morning knowledge.[1]

Am I asked whether the thoughts clothe themselves in words? I answer, Yes, always; but they are apt to be instantly forgotten. Never was truer fable than that of the Sibyl's writing on leaves which the wind scatters. The difference between men is that in one the memory with inconceivable swiftness flies after and recollects the flying leaves, — flies on wing as fast as that mysterious whirlwind, and the envious Fate is baffled.

This command of old facts, the clear beholding at will of what is best in our experience, is our splendid privilege. "He who calls what is vanished back again into being enjoys a bliss like that of creating," says Niebuhr. The memory plays a great part in settling the intellectual rank of men. We estimate a man by how much he remembers. A seneschal of Parnassus is Mnemosyne. This power will alone make a man remarkable; and it is found in all good wits. Therefore the poets represented the Muses as the daughters of Memory, for the power exists in some marked and eminent degree in men of an ideal determination. Quintilian reckoned it the measure of genius. *Tantum ingenii quantum memoriæ.*

We are told that Boileau having recited to

Daguesseau one day an epistle or satire he had just been composing, Daguesseau tranquilly told him he knew it already, and in proof set himself to recite it from end to end. Boileau, astonished, was much distressed until he perceived that it was only a feat of memory.

The mind disposes all its experience after its affection and to its ruling end; one man by puns and one by cause and effect, one to heroic benefit and one to wrath and animal desire. This is the high difference, the quality of the association by which a man remembers. In the minds of most men memory is nothing but a farm-book or a pocket-diary. On such a day I paid my note; on the next day the cow calved; on the next I cut my finger; on the next the banks suspended payment. But another man's memory is the history of science and art and civility and thought; and still another deals with laws and perceptions that are the theory of the world.

This thread or order of remembering, this classification, distributes men, one remembering by shop-rule or interest; one by passion; one by trifling external marks, as dress or money. And one rarely takes an interest in how the facts really stand, in the order of cause and effect, without self-reference. This is an intellectual man. Nature interests him; a plant, a fish, time, space, mind, being, in their own method and law. Napoleon is such, and that saves him.

But this mysterious power that binds our life together has its own vagaries and interruptions. It sometimes occurs that Memory has a personality of its own, and volunteers or refuses its informations at its will, not at mine. One sometimes asks himself, Is it possible that it is only a visitor, not a resident? Is it some old aunt who goes in and out of the house, and occasionally recites anecdotes of old times and persons which I recognize as having heard before, and she being gone again I search in vain for any trace of the anecdotes?

We can help ourselves to the *modus* of mental processes only by coarse material experiences. A knife with a good spring, a forceps whose lips accurately meet and match, a steel-trap, a loom, a watch, the teeth or jaws of which fit and play perfectly, as compared with the same tools when badly put together, describe to us the difference between a person of quick and strong perception, like Franklin or Swift or Webster or Richard Owen, and a heavy man who witnesses the same facts or shares experiences like theirs. 'T is like the impression made by the same stamp in sand or in wax. The way in which Burke or Sheridan or Webster or any orator surprises us is by his always having a sharp tool that fits the present use. He has an old story, an odd circumstance, that illustrates the point he is now proving, and is better than an argument. The more he is heated, the wider he sees; he seems to remember all he ever knew; thus certifying us that he is in the habit of seeing better than other people; that what his mind grasps it does not let go. 'T is the bull-dog bite; you must cut off the head to loosen the teeth.

We hate this fatal shortness of Memory, these docked men whom we behold. We gathered up what a rolling snow-ball as we came along,—much of it professedly for the future, as capital stock of knowledge. Where is it now? Look behind you. I cannot see that your train is any longer than it was in childhood. The facts of the last two or three days or weeks are all you have with you,—the reading of the last month's books. Your conversation, action, your face and manners report of no more, of no greater wealth of mind. Alas! you have lost something for everything you have gained, and cannot grow. Only so much iron will the loadstone draw; it gains new particles all the way as you move it, but one falls off for every one that adheres.

As there is strength in the wild horse which is never regained when he is once broken by training, and as there is a sound sleep of children and of savages, profound as the hibernation of bears, which never visits the eyes of civil gentlemen and ladies, so there is a wild memory in children and youth which makes what is early learned impossible to forget; and perhaps in the beginning of the world it had most vigor. Plato deplores writing as a barbarous invention which would weaken the memory by disuse. The Rhapsodists in Athens it seems could recite at once any passage of Homer that was desired.

If writing weakens the memory, we may say as much and more of printing. What is the newspaper but a sponge or invention for oblivion? the rule being that for every fact added to the memory, one is crowded out, and that only what the affection animates can be remembered.

The mind has a better secret in generalization than merely adding units to its list of facts. The reason of the short memory is shallow thought.[1] As deep as the thought, so great is the attraction. An act of the understanding will marshal and concatenate a few facts; a principle of the reason will thrill and magnetize and redistribute the whole world.

But defect of memory is not always want of genius. By no means. It is sometimes owing to excellence of genius. Thus men of great presence of mind who are always equal to the occasion do not need to rely on what they have stored for use, but can think in this moment as well and deeply as in any past moment, and if they cannot remember the rule they can make one. Indeed it is remarked that inventive men have bad memories. Sir Isaac Newton was embarrassed when the conversation turned on his discoveries and results; he could not recall them; but if he was asked why things were so or so, he could find the reason on the spot.

A man would think twice about learning a new science or reading a new paragraph, if he believed the magnetism was only a constant amount, and that he lost a word or a thought for every word he gained. But the experience is not quite so bad. In reading a foreign language, every new word mastered is a lamp lighting up related words and so assisting the memory. Apprehension of the whole sentence aids to fix the precise meaning of a particular word, and what familiarity has been acquired with the genius of the language, and the writer, helps in fixing the exact meaning of the sentence. So is it with every fact in a new science: they are mutually explaining, and each one adds transparency to the whole mass.

The damages of forgetting are more than compensated by the large values which new thoughts and knowledge give to what we already know. If new impressions sometimes efface old ones, yet we steadily gain insight; and because all Nature has one law and meaning,—part corresponding to part,—all we have known aids us continually to the knowledge of the rest of Nature. Thus, all the facts in this chest of memory are property at interest. And who shall set a boundary to this mounting value? Shall we not on higher stages of being remember and understand our early history better?

They say in Architecture, "An arch never sleeps;" I say, the Past will not sleep, it works still. With every new fact a ray of light shoots up from the long buried years. Who can judge the new book? He who has read many books. Who, the new assertion? He who has heard many the like. Who, the new man? He that has seen men. The experienced and cultivated man is lodged in a hall hung with pictures which every new day retouches, and to which every step in the march of the soul adds a more sublime perspective.

We learn early that there is great disparity of value between our experiences; some thoughts perish in the using. Some days are bright with thought and sentiment, and we live a year in a day.[1] Yet these best days are not always those which memory can retain. This water once spilled cannot be gathered. There are more inventions in the thoughts of one happy day than ages could execute, and I suppose I speak the sense of most thoughtful men when I say, I would rather have a perfect recollection of all I have thought and felt in a day or a week of high activity than read all the books that have been published in a century.

The memory is one of the compensations which Nature grants to those who have used their days well; when age and calamity have bereaved them of their limbs or organs, then they retreat on mental faculty and concentrate on that. The poet, the philosopher, lamed, old, blind, sick, yet disputing the ground inch by inch against fortune, finds a strength against the wrecks and decays sometimes more invulnerable than the heyday of youth and talent.

I value the praise of Memory. And how does memory praise? By holding fast the best. A thought takes its true rank in the memory by surviving other thoughts that were once preferred. Plato remembered Anaxagoras by one of his sayings. If we recall our own favorites, we shall usually find that it is for one crowning act or thought that we hold them dear.

Have you not found memory an apotheosis or deification? The poor short lone fact dies at the birth. Memory catches it up into her heaven, and bathes it in immortal waters. Then a thousand times over it lives and acts again, each time transfigured, ennobled. In solitude, in darkness, we tread over again the sunny walks of youth; confined now in populous streets you behold again the green fields, the shadows of the gray birches; by the solitary river hear again the joyful voices of early companions, and vibrate anew to the tenderness and dainty music of the poetry your boyhood fed upon. At this hour the stream is still flowing, though you hear it not; the plants are still drinking their accustomed life and repaying it with their beautiful forms. But you need not wander thither. It flows for you, and they grow for you, in the returning images of former summers. In low or bad company you fold yourself in your cloak,[1] withdraw yourself entirely from all the doleful circumstance, recall and surround yourself with the best associates and the fairest hours of your life: —

"Passing sweet are the domains of tender memory."[2]

You may perish out of your senses, but not out of your memory or imagination.

The memory has a fine art of sifting out the pain and keeping all the joy. The spring days when the bluebird arrives have usually only few hours of fine temperature, are sour and unlovely; but when late in autumn we hear rarely a bluebird's notes they are sweet by reminding us of the spring.[3] Well, it is so with other tricks of memory. Of the most romantic fact the memory is more romantic; and this power of sinking the pain of any experience and of recalling the saddest with tranquillity, and even with a wise pleasure, is familiar. The memory is as the affection. Sampson Reed says, "The true way to store the memory is to develop the affections." A *souvenir* is a token of love. *Remember me* means, Do not cease to love me.

We remember those things which we love and those things which we hate. The memory of all men is robust on the subject of a debt due to them, or of an insult inflicted on them. "They can remember," as Johnson said, "who kicked them last."

Every artist is alive on the subject of his art. The Persians say, "A real singer will never forget the song he has once learned." Michael Angelo, after having once seen a work of any other artist, would remember it so perfectly that if it pleased him to make use of any portion thereof, he could do so, but in such a manner that none could perceive it.

We remember what we understand, and we understand best what we like; for this doubles our power of attention, and makes it our own. Captain John Brown, of Ossawatomie, said he had in Ohio three thousand sheep on his farm, and could tell a strange sheep in his flock as soon as he saw its face. One of my neighbors, a grazier, told me that he should know again every cow, ox, or steer that he ever saw. Abel Lawton knew every horse that went up and down through Concord to the towns in the county. And in higher examples each man's memory is in the line of his action.

Nature trains us on to see illusions and prodigies with no more wonder than our toast and omelet at breakfast. Talk of memory and cite me these fine examples of Grotius and Daguesseau, and I think how awful is that power and what privilege and tyranny it must confer. Then I come to a bright school-girl who remembers all she hears, carries thousands of nursery rhymes and all the poetry in all the readers, hymn-books, and pictorial ballads in her mind; and 't is a mere drug. She carries it so carelessly, it seems like the profusion of hair on the shock heads of all the village boys and village dogs; it grows like grass. 'T is a bushel-basket memory of all unchosen knowledge, heaped together in a huge hamper, without method, yet securely held, and ready to come at call; so that an old scholar, who knows what to do with a memory, is full of wonder and pity that this magical force should be squandered on such frippery.

He is a skilful doctor who can give me a recipe for the cure of a bad memory. And yet we have some hints from experience on this subject. And first, *health*. It is found that we remember best when the head is clear, when we are thoroughly awake. When the body is in a quiescent state in the absence of the passions, in the moderation of food, it yields itself a willing medium to the intellect. For the true river Lethe is the body of man, with its belly and uproar of appetite and mountains of indigestion and bad humors and quality of darkness. And for this reason, and observing some mysterious continuity of mental operation during sleep or when our will is suspended, 't is an old rule of scholars, that which Fuller records, "'T is best knocking in the nail over-night and clinching it next morning." Only I should give extension to this rule and say, Yes, drive the nail this week and clinch it the next, and drive it this year and clinch it the next.

But Fate also is an artist. We forget also according to beautiful laws. Thoreau said, "Of what significance are the things you can forget. A little thought is sexton to all the world."

We must be severe with ourselves, and what we wish to keep, we must once thoroughly possess. Then the thing seen will no longer be what it was, a mere sensuous object before the eye or ear, but a reminder of its law, a possession for the intellect. Then we relieve ourselves of all task in the matter, we put the *onus* of being remembered on the object, instead of on our will. We shall do as we do with all our studies, prize the fact or the name of the person by that predominance it takes in our mind after near acquaintance. I have several times forgotten the name of Flamsteed, never that of Newton; and can drop easily many poets out of the Elizabethan chronology, but not Shakspeare.

We forget rapidly what should be forgotten. The *universal* sense of fables and anecdotes is marked by our tendency to forget name and date and geography. "How in the right are children," said Margaret Fuller, "to forget name and date and place."

You cannot overstate our debt to the past, but has the present no claim? This past memory is the baggage, but where is the troop? The divine gift is not the old but the new. The divine is the instant life that receives and uses, the life that can well bury the old in the omnipotency with which it makes all things new.[1]

The acceleration of mental process is equivalent to the lengthening of life. If a great many thoughts pass through your mind, you will believe a long time has elapsed, many hours or days. In dreams a rush of many thoughts, or seeming experiences, of spending hours and going through a great variety of actions and companies, and when we start up and look at the watch, instead of a long night we are surprised to find it was a short nap. The opium-eater says, "I sometimes seemed to have lived seventy or a hundred years in one night." You know what is told of the experience of some persons who have been recovered from drowning. They relate that their whole life's history seemed to pass before them in review. They remembered in a moment all that they ever did.

If we occupy ourselves long on this wonderful faculty, and see the natural helps of it in the mind, and the way in which new knowledge calls upon old knowledge — new giving undreamed-of value to old; every relation and suggestion, so that what one had painfully held by strained attention and recapitulation now falls into place and is clamped and locked by inevitable connection as a planet in its orbit (every other orb, or the law or system of which it is a part, being a perpetual reminder), — we cannot fail to draw thence a sublime hint that thus there must be an endless increase in the power of memory only through its use; that there must be a proportion between the power of memory and the amount of knowables; and since the Universe opens to us, the reach of the memory must be as large.

With every broader generalization which the mind makes, with every deeper insight, its retrospect is also wider. With every new insight into the duty or fact of to-day we come into new possession of the past.

When we live by principles instead of traditions, by obedience to the law of the mind instead of by passion, the Great Mind will enter into us, not as now in fragments and detached thoughts, but the light of to-day will shine backward and forward.

Memory is a presumption of a possession of the future. Now we are halves, we see the past but not the future, but in that day will the hemisphere complete itself and foresight be as perfect as aftersight.

II

THE CELEBRATION OF INTELLECT

AN ADDRESS DELIVERED BEFORE THE STUDENTS OF TUFTS COLLEGE, JULY 10, 1861

By Sybarites beguiled,
He shall no task decline;
Merlin's mighty line
Extremes of nature reconciled —
Bereaved a tyrant of his will,
And made the lion mild.

I KNOW the mighty bards,
I listen when they sing,
And now I know
The secrêt store
Which these explore
When they with torch of genius pierce
The tenfold clouds that cover
The riches of the universe
From God's adoring lover.
And if to me it is not given
To fetch one ingot hence
Of the unfading gold of Heaven
His merchants may dispense,
Yet well I know the royal mine
And know the sparkle of its ore,
Know Heaven's truths from lies that shine —
Explored, they teach us to explore.

THE CELEBRATION OF INTELLECT

I CANNOT consent to wander from the duties of this day into the fracas of politics. The brute noise of cannon has, I know, a most poetic echo in these days when it is an instrument of freedom and the primal sentiments of humanity. Yet it is but representative and a far-off means and servant: but here in the college we are in the presence of the constituency and the principle itself. Here is, or should be, the majesty of reason and the creative cause; and it were a compounding of all gradation and reverence to suffer the flash of swords and the boyish strife of passion and the feebleness of military strength to intrude on this sanctity and omnipotence of Intellectual Law. Against the heroism of soldiers I set the heroism of scholars, which consists in ignoring the other. You shall not put up in your Academy the statue of Cæsar or Pompey, of Nelson or Wellington, of Washington or Napoleon, of Garibaldi, but of Archimedes, of Milton, of Newton. Archimedes disdained to apply himself to the useful arts, only to the liberal or the causal arts. Hiero the king reproached him with his barren studies. Like Thales, he was willing to show him that he was quite able in rude matters, if he could condescend to them, and he conducted the defence of Syracuse against the Romans. Then he returned to his geometry; and when the Roman soldier, at the sack of Syracuse, broke into his study, the philosopher could not rise from his chair and his diagram, and took his death without resistance. Michael Angelo gave himself to art, despising all meaner pursuits. When the war came to his own city, he lent his genius, and defended Florence as long as he was obeyed. Milton congratulates the Parliament that, whilst London is besieged and blocked, the Thames infested, inroads and excursions round, and battle oft rumored to be marching up to her walls and suburb trenches, — yet then are the people, or the greater part, more than at other times wholly taken up with the study of highest and most important matters to be reformed, — they reasoning, reading, inventing, discoursing, even to a rarity and admiration, things not before discoursed or written, and the fact argues a just confidence in the grandeur and self-subsistency of the cause of religious liberty which made all material war an impertinence.

For either science and literature is a hypocrisy, or it is not. If it be, then resign your charter to the Legislature, turn your college into barracks and warehouses, and divert the funds of your founders into the stock of a rope-walk or a candle-factory, a tan-yard or some other undoubted conveniency for the surrounding population. But if the intellectual interest be, as I hold, no hypocrisy, but the only reality, — then it behooves us to enthrone it, obey it; and give it possession of us and ours; to give, among other possessions, the college into its hand casting down every idol, every pretender, every hoary lie, every dignified blunder that has crept into its administration.

At this season, the colleges keep their anniversaries, and in this country where education is a primary interest, every family has a representative in their halls, a son, a brother, or one of our own kindred is there for his training. But even if we had no son or friend therein, yet the college is part of the community, and it is there for us, is training our teachers, civilizers and inspirers. It is essentially the most radiating and public of agencies, like, but better than, the light-house, or the alarm-bell, or the sentinel who fires a signal-cannon, or the telegraph which speeds the local news over the land. Besides, it deals with a force which it cannot monopolize or confine; cannot give to those who come to it and refuse to those outside. I have no doubt of the force, and for me the only question is, whether the force is inside.

This power which it deals is dear to all. If the colleges were better, if they had any monopoly of it, nay, if they really had it, had the power of imparting valuable thought, creative principles, truths which become powers, thoughts which become talents, — if they could cause that a mind not profound should become profound, — we should all rush to their gates: instead of contriving inducements to draw students, you would need to set police at the gates to keep order in the in-rushing multitude.

These are giddy times, and, you say, the college will be deserted. No, never was it so much needed. But I say, those were the giddy times which went before these, and the new times are the times of arraignment, times of trial and times of judgment. 'T is because the college was false to its trust, because the scholars did not learn and teach, because they were traders and left their altars and libraries and worship of truth and played the sycophant to presidents and generals and members of Congress, and gave degrees and literary and social honors to those whom they ought to have rebuked and exposed, incurring the contempt of those whom they ought to have put in fear; then the college is suicidal; ceases to be a school; power oozes out of it just as fast as truth does; and instead of overawing the strong, and upholding the good, it is a hospital for decayed tutors.

This Integrity over all partial knowledge and skill, homage to truth — how rare! Few men wish to know how the thing really stands, what is the law of it without reference to persons. Other men are victims of their means — sanity consists in not being subdued by your means.

Two men cannot converse together on any topic without presently finding where each stands in moral judgment; and each learns whether the other's view commands, or is commanded by, his own. I presently know whether my companion has more candor or less, more hope for men or less, whether his sense of duty is more or less severe and his generosity larger than mine; whether he stands for ideal justice, or for a timorous expediency.

Society is always idolatrous and exaggerates the merits of those who work to vulgar ends.

But genius may be known by its probity. Never was pure valor — and almost I might say, never pure ability — shown in a bad cause. For ambition makes insane.[1]

Society is always taken by surprise at any new example of common sense and of simple justice, as at a wonderful discovery. Thus, at Mr. Rarey's mode of taming a horse by kindness, or Garibaldi's emancipation of Italy for Italy's sake; at the introduction of gentleness into insane asylums, and of cleanliness and comfort into penitentiaries. A farmer wished to buy an ox. The seller told him how well he had treated the animal. "But," said my farmer, "I asked the ox, and the ox showed me by marks that could not lie that he had been abused." We affect to slight England and Englishmen. But I note that we had a vast self-esteem on the subject of Bunker Hill, Yorktown and New Orleans. We should not think it much to beat Indians or Mexicans, — but to beat English! The English newspapers and some writers of reputation disparage America. Meantime I note that the British people are emigrating hither by thousands, which is a very sincere, and apt to be a very seriously considered expression of opinion. The emigration into America of British, as well as of Continental people, is the eulogy of America by the most competent and sincere arbiters. The hater of property and of government takes care to have his warranty-deed recorded; and the book written against fame and learning has the author's name on the title-page. . . .

Gentlemen, I too am an American, and value practical talent. I love results and hate abortions. I delight in people who can do things. I value talent, — perhaps no man more. I value dearly the poet who knows his art so well that, when his voice vibrates, it fills the hearer with sympathetic song, just as a powerful note of an organ sets all tuned strings in its neighborhood in accordant vibration, — the novelist with his romance, the architect with his palace, the composer with his score. I wish you to be eloquent, to grasp the bolt and to hurl it home to the mark. I wish to see that Mirabeau who knows how to seize the heart-strings of the people and drive their hands and feet in the way he wishes them to go, to fill them with himself, to enchant men so that their will and purpose is in abeyance and they serve him with a million hands just as implicitly as his own members obey him. But I value it more when it is legitimate, when the talent is in true order, subject to genius, subject to the total and native sentiment of the man, and therefore in harmony with the public sentiment of mankind. Such is the patriotism of Demosthenes, of Patrick Henry and of what was best in Cicero and Burke; not an ingenious special pleading, not the making a plausible case, but strong by the strength of the facts themselves. Then the orator is still one of the audience, persuaded by the same reasons which persuade them; not a ventriloquist, not a juggler, not a wire-puller paid to manage the lobby and caucus.[1]

In Demosthenes is this realism of genius. He wins his cause honestly. His doctrine is self-reliance. "If it please you to note it, my counsels to you are not such whereby I should grow great among you, and you become little among the Grecians; but they be of that nature as is sometimes not good for me to give, but are always good for you to follow."

You, gentlemen, are selected out of the great multitude of your mates, out of those who begun life with you, set apart through some strong persuasion of your own, or of your friends, that you were capable of the high privilege of thought. Need enough there is of such a band of priests of intellect and knowledge; and great is the office, and well deserving and well paying the last sacrifices and the highest ability. But I wish this were a needless task, to urge upon you scholars the claims of thought and learning. The order of the world educates with care the senses and the understanding.[1] . . .

Men are as they think. A certain quantity of power belongs to a certain quantity of truth. And the man who knows any truth not yet discerned by other men is master of all other men, so far as that truth and its wide relations are concerned. Do you suppose that the thunderbolt falls short? Do you imagine that a lie will nourish and work like a truth? . . . The whole battle is fought in a few heads. A little finer order, a larger angle of vision, commands centuries of facts and millions of thoughtless people. It reverses all rank; "he who discriminates is the father of his father." . . .

And yet the world is not saved. With this divine oracle, we somehow do not get instructed. Here are still perverse millions full of passion, crime and blood. Here are bad governors and bad subjects. Nay, in the class called intellectual the men are no better than the uninstructed. They use their wit and learning in the service of the Devil. There are bad books and false teachers and corrupt judges; and in the institutions of education a want of faith in their own cause. Nay, it happens often that the well-bred and refined, the inhabitants of cities, dwelling amidst colleges, churches, and scientific museums, lectures, poets, libraries, newspapers, and other aids supposed intellectual are more vicious and malignant than the rude country people, and need to have their corrupt voting and violence corrected by the cleaner and wiser suffrages of poor farmers. The poet does not believe in his poetry. Men are ashamed of their intellect.[1] . . .

Instinct is the name for the potential wit, that feeling which each has that what is done by any man or agent is done by the same wit as his. He looks at all men as his representatives, and is glad to see that his wit can work at that problem as it ought to be done, and better than he could do it; whether it be to build, engineer, carve, paint, sing, heal, or compute, or play chess, or ride, or swim. We feel as if one man wrote all the books, painted, built, in dark ages, and we are sure we can do more than ever was done. It was the same mind that built the world.

The Understanding is the name we give to

the low, limitary power working to short ends, to daily life in house and street. This is the power which the world of men adopt and educate. He is the calculator, he is the merchant, the politician, the worker in the useful; he works by shifts, by compromise, by statute, by bribes. All his activities are to short, personal ends, and he is apt to be a talker, a boaster, a busy-body.

Will you let me say to you what I think is the organic law of learning? It is to observe the order, to keep down the talent, to enthrone the Instinct. There must be the perpetual rallying and self-recovery; each talent links itself so fast with self-love and with petty advantage that it loses sight of its obedience, which is beautiful, and sets up for itself, and makes confusion. Falsehood begins as soon as it disobeys, it works for show, and for the shop, and the greater it grows, the more is the mischief and misleading, so that presently all is wrong, talent is mistaken for genius, dogma or system for truth.[1] . . .

Now the idea of a college is an assembly of such men, obedient each to this pure light, and drawing from it illumination to that science or art to which his constitution and affections draw him. And the very highest advantage which a young man of good mind can meet is to find such a teacher. No books, no aids, laboratory, apparatus, prizes, can compare with this. Here is sympathy; here is an order that corresponds to that in his own mind, and in all sound minds, and the hope and impulse imparted. And education is what it should be, a delightful unfolding of the faculties in right order.

I could heartily wish it were otherwise, but there is a certain shyness of genius, of free thought, of a master of art in colleges, which is as old as the rejection of Molière by the French Academy, of Bentley by the pedants of his time, and only the other day, of Arago; in Oxford, the recent rejection of Max Müller. . . . If the truth must be told, thought is as rare in colleges as in cities. The necessity of a mechanical system is not to be denied. Young men must be classed and employed, not according to the secret needs of each mind but by some available plan that will give weekly and annual results; and a little violence must be done to private genius to accomplish this. Then genius is always its own law, and must be a little impatient and rebellious to this rule, so that, of necessity, a certain hostility and jealousy of genius grows up in the masters of routine, and unless, by rare good fortune, the professor has a generous sympathy with genius and takes care to interpose a certain relief and cherishing and reverence for the wild poet and dawning philosopher he has detected in his classes, that will happen which has happened so often, that the best scholar, he for whom colleges exist, finds himself a stranger and an orphan therein. 'T is precisely analogous to what befalls in religious societies. In the romance Spiridion a few years ago, we had what it seems was a piece of accurate autobiography, the story of a young saint who comes into a convent for her education, and not falling into the system and the little parties in the convent, but inspired with an enthusiasm which finds nothing there to feed it, it turns out in a few days that every hand is against this young votary. Piety in a convent accuses every one, from the novice to the abbess. What right have you to be better than your neighbor? Piety comes to be regarded as a spy and a rebel. . . . And how often we have had repeated the trials of the young man who made no figure at college because his own methods were new and extraordinary, and who only prospered at last because he forsook theirs and took his own.[1]

It is true that the University and the Church, which should be counterbalancing institutions to our great material institutions of trade and of territorial power, do not express the sentiment of the popular politics and the popular optimism, whatever it be. Harvard College has no voice in Harvard College, but State Street votes it down on every ballot. Everything will be permitted there which goes to adorn Boston Whiggism, — is it geology, astronomy, poetry, antiquities, art, rhetoric. But that which it exists for, to be a fountain of novelties out of heaven, a Delphos uttering warning and ravishing oracles to lift and lead mankind, — *that* it shall not be permitted to do or to think of.[1] On the contrary, every generosity of thought is suspect and gets a bad name. And all the youth come out decrepit citizens;[2] not a prophet, not a poet, not a *daimon*, but is gagged and stifled or driven away. All that is sought in the instruction is drill; tutors, not inspirers.

I conceive that a college should have no mean ambition, but should aim at a reverent discipline and invitation of the soul, that here, if nowhere else in the world, genius should find its home; here Imagination should be greeted with the problems in which it delights; the noblest tasks to the Muse proposed and the most cordial and honoring rewards; here the highest duties be urged, and enthusiasm for liberty and wisdom should breed enthusiasm and form heroes for the state. The College should hold the profound thought, and the Church the great heart to which the nation should turn, and these two should be counterbalancing to the bad politics and selfish trade. But there is but one institution, and not three. The Church and the College now take their tone from the City, and do not dictate their own. You all well know the downward tendency in literature, the facility with which men renounce their youthful aims and say, the labor is too severe, the prize too high for me; and they accept the employments of the market. . . .

Ah, gentlemen, it's only a dream of mine, and perhaps never will be true, — but I thought a college was a place not to train talents, not to train attorneys, and those who say what they please, but to adorn Genius, which only speaks truth, and after the way which truth uses, namely, Beauty; a college was to teach you geometry, or the lovely laws of space and figure; chemistry, botany, zoölogy, the streaming of thought into form, and the precipitation of atoms which Nature is.

This, then, is the theory of Education, the happy meeting of the young soul, filled with the desire, with the living teacher who has already made the passage from the centre forth, step by step, along the intellectual roads to the theory and practice of special science. Now if there be genius in the scholar, that is, a delicate sensibility to the laws of the world, and the power to express them again in some new form, he is made to find his own way. He will greet joyfully the wise teacher, but colleges and teachers are no wise essential to him; he will find teachers everywhere.

I would have you rely on Nature ever, — wise, omnific, thousand-handed Nature, equal to each emergency, which can do very well without colleges, and, if the Latin, Greek, Algebra or Art were in the parents, it will be in the children, without being pasted on.

If your college and your literature are not felt, it is because the truth is not in them. When you say the times, the persons are prosaic, where is the feudal, or the Saracenic, or Egyptian architecture? where the romantic manners? where the Romish or the Calvinistic religion, which made a kind of poetry in the air for Milton, or Byron, or Belzoni? but to us it is barren, — you expose your atheism. Is a railroad, or a shoe-factory, or an insurance office, bank or bakery outside of the system and connection of things, or further from God than a sheep-pasture or a clam-bank? Is chemistry suspended? Do not the electricities and the imponderable influences play with all their magic undulations? Do not gravity and polarity keep their unerring watch on a needle and thread, on a cobbler's lapstone or a switchman's turntable as on the moon's orbit? Only bring a deep observer, and he will make light of the new shop or old cathedral — all one to him — or new circumstances that afflict you. He will find the circumstances not altered; as deep a cloud of mystery on the cause, as dazzling a glory on the invincible law. Is it so important whether a man wears a shoe-buckle or ties his shoe-lappet with a string? . . . Bring the insight, and he will find as many beauties and heroes and astounding strokes of genius close by him as Shakspeare or Æschylus or Dante beheld. It was in a beggarly heath farm, it was in a mean country inn that Burns found his fancy so sprightly. You find the times and places mean. My friend, stretch a few threads over a common Æolian harp, and put it in your window, and listen to what it says of times and the heart of Nature. I do not think that you will believe that the miracle of Nature is less, the chemical power worn out. Watch the breaking morning, the enchantments of the sunset.

If I had young men to reach, I should say to them, Keep the intellect sacred. Revere it. Give all to it. Its oracles countervail all. Attention is its acceptable prayer. Sit low and wait long; and know that, next to being its minister, like Aristotle, and perhaps better than that, is the profound reception and sympathy, without ambition which secularizes and trades it. Go sit with the Hermit in you, who knows more than you do. You will find life enhanced, and doors opened to grander entertainments. Yet all comes easily that he does, as snow and vapor, heat, wind and light. Power costs nothing to the powerful. I should say to them, Do what you can do. He that draws on his own talent cannot be overshadowed or supplanted.[1] . . . Homage to truth discriminates good and evil. Power never departs from it.

Our colleges may differ much in the scale of requirements, and the examination for admission and the examination for degrees and honors may be lax in this college and severe in that, and you may find facilities, translations, syllabuses and tutors here or there to coach you through, but 't is very certain that an examination is yonder before us and an examining committee that cannot be escaped nor deceived, that every scholar is to be put fairly on his own powers and must hear the questions proposed, and answer them by himself, and receive honor or dishonor according to the fidelity shown. For the men and women of your time, the circle of your friends and employers, your conditions, the invisible world, are the interrogators.[1] . . .

When the great painter was told by a dauber, "I have painted five pictures whilst you have made one," he replied, "*Pingo in æternitatem.*" "Study for eternity smiled on me," says Van Helmont. And it were a good rule to read some lines at least every day that shall not be of the day's occasion or task, but of study for eternity.

I have detained you too long; but it is the privilege of the moral sentiment to be every moment new and commanding, and old men cannot see the powers of society, the institutions, the laws under which they have lived, passing, or soon to pass, into the hands of you and your contemporaries, without an earnest wish that you have caught sight of your high calling, your vast possibilities and inspiring duties.

III

COUNTRY LIFE

THE air is wise, the wind thinks well,
And all through which it blows;
If plant or brain, if egg or shell,
Or bird or biped knows.

What boots it here of Thebes or Rome,
Or lands of Eastern day?
In forests I am still at home
And there I cannot stray.

KEEN ears can catch a syllable,
As if one spoke to another,
In the hemlocks tall, untamable,
And what the whispering grasses smother.

Wonderful verse of the gods,
Of one import, of varied tone;
They chant the bliss of their abodes
To man imprisoned in his own.

COUNTRY LIFE

THE Teutonic race have been marked in all ages by a trait which has received the name of Earth-hunger, a love of possessing land. It is not less visible in that branch of the family which inhabits America. Nor is it confined to farmers, speculators, and filibusters, or conquerors. The land, the care of land, seems to be the calling of the people of this new country, of those, at least, who have not some decided bias, driving them to a particular craft, as a born sailor or machinist. The capable and generous, let them spend their talent on the land. Plant it, adorn it, study it, it will develop in the cultivator the talent it requires.

The avarice of real estate native to us all covers instincts of great generosity, namely, all that is called the love of Nature, comprising the largest use and the whole beauty of a farm or landed estate. Travel and walking have this apology, that Nature has impressed on savage men periodical or secular impulses to emigrate, as upon lemmings, rats and birds. The Indians go in summer to the coast, for fishing; in winter, to the woods. The nomads wander over vast territory, to find their pasture. Other impulses hold us to other habits. As the increasing population finds new values in the ground, the nomad life is given up for settled homes. But the necessity of exercise and the nomadic instinct are always stirring the wish to travel, and in the spring and summer, it commonly gets the victory. Chaucer notes of the month of April,

> "Than longen folk to goon on pilgrymages,
> And palmers for to seken straunge strondes,
> To ferne halwes, couthe in sondry londes."[1]

And, in the country, Nature is always inviting to the compromise of walking as soon as we are released from severe labor. Linnæus, early in life, read a discourse at the University of Upsala on the necessity of travelling in one's own country, based on the conviction that Nature was inexhaustibly rich, and that in every district were swamps, or beaches, or rocks, or mountains, which were now nuisances, but, if explored, and turned to account, were capable of yielding immense benefit. At Upsala, therefore, he instituted what were called *herborizations:* he summoned his class to go with him on excursions on foot into the country, to collect plants and insects, birds and eggs. These parties started at seven in the morning, and stayed

The Emerson House about 1852

out till nine in the evening; the Professor was generally attended by two hundred students, and, when they returned, they marched through the streets of Upsala in a festive procession, with flowers in their hats, to the music of drums and trumpets, and with loads of natural productions collected on the way.

Let me remind you what this walker found in his walks. He went into Oland, and found that the farms on the shore were perpetually encroached on by the sea, and ruined by blowing sand. He discovered that the *arundo arenaris*, or beach-grass, had long firm roots, and he taught them to plant it for the protection of their shores. In Tornea, he found the people suffering every spring from the loss of their cattle, which died by some frightful distemper, to the number of fifty or a hundred in a year. Linnæus walked out to examine the meadow into which they were first turned out to grass, and found it a bog, where the water-hemlock grew in abundance, and had evidently been cropped plentifully by the animals in feeding. He found the plant also dried in their cut hay. He showed them that the whole evil might be prevented by employing a woman for a month to eradicate the noxious plants. When the shipyards were infested with rot, Linnæus was sent to provide some remedy. He studied the insects that infested the timber, and found that they laid their eggs in the logs within certain days in April and he directed that during ten days, at that time of the year, the logs should be immersed under the water, which being done, the timber was found to be uninjured.

He found that the gout, to which he was subject, was cured by wood-strawberries. He had other remedies. When Kalm returned from America, Linnæus was laid up with severe gout. But the joy in his return, and the curiosity to see his plants, restored him instantly, and he found an old friend as good as the treatment by wood-strawberries. He learned the secret of making pearls in the river-pearl mussel. He found out that a terrible distemper which sometimes proves fatal in the north of Europe, was occasioned by an animalcule, which he called *Furia infernalis*, which falls from the air on the face, or hand, or other uncovered part, burrows into it, multiplies and kills the sufferer. By timely attention, it is easily extracted.

He examined eight thousand plants; and examined fishes, insects, birds, quadrupeds; and distributed the animal, vegetable and mineral kingdoms. And if, instead of running about in the hotels and theatres of Europe, we would, manlike, see what grows, or might grow, in Massachusetts, stock its gardens, drain its bogs, plant its miles and miles of barren waste with oak and pine, and following what is usually the natural suggestion of these pursuits, ponder the moral secrets which, in her solitudes, Nature has to whisper to us, we were better patriots and happier men.

We have the finest climate in the world, for this purpose, in Massachusetts. If we have coarse days, and dogdays, and white days, and days that are like ice-blinks, we have also yellow days, and crystal days, — days which are neither hot nor cold, but the perfection of temperature. New England has a good climate, — yet, in choosing a farm, we like a southern exposure, whilst Massachusetts, it must be owned, is on the northern slope, towards the Arctic circle, and the Pole. Our climate is a series of surprises, and among our many prognostics of the weather, the only trustworthy one that I know is that, when it is warm, it is a sign that it is going to be cold. The climate needs, therefore, to be corrected by a little anthracite coal, — a little coal indoors, during much of the year, and thick coats and shoes must be recommended to walkers. I own I prefer the solar to the polar climates. "I have no enthusiasm for Nature," said a French writer, "which the slightest chill will not instantly destroy."

But we cannot overpraise the comfort and the beauty of the climate in the best days of the year. In summer, we have for weeks a sky of Calcutta, yielding the richest growth, maturing plants which require strongest sunshine, and scores of days when the heat is so rich, and yet so tempered, that it is delicious to live.

The importance to the intellect of exposing the body and brain to the fine mineral and imponderable agents of the air makes the chief interest in the subject. "So exquisite is the structure of the cortical glands," said the old physiologist Malpighi, "that when the atmosphere is ever so slightly vitiated or altered, the brain is the first part to sympathize and to undergo a change of state." We are very sensible of this, when, in midsummer, we go to the seashore, or to mountains, or when, after much confinement to the house, we go abroad into the landscape, with any leisure to attend to its soothing and expanding influences. The power of the air was the first explanation offered by the early philosophers of the mutual understanding that men have. "The air," said Anaximenes, "is the soul, and the essence of life. By breathing it, we become intelligent, and, because we breathe the same air, understand one another." Plutarch thought it contained the knowledge of the future. "If it be true that souls are naturally endowed with the faculty of prediction, and that the chief cause that excites that faculty is a certain temperature of air and winds," etc. Even Lord Bacon said, "The Stars inject their imagination or influence into the air."

The air that we breathe is an exhalation of all the solid material of the globe. . . . It is the last finish of the work of the Creator. We might say, the Rock of Ages dissolves himself into the mineral air to build up this mystic constitution of man's mind and body.

Walking has the best value as gymnastics for the mind. "You shall never break down in a speech," said Sydney Smith, "on the day on which you have walked twelve miles." In the English universities, the reading men are daily performing their punctual training in the boat-clubs, or a long gallop of many miles in the saddle, or, taking their famed "constitutionals," walks of eight and ten miles. "Walking," said

Rousseau, "has something which animates and vivifies my ideas." And Plato said of exercise that "it would almost cure a guilty conscience." "For the living out of doors, and simple fare, and gymnastic exercises, and the morals of companions, produce the greatest effect on the way of virtue and of vice."

Few men know how to take a walk. The qualifications of a professor are endurance, plain clothes, old shoes, an eye for Nature, good humor, vast curiosity, good speech, good silence and nothing too much. If a man tells me that he has an intense love of Nature, I know, of course, that he has none. Good observers have the manners of trees and animals, their patient good sense, and if they add words, 't is only when words are better than silence. But a loud singer, or a story-teller, or a vain talker profanes the river and the forest, and is nothing like so good company as a dog.

There is also an effect on beauty. . . . De Quincey said, "I have seen Wordsworth's eyes sometimes affected powerfully in this respect. His eyes are not under any circumstances bright, lustrous or piercing, but, after a long day's toil in walking, I have seen them assume an appearance the most solemn and spiritual that it is possible for the human eye to wear. The light which resides in them is at no time a superficial light, but, under favorable accidents, it is a light which seems to come from depths below all depths; in fact, it is more truly entitled to be held 'the light that never was on land or sea,' a light radiating from some far spiritual world, than any that can be named." But De Quincey prefixes to this description of Wordsworth a little piece of advice, which I wonder has not attracted more attention. "The depth and subtlety of the eyes varies exceedingly with the state of the stomach, and, if young ladies were aware of the magical transformations which can be wrought in the depth and sweetness of the eye by a few weeks' exercise, I fancy we should see their habits in this point altered greatly for the better."

For walking, you must have a broken country. In Illinois, everybody rides. There is no good walk in that state. The reason is, a square yard of it is as good as a hundred miles. You can distinguish from the cows a horse feeding, at the distance of five miles, with the naked eye. Hence, you have the monotony of Holland, and when you step out of the door can see all that you will have seen when you come home. In

Massachusetts, our land is agreeably broken, and is permeable like a park, and not like some towns in the more broken country of New Hampshire, built on three or four hills having each one side at forty-five degrees and the other side perpendicular: so that if you go a mile, you have only the choice whether you will climb the hill on your way out or on your way back. The more reason we have to be content with the felicity of our slopes in Massachusetts, undulating, rocky, broken and surprising, but without this alpine inconveniency. Twenty years ago in Northern Wisconsin the pinery was composed of trees so big, and so many of them, that it was impossible to walk in the country, and the traveller had nothing for it but to wade in the streams. One more inconveniency, I remember, they showed me in Illinois, that, in the bottom lands, the grass was fourteen feet high. We may well enumerate what compensating advantages we have over that country, for 't is a commonplace, which I have frequently heard spoken in Illinois, that it was a manifest leading of the Divine Providence that the New England states should have been first settled, before the Western country was known, or they would never have been settled at all.

The privilege of the countryman is the culture of the land, the laying out of grounds and gardens, the orchard and the forest. The Rosaceous tribe in botany, including the apple, pear, peach and cherry, are coeval with man. The apple is our national fruit. In October, the country is covered with its ornamental harvests. The American sun paints itself in these glowing balls amid the green leaves, the social fruit, in which Nature has deposited every possible flavor; whole zones and climates she has concentrated into apples. I am afraid you do not understand values. Look over the fence at the farmer who stands there. He makes every cloud in the sky, and every beam of the sun, serve him. His trees are full of brandy. He saves every drop of sap, as if it were wine. A few years ago those trees were whipsticks. Now, every one of them is worth a hundred dollars. Observe their form; not a branch nor a twig is to spare. They look as if they were arms and fingers, holding out to you balls of fire and gold. One tree yields the rent of an acre of land. Yonder pear has every property which should belong to a tree. It is hardy, and almost immortal. It accepts every species of nourishment, and yet could live, like an Arab, on air and water.

It grows like the ash Ygdrasil. It seems to me much that I have brought a skilful chemist into my ground, and keep him there overnight, all day, all summer, for an art he has, out of all kinds of refuse rubbish to manufacture Virgaliens, Bergamots, and Seckels, in a manner which no confectioner can approach, and his method of working is no less beautiful than the result.

In old towns there are always certain paradises known to the pedestrian, old and deserted farms, where the neglected orchard has been left to itself, and whilst some of its trees decay, the hardier have held their own. I know a whole district, Estabrook Farm, made up of wide, straggling orchards, where the apple-trees strive with and hold their ground against the native forest-trees: the apple growing with profusion that mocks the pains taken by careful cockneys, who come out into the country, plant young trees and watch them dwindling. Here, no hedges are wanted; the wide distance from any population is fence enough: the fence is a mile wide. Here are varieties of apple not found in Downing or Loudon. The "Tartaric" variety, and "Cow-apple," and the "Bite-me-if-you-dare," the "Beware-of-this." Apples of a kind which I remember in boyhood, each containing a barrel of wind and half a barrel of cider. But there was a contest between the old orchard and the invading forest-trees, for the possession of the ground, of the whites against the Pequots, and if the handsome savages win, we shall not be losers.[1] . . .

According to the common estimate of farmers, the wood-lot yields its gentle rent of six per cent., without any care or thought, when the owner sleeps or travels, and it is subject to no enemy but fire. Evelyn quotes Lord Caernarvon's saying, "Wood is an excrescence of the earth provided by God for the payment of debts."

When Nero advertised for a new luxury, a walk in the woods should have been offered. 'T is one of the secrets for dodging old age. For Nature makes a like impression on age as on youth. Then I recommend it to people who are growing old, against their will. A man in that predicament, if he stands before a mirror, or among young people, is made quite too sensible of the fact; but the forest awakes in him the same feeling it did when he was a boy, and he may draw a moral from the fact that 't is the old trees that have all the beauty and grandeur. I admire the taste which makes the avenue to a house, were the house never so small, through a wood; besides the beauty, it has a positive effect on manners, as it disposes the mind of the inhabitant and of his guests to the deference due to each. Some English reformers[1] thought the cattle made all this wide space necessary between house and house, and that, if there were no cows to pasture, less land would suffice. But a cow does not need so much land as the owner's eyes require between him and his neighbor.

Our Aryan progenitors in Asia celebrated the winds as the conveying Maruts, "traversers of places difficult of access. Stable is their birth-place in the sky, but they are agitators of heaven and earth, who shake all around like the top of a tree. Because they drive the clouds, they have harnessed the spotted deer to their chariot; they are coming with weapons, war-cries and decorations. I hear the cracking of the whips in their hands. I praise their sportive resistless strength. They are the generators of speech. They drive before them in their course the long, vast, uninjurable, rain-retaining cloud. Wherever they pass, they fill the way with clamor. Every one hears their noise. The lightning roars like a parent cow that bellows for its calf, and the rain is set free by the Maruts. Maruts, as you have vigor, invigorate mankind! Aswins (Waters), long-armed, good-looking Aswins! bearers of wealth, guides of men, harness your car! Ambrosia is in you, in you are medicinal herbs." The Hindoos called fire Agni, born in the woods, bearer of oblations, smoke-bannered and light-shedding, lord of red coursers; the guest of man; protector of people in villages; the sacrificer visible to all, thousand-eyed, all-beholding, of graceful form and whose countenance is turned on all sides.

What uses that we know belong to the forest, and what countless uses that we know not! How an Indian helps himself with fibre of milkweed, or withe-bush, or wild hemp, or root of spruce, black or white, for strings; making his bow of hickory, birch, or even a fir-bough, at a pinch; hemlock bark for his roof, hair-moss or fern for his bed. He goes to a white birch-tree, and can fit his leg with a seamless boot, or a hat for his head. He can draw sugar from the maple, food and antidotes from a hundred plants. He knows his way in a straight line from watercourse to watercourse, and you cannot lose him in the woods. He consults by way of natural compass, when he travels: (1) large pine-trees, which bear more numerous branches on their southern side; (2) ant-hills, which have grass on their south and whortleberries on the north; (3) aspens, whose bark is rough on the north and smooth on the south side. All his knowledge is for use, and it only appears in use, whilst white men have theirs also for talking purposes.

I am a very indifferent botanist, but I admire that perennial four-petalled flower, which has one gray petal, one green, one red, and one white. I think sometimes how many days could Methuselah go out and find something new! In January the new snow has changed the woods so that he does not know them; has built sudden cathedrals in a night. In the familiar forest he finds Norway and Russia in the masses of overloading snow which break all that they cannot bend. In March, the thaw, and the sounding of the south wind, and the splendor of the icicles. On the pond there is a cannonade of a hundred guns, but it is not in honor of election of any President. He went forth again after the rain; in the cold swamp, the buds are swollen, the *ictodes* prepares its flower, and the mallows and mouse-ear. The mallows the Greeks held sacred as giving the first sign of the sympathy of the earth with the celestial influences. The next day the Hylas were piping in every pool, and a new activity among the hardy birds, the premature arrival of the bluebird, and the first northward flight of the geese, who cannot keep their joy to themselves, and fly low over the farms. In May, the bursting of the leaf, — the oak and maple are red with the same colors on the new leaf which they will resume in autumn when it is ripe. In June, the miracle works faster,[1]

> Painting with white and red the moors
> To draw the nations out of doors.

Man feels the blood of thousands in his body, and pumps the sap of all this forest through his arteries; the loquacity of all birds in the morning; and the immensity of life seems to make the world deep and wide. In August, when the corn is grown to be a resort and protection to woodcocks and small birds, and when the leaves whisper to each other in the wind, we observe already that the leaf is sere, that a change has passed on the landscape. The world has nothing to offer more rich or entertaining than the days which October always brings us, when, after the first frosts, a steady shower of gold falls in the strong south wind from the chestnuts, maples and hickories: all the trees are wind-harps, filling the air with music; and all men become poets, and walk to the measure of rhymes they make or remember. The dullest churl begins to quaver. The forest in its coat of many colors reflects its varied splendor through the softest haze. The witch-hazel blooms to mark the last hour arrived, and that Nature has played out her summer score. The dry leaves rustle so loud, as we go rummaging through them, that we can hear nothing else. The leaf in our dry climate gets fully ripe, and, like the fruit when fully ripe, acquires fine color, whilst, in Europe, the damper climate decomposes it too soon.

But the pleasures of garden, orchard and wood must be alternated. We know the healing effect on the sick of change of air, — the action of new scenery on the mind is not less fruitful. We must remember that man is a natural nomad, and his old propensities will stir at midsummer, and send him, like an Indian, to the sea. The influence of the ocean on the love of liberty, I have mentioned elsewhere. Its power on the mind in sharpening the perceptions has made the sea the famous educator of our race.

The history of the world, — what is it but the doings about the shores of the Mediterranean Sea, and the Atlantic? . . .

What freedom of grace has the sea with all this might! . . . The freedom makes the observer feel as a slave. Our expression is so thin and cramped! Can we not learn here a generous eloquence? This was the lesson our starving poverty wanted. . . . At Niagara, I have noticed, that, as quick as I got out of the wetting of the Fall, all the grandeur changed into beauty. You cannot keep it grand, 't is so quickly beautiful; and the sea gave me the same experience. 'T is great and formidable, when you lie down in it, among the rocks. But, on the shore, at one rod's distance, 't is changed into a beauty as of gems and clouds. Shores in sight of each other in a warm climate make boat-builders; and whenever we find a coast broken up into bays and harbors, we find an instant effect on the intellect and industry of the people.[1]

On the seashore the play of the Atlantic with the coast! What wealth is here! Every wave is a fortune; one thinks of Etzlers and great projectors who will yet turn all this waste strength to account: what strength and fecundity, from the sea-monsters, hugest of animals, to the primary forms of which it is the immense cradle, and the phosphorescent infusories ; — it is one vast rolling bed of life, and every sparkle is a fish. What freedom and grace with all this might ! The seeing so excellent a spectacle is a certificate to the mind that all imaginable good shall yet be realized. The sea is the chemist that dissolves the mountain and the rock ; pulverizes old continents, and builds new ; — forever redistributing the solid matter of the globe ; and performs an analogous office in perpetual new transplanting of the races of men over the surface, the Exodus of nations. We may well yield us for a time to its lessons. But the nomad instinct, as I said, persists to drive us to fresh fields and pastures new. Indeed the variety of our moods has an answering variety in the face of the world, and the sea drives us back to the hills.

Dr. Johnson said of the Scotch mountains, " The appearance is that of matter incapable of form or usefulness, dismissed by Nature from her care." The poor blear-eyed doctor was no poet. Like Charles Lamb, he loved the sweet security of streets. It was said of him that " he preferred the Strand to the Garden of the Hesperides." But this is not the experience of imaginative men, nor of men with good eyes and susceptible organizations. "For my own part," says Linnæus, "I have enjoyed good health, except a slight languor, but as soon as I got upon the Norway Alps I seemed to have acquired a new existence. I felt as if relieved from a heavy burden. Then, spending a few days in the low country of Norway, though without committing the least excess, my languor or heaviness returned. When I again ascended the Alps, I revived as before." And he celebrates the health and performance of the Laps as the best walkers of Europe. "Not without admiration, I have watched my two Lap companions, in my journey to Finmark, one, my conductor, the other, my interpreter. For after having climbed the Alps, whilst I, a youth of twenty-five years, was spent and tired, like one dead, and lay down as if to die in those ends of the world, these two old men, one fifty, one seventy years, running and playing like boys, felt none of the inconveniences of the road, although they were both loaded heavily enough with my baggage. I saw men more than seventy years old put their heel on their own neck, without any exertion. O holy simplicity of diet, past all praise!" [1]

But beside their sanitary and gymnastic benefit, mountains are silent poets, and a view from a cliff over a wide country undoes a good deal of prose, and reinstates us wronged men in our rights. The imagination is touched. There is some pinch and narrowness to us, and we are glad to see the world, and what amplitudes it has, of meadow, stream, upland, forest and sea, which yet are lanes and crevices to the great space in which the world shines like a cockboat in the sea.

Of the finer influences, I shall say that they are not less positive, if they are indescribable. If you wish to know the shortcomings of poetry and language, try to reproduce the October picture to a city company, — and see what you make of it.[1] There is somewhat finer in the sky than we have senses to appreciate. It escapes us, and yet is only just beyond our reach. Is all this beauty to perish? Where is he who is to save the perfect moment, and cause that this beauty shall not be lost? Where is he who has senses fine enough to catch the inspiration of the landscape? The mountains in the horizon acquaint us with finer relations to our friends than any we sustain.

I think 't is the best of humanity that goes

out to walk. In happy hours, I think all affairs may be wisely postponed for this walking. Can you hear what the morning says to you, and believe *that?* Can you bring home the summits of Wachusett, Greylock, and the New Hampshire hills? the Savin groves of Middlesex? the sedgy ripples of the old Colony ponds? the sunny shores of your own bay, and the low Indian hills of Rhode Island? the savageness of pine-woods? Can you bottle the efflux of a June noon, and bring home the tops of Uncanoonuc? The landscape is vast, complete, alive. We step about, dibble and dot, and attempt in poor linear ways to hobble after those angelic radiations. The gulf between our seeing and our doing is a symbol of that between faith and experience. . . .

Our schools and colleges strangely neglect the general education of the eye. Every acquisition we make in the science of beauty is so sweet that I think it is cheaply paid for by what accompanies it, of course, the prating and affectation of connoisseurship. The facts disclosed by Winkelmann, Goethe, Bell, Greenough, Ruskin, Garbett, Penrose, are joyful possessions, which we cannot spare, and which we rank close beside the disclosures of natural history. There are probably many in this audience who have tried the experiment on a hilltop, and many who have not, of bending the head so as to look at the landscape with your eyes upside down. What new softness in the picture! It changes the landscape from November into June. My companion and I remarked from the hilltop the prevailing sobriety of color, and agreed that russet was the hue of Massachusetts, but on trying this experiment of inverting the view he said, "There is the Campagna! and Italy is Massachusetts upside down." The effect is remarkable, and perhaps is not explained. An ingenious friend of mine suggested that it was because the upper part of the eye is little used, and therefore retains more susceptibility than the lower, and returns more delicate impressions.

Dr. Johnson said, "Few men know how to take a walk," and it is certain that Dr. Johnson was not one of the few. It is a fine art, requiring rare gifts and much experience. No man is suddenly a good walker. Many men begin with good resolution, but they do not hold out, and I have sometimes thought it would be well to publish an Art of Walking, with Easy Lessons for Beginners. These we call apprentices. Those who persist from year to year, and obtain at last an intimacy with the country, and know all the good points within ten miles, with the seasons for visiting each, know the lakes, the hills, where grapes, berries and nuts, where the rare plants are; where the best botanic ground; and where the noblest landscapes are seen, and are learning all the time; — these we call professors. . . .

Nature kills egotism and conceit; deals strictly with us; and gives sanity; so that it was the practice of the Orientals, especially of the Persians, to let insane persons wander at their own will out of the towns, into the desert, and, if they liked, to associate with wild animals. In their belief, wild beasts, especially gazelles, collect around an insane person, and live with him on a friendly footing. The patient found something curative in that intercourse, by which he was quieted, and sometimes restored. But there are more insane persons than are called so, or are under treatment in hospitals. The crowd in the cities, at the hotels, theatres, card-tables, the speculators who rush for investment, at ten per cent., twenty per cent., cent. per cent., are all more or less mad, — I need not say it now in the crash of bankruptcy; — these point the moral, and persuade us to seek in the fields the health of the mind.

I hold all these opinions on the power of the air to be substantially true. The poet affirms them; the religious man, going abroad, affirms them; the patriot on his mountains or his prairie affirms them; the contemplative man affirms them.

Nature tells everything once. Our microscopes are not necessary. She shows every fact in large bodies somewhere. On the seashore, she reveals to the eye, by the sea-line, the true curve of the globe. It does not need a barometer to find the height of mountains. The line of snow is surer than the barometer: and the zones of plants, the savin, the pine, vernal gentian, plum, linnæa and the various lichens and grapes are all thermometers which cannot be deceived, and will not lie. They are instruments by the best maker. The earthquake is the first chemist, goldsmith and brazier: he wrought to purpose in craters, and we borrowed the hint in crucibles. When I look at natural structures, as at a tree, or the teeth of a shark, or the anatomy of an elephant, I know that I am seeing an architecture and carpentry which has no sham, is solid and conscientious, which perfectly answers its end, and has nothing to spare. But in all works of human art there is deduction to be made for blunder and falsehood. Therefore Goethe, whose whole life was a study of the theory of art, said no man should be admitted to his Republic, who was not versed in Natural History.

The college is not so wise as the mechanic's shop, nor the quarter-deck as the forecastle. Witness the insatiable interest of the white man about the Indian, the trapper, the hunter and sailor. In a water-party in which many scholars joined, I noted that the skipper of the boat was much the best companion. The scholars made puns. The skipper saw instructive facts on every side, and there was no trifle to him. How startling are the hints of wit we detect in the horse and dog, and in the wild animals! By what compass the geese steer, and the herring migrate, we would so gladly know. What the dog knows, and how he knows it, piques us more than all we heard from the chair of metaphysics.

Is it not an eminent convenience to have in your town a person who knows where arnica grows, or sassafras, or pennyroyal, and the mints, or the scented goldenrod, or punk for slow-match; or the slippery-elm, or wild cherries, or wild pears? Where are the best hazelnuts, chestnuts and shagbarks? Where the white grapes? Where are the choice apple-trees? And what are the poisons? Where is the Norway pine, where the beech, where the epigæa, the linnæa, or sanguinaria, or orchis pulcherrima, or sundew, or laurus benzoin, or pink huckleberry? where trout, woodcocks, wild bees, pigeons, where the bittern (stake-driver) can be seen and heard, where the Wilson's plover can be seen and heard?

The true naturalist can go wherever woods or waters go; almost where a squirrel or a bee can go, he can; and no man is asked for leave. Sometimes the farmer withstands him in crossing his lots, but 't is to no purpose; the farmer could as well hope to prevent the sparrows or tortoises. It was their land before it was his, and their title was precedent. My naturalist knew what was on their land, and the farmers did not, and sometimes he brought them ostentatiously gifts of flowers, fruits or rare shrubs they would gladly have paid a price for, and did not tell them that he gathered them in their own woods. Moreover the very time at which he used their land and water (for his boat glided like a trout everywhere unseen) was in hours when they were sound asleep. Before the sun was up, he went up and down to survey his possessions, and passed onward and left them, before the second owners, as he called them, were awake.

If we should now say a few words on the advantages that belong to the conversation with Nature, I might set them so high as to make it a religious duty. 'T is the greatest use and the greatest beauty. 'T is the lesson we were put hither to learn. What truth, and what elegance belong to every fact of Nature, we know. And the study of them awakens the like truth and elegance in the student. One thing, the lover of Nature cannot tell the best thing he knows.[1] . . .

What alone possesses interest for us is the *naturel* of each man. This is that which is the saliency, or principle of levity, the antagonist of matter and gravitation, and as good as they. This is forever a surprise, and engaging, and lovely. We can't be satiated with knowing it, and about it. It is related to the purest of the world, to gravity, the growth of grass, and the angles of crystals. Nature speaks to the imagination; first, through her grand style, — the hint of immense force and unity which her works convey; second, because her visible productions and changes are the nouns of language, and our only means of uttering the invisible thought. Every new perception of the method and beauty of Nature gives a new shock of surprise and pleasure; and always for this double reason: first, because they are so excellent in their primary fact, as frost, or cloud, or fire, or animal; and, secondly, because we have an instinct that they express a grander law.

'T is not easy to say again what Nature says to us. But it is the best part of poetry, merely to name natural objects well. A farmer's boy finds delight in reading the verses under the Zodiacal vignettes in the Almanac. What is the merit of Thomson's Seasons but copying a few of the pictures out of this vast book into words, without a hint of what they signify, and the best passages of great poets, old and new, are often simple enumerations of some features of landscape. And as man is the object of Nature, what we study in Nature is man. 'T is true, that man only interests us. We are not to be imposed upon by the apparatus and the nomenclature of the physiologist. Agassiz studies year after year fishes and fossil anatomy of saurian, and lizard, and pterodactyl. But whatever he says, we know very well what he means. He pretends to be only busy with the foldings of the yolk of a turtle's egg. I can see very well what he is driving at; he means men and women. He talks about lizard, shell-fish and squid, he means John and Mary, Thomas and Ann. For Nature is only a mirror in which man is reflected colossally. Swedenborg or Behman or Plato tried to decipher this hieroglyphic, and explain what rock, what sand, what wood, what fire signified in regard to man.

They may have been right or wrong in any particulars of their interpretation, but it is only our ineradicable belief that the world answers to man, and part to part, that gives any interest in the subject. If we believed that Nature was foreign and unrelated, — some rock on which souls wandering in the Universe were shipwrecked, we should think all exploration of it frivolous waste of time. No, it is bone of our bone, flesh of our flesh, made of us, as we of it. External Nature is only a half. The geology, the astronomy, the anatomy, are all good, but 't is all a half, and — enlarge it by astronomy never so far — remains a half. It requires a will as perfectly organized, — requires man. Astronomy is a cold, desert science, with all its pompous figures, — depends a little too much on the glass-grinder, too little on the mind. 'T is of no use to show us more planets and systems. We know already what matter is, and more or less of it does not signify. He can dispose in his thought of more worlds, just as readily as of few, or one. It is his relation to one, to the first, that imports. Nay, I will say, of the two facts, the world and man, man is by much the larger half.

I know that the imagination . . . is a coy, capricious power, and does not impart its secret to inquisitive persons. Sometimes a parlor in which fine persons are found, with beauty, culture and sensibility, answers our purpose still better. Striking the electric chain with which we are darkly bound, but that again is Nature, and there we have again the charm which landscape gives us, in a finer form; but the persons must have had the influence of Nature, must know her simple, cheap pleasures, must know what Pindar means when he says that "water is the best of things," and have manners that speak of reality and great elements, or we shall know no Olympus.

Matter, how immensely soever enlarged by the telescope, remains the lesser half. The very science by which it is shown to you argues the force of man. Nature is vast and strong, but as soon as man knows himself as its interpreter, knows that Nature and he are from one source, and that he, when humble and obedient, is nearer to the source, then all things fly into place, then is there a rider to the horse, an organized will, then Nature has a lord.

IV

CONCORD WALKS

Not many men see beauty in the fogs
Of close, low pine-woods in a river town;
Yet unto me not morn's magnificence
Nor the red rainbow of a summer's eve,
Nor Rome, nor joyful Paris, nor the halls
Of rich men, blazing hospitable light,
Nor wit, nor eloquence, — no, nor even the song
Of any woman that is now alive, —
Hath such a soul, such divine influence,
Such resurrection of the happy past,
As is to me when I behold the morn
Ope in such low, moist roadside, and beneath
Peep the blue violets out of the black loam.

THERE is no rood has not a star above it;
The cordial quality of pear or plum
Ascends as gladly in a single tree
As in broad orchards resonant with bees;
And every atom poises for itself,
And for the whole. The gentle deities
Showed me the love of color and of sounds,
The innumerable tenements of beauty,
The miracle of generative force,
Far-reaching concords of astronomy
Felt in the plants and in the punctual birds;
Better, the linkèd purpose of the whole.

CONCORD WALKS

WHEN I bought my farm, I did not know what a bargain I had in the bluebirds, bobolinks and thrushes, which were not charged in the bill; as little did I guess what sublime mornings and sunsets I was buying — what reaches of landscape, and what fields and lanes for a tramp. Neither did I fully consider what an indescribable luxury is our Indian river, the Musketaquid, — which runs parallel with the village street and to which every house on that long street has a back door, which leads down through the garden to the river-bank, when a skiff, or a dory, gives you, all summer, access to enchantments, new every day, and all winter, to miles of ice for the skater.[1] And because our river is no Hudson or Mississippi I have a problem long waiting for an engineer, — this, — to what height I must build a tower in my garden that shall show me the Atlantic Ocean from its top — the ocean twenty miles away.

Still less did I know what good and true neighbors I was buying, men of thought and virtue, some of them now known the country through for their learning, or subtlety, or active or patriotic power, but whom I had the pleasure of knowing long before the Country did; and of other men not known widely but known at home, farmers, — not doctors of laws but doctors of land, skilled in turning a swamp or a sand-bank into a fruitful field, and, when witch-grass and nettles grew, causing a forest of apple-trees or miles of corn and rye to thrive.

I did not know what groups of interesting school-boys and fair school-girls were to greet me in the highway, and to take hold of one's heart at the School Exhibitions.[1]

"Little joy has he who has no garden," said Saadi. Montaigne took much pains to be made a citizen of Rome; and our people are vain, when abroad, of having the freedom of foreign cities presented to them in a gold box. I much prefer to have the freedom of a garden presented me. When I go into a good garden, I think, if it were mine, I should never go out of it. It requires some geometry in the head to lay it out rightly, and there are many who can enjoy to one that can create it.

Linnæus, who was professor of the Royal Garden at Upsala, took the occasion of a public ceremony to say, "I thank God, who has ordered my fate, that I live in this time, and so ordered it that I live happier than the king of the Persians. You know, fathers and citizens, that I live entirely in the Academy Garden; here is my Vale of Tempe, say rather my Elysium. I possess here all that I desire of the spoils of the East and the West, and, unless I am very much mistaken, what is far more beautiful than Babylonian robes, or vases of the Chinese. Here I learn what I teach. Here I admire the wisdom of the Supreme Artist, disclosing Himself by proofs of every kind, and show them to others." Our people are learning that lesson year by year. As you know, nothing in Europe is more elaborately luxurious than the costly gardens, — as the Boboli at Florence, the Borghese, the Orsini at Rome, the Villa d' Este at Tivoli; with their greenhouses, conservatories, palm-houses, fish-ponds, sculptured summer-houses and grottoes; but without going into the proud niceties of an European garden, there is happiness all the year round to be had from the square fruit-gardens which we plant in the front or rear of every farmhouse. In the orchard, we build monuments to Van Mons[1] annually.

The place where a thoughtful man in the country feels the joy of eminent domain is in his wood-lot. If he suffer from accident or low spirits, his spirits rise when he enters it. He can spend the entire day therein, with hatchet or pruning-shears, making paths, without remorse of wasting time. He can fancy that the birds know him and trust him, and even the trees make little speeches or hint them. Then he remembers that Allah in his allotment of life "does not count the time which the Arab spends in the chase." [1]

If you can add to the garden a noble luxury, let it be an arboretum. In the arboretum you should have things which are of a solitary excellence, and which people who read of them are hungry to see. Thus plant the *Sequoia Gigantea*, give it room, and set it on its way of ten or fifteen centuries. Bayard Taylor planted two — one died, but I saw the other looking well. Plant the Banian, the Sandal-tree, the Lotus, the Upas, Ebony, Century Aloes, the Soma of the Vedas — *Asclepias Viminalis*, the Mandrake and Papyrus, Dittany, Asphodel, Nepenthe, Hæmony, Moly, Spikenard, Amomum.[2] Make a calendar — your own — of the year, that you may never miss your favorites in their month. As Linnæus made a dial of plants, so shall you of all the objects that guide your walks.

Learn to know the conspicuous planets in

the heavens, and the chief constellations. Thus do not forget the 14th of November, when the meteors come, and on some years drop into your house-yard like sky-rockets. And 't is worth remarking, what a man may go through life without knowing, that a common spy-glass, which you carry in your pocket, will show the satellites of Jupiter, and turned on the Pleiades, or Seven Stars, in which most eyes can only count six, — will show many more, — a telescope in an observatory will show two hundred. How many poems have been written, or, at least attempted, on the lost Pleiad! for though that pretty constellation is called for thousands of years the "Seven Stars," most eyes can only count six.

Horses and carriages are costly toys, but the word park always charms me. I could not find it in my heart to chide the citizen who should ruin himself to buy a patch of heavy oak timber. I admire the taste which makes the avenue to the house — were the house never so small — through a wood; — as it disposes the mind of the inhabitant and of his guest to the deference due to each.

There are two companions, with one or other

of whom 't is desirable to go out on a tramp. One is an artist, that is, who has an eye for beauty. If you use a good and skilful companion, you shall see through his eyes; and, if they be of great discernment, you will learn wonderful secrets. In walking with Allston, you shall see what was never before shown to the eye of man. And as the perception of beauty always exhilarates, if one is so happy as to find the company of a true artist, he is a perpetual holiday and benefactor, and ought only to be used like an oriflamme or a garland, for feasts and May-days, and parliaments of wit and love.

The other is a naturalist, for the reason that it is much better to learn the elements of geology, of botany, of ornithology and astronomy by word of mouth from a companion than dully from a book. There is so much, too, which a book cannot teach which an old friend can. A man should carry Nature in his head — should know the hour of the day or night, and the time of the year, by the sun and stars; should know the solstice and the equinox, the quarter of the moon and the daily tides.[1]

This is my ideal of the powers of wealth. Find out what lake or sea Agassiz wishes to explore, and offer to carry him there, and he will make you acquainted with all its fishes: or what district Dr. Gray has not found the plants of, — carry him; or when Dr. Wyman wishes to find new anatomic structures or fossil remains; or when Dr. Charles Jackson or Mr. Hall would study chemistry or mines; and you secure the best company and the best teaching with every advantage.[1]

But the countryman, as I said, has more than he paid for; the landscape is his. I am sorry to say the farmers seldom walk for pleasure. It is a fine art; — there are degrees of proficiency, and we distinguish the professors of that science from the apprentices. But there is a manifest increase in the taste for it. 'T is the consolation of mortal men. It is an old saying that physicians or naturalists are the only professional men who continue their tasks out of study-hours; and the naturalist has no barren places, no winter, and no night, pursuing his researches in the sea, in the ground, in barren moors, in the night even, because the woods exhibit a whole new world of nocturnal animals; in winter, because, remove the snow a little, a multitude of plants live and grow, and there is a perpetual push of buds, so that it is impossible to say when vegetation begins. I think no pursuit has more breath of immortality in it.

I admire in trees the creation of property so clean of tears, or crime, or even care. No lesson of chemistry is more impressive to me than this chemical fact that "Nineteen twentieths of the timber are drawn from the atmosphere." We knew the root was sucking juices from the ground. But the top of the tree is also a tap-root thrust into the public pocket of the atmosphere. This is a highwayman, to be sure. And I am always glad to remember that in proportion to the foliation is the addition of wood. Then they grow, when you wake and when you sleep, at nobody's cost, and for everybody's comfort. Lord Abercorn, when some one praised the rapid growth of his trees, replied, "Sir, they have nothing else to do!"

That uncorrupted behavior which we admire in the animals, and in young children, belongs also to the farmer, the hunter, the sailor, the man who lives in the presence of Nature. Cities force the growth and make him talkative and entertaining, but they make him artificial. What alone possesses interest for us is the *naturel* of each, that which is constitutional to him only. This is forever a surprise, and engaging, and lovely; we can't be satiated with knowing it, and about it, and this is that which the conversation with Nature goes to cherish and to guard.

The man finds himself expressed in Nature. Yet when he sees this annual reappearance of beautiful forms, the lovely carpet, the lovely tapestry of June, he may well ask himself the special meaning of the hieroglyphic, as well as the sense and scope of the whole — and there is a general sense which the best knowledge of the particular alphabet leaves unexplained.[1]

him only. This is forever a surprise, and engaging and novel; we can't be satisfied with knowing it, and about it, and this is that which our conversation with Nature gives to cherish and to gratify.

The man finds himself expressed in Nature. Yet when he sees the annual reappearance of beautiful forms, the lovely carpet, the lovely tapestry of June, he may well ask himself the special meaning of the hieroglyphic as well as the sense and scope of the whole — and there is a general sense which the best knowledge of the particular alphabet leaves unexplained.

V

BOSTON

"WE are citizens of two fair cities," said the Genoese gentle man to a Florentine artist, "and if I were not a Genoese, I should wish to be Florentine." "And I," replied the artist, "if I were not Florentine —" "You would wish to be Genoese," said the other. "No," replied the artist, "I should wish to be Florentine."

THE rocky nook with hilltops three
Looked eastward from the farms,
And twice each day the flowing sea
Took Boston in its arms.

. . . .

The sea returning day by day
Restores the world-wide mart;
So let each dweller on the Bay
Fold Boston in his heart.

Let the blood of her hundred thousands
Throb in each manly vein,
And the wits of all her wisest
Make sunshine in her brain.

And each shall care for other,
And each to each shall bend,
To the poor a noble brother,
To the good an equal friend.

A blessing through the ages thus
Shield all thy roofs and towers!
GOD WITH THE FATHERS, SO WITH US,
Thou darling town of ours!

BOSTON

THE old physiologists said, "There is in the air a hidden food of life;" and they watched the effect of different climates. They believed the air of mountains and the seashore a potent predisposer to rebellion. The air was a good republican, and it was remarked that insulary people are versatile and addicted to change, both in religious and secular affairs.

The air that we breathe is an exhalation of all the solid material globe. An aërial fluid streams all day, all night, from every flower and leaf, from every water and soil, from every rock ledge; and from every stratum a different aroma and air according to its quality. According to quality and according to temperature, it must have effect on manners.[1]

There is the climate of the Sahara: a climate where the sunbeams are vertical; where is day after day, sunstroke after sunstroke, with a frosty shadow between. "There are countries," said Howell, "where the heaven is a fiery furnace or a blowing bellows, or a dropping sponge, most parts of the year." Such is the assimilating force of the Indian climate that Sir Erskine Perry says "the usage and opinion of the Hindoos so invades men of all castes and colors who deal with them that all take a Hindoo tint. Parsee, Mongol, Afghan, Israelite, Christian, have all passed under this influence and exchanged a good part of their patrimony of ideas for the notions, manner of seeing and habitual tone of Indian society." He compares it to the geologic phenomenon which the black soil of the Dhakkan offers, — the property, namely, of assimilating to itself every foreign substance introduced into its bosom.

How can we not believe in influences of climate and air, when, as true philosophers, we must believe that chemical atoms also have their spiritual cause why they are thus and not other; that carbon, oxygen, alum and iron, each has its origin in spiritual nature?

Even at this day men are to be found superstitious enough to believe that to certain spots on the surface of the planet special powers attach, and an exalted influence on the genius of man. And it appears as if some localities of the earth, through wholesome springs, or as the *habitat* of rare plants and minerals, or through ravishing beauties of Nature, were preferred before others. There is great testimony of

Boston Common in 1810

discriminating persons to the effect that Rome is endowed with the enchanting property of inspiring a longing in men there to live and there to die.[1]

Who lives one year in Boston ranges through all the climates of the globe. And if the character of the people has a larger range and greater versatility, causing them to exhibit equal dexterity in what are elsewhere reckoned incompatible works, perhaps they may thank their climate of extremes, which at one season gives them the splendor of the equator and a touch of Syria, and then runs down to a cold which approaches the temperature of the celestial spaces.

It is not a country of luxury or of pictures; of snows rather, of east winds and changing skies; visited by icebergs, which, floating by, nip with their cool breath our blossoms. Not a luxurious climate, — but wisdom is not found with those who dwell at their ease. Give me a climate where people think well and construct well, — I will spend six months there, and you may have all the rest of my years.

What Vasari said, three hundred years ago, of the republican city of Florence might be said of Boston; "that the desire for glory and honor is powerfully generated by the air of that place, in the men of every profession; whereby all who possess talent are impelled to struggle that they may not remain in the same grade with those whom they perceive to be only men like themselves, even though they may acknowledge such indeed to be masters; but all labor by every means to be foremost."

We find no less stimulus in our native air; not less ambition in our blood, which Puritanism has not sufficiently chastised; and at least an equal freedom in our laws and customs, with as many and as tempting rewards to toil; with so many philanthropies, humanities, charities, soliciting us to be great and good.

New England is a sort of Scotland. 'T is hard to say why. Climate is much; then, old accumulation of the means, — books, schools, colleges, literary society; — as New Bedford is not nearer to the whales than New London or Portland, yet they have all the equipments for a whaler ready, and they hug an oil-cask like a brother.

I do not know that Charles River or Merrimac water is more clarifying to the brain than the Savannah or Alabama rivers, yet the men that drink it get up earlier, and some of the morning light lasts through the day. I notice that they who drink for some little time of the Potomac water lose their relish for the water of the Charles River, of the Merrimac and the Connecticut, — even of the Hudson. I think the Potomac water is a little acrid, and should be corrected by copious infusions of these provincial streams.

Of great cities you cannot compute the influences. In New York, in Montreal, New Orleans and the farthest colonies, — in Guiana, in Guadaloupe, — a middle-aged gentleman is just embarking with all his property to fulfil the dream of his life and spend his old age in Paris; so that a fortune falls into the massive wealth of that city every day in the year. Astronomers come because there they can find apparatus and companions. Chemist, geologist, artist, musician, dancer, because there only are grandees and their patronage, appreciators and patrons. Demand and supply run into every invisible and unnamed province of whim and passion.

Each great city gathers these values and delights for mankind, and comes to be the brag of its age and population. The Greeks thought him unhappy who died without seeing the statue of Jove at Olympia. With still more reason, they praised Athens, the "Violet City." It was said of Rome in its proudest days, looking at the vast radiation of the privilege of Roman citizenship through the then-known world,— "the extent of the city and of the world is the same" (*spatium et urbis et orbis idem*). London now for a thousand years has been in an affirmative or energizing mood; has not stopped growing. Linnæus, like a naturalist, esteeming the globe a big egg, called London the *punctum saliens* in the yolk of the world.

This town of Boston has a history. It is not an accident, not a windmill, or a railroad station, or cross-roads tavern, or an army-barracks grown up by time and luck to a place of wealth; but a seat of humanity, of men of principle, obeying a sentiment and marching loyally whither that should lead them; so that its annals are great historical lines, inextricably national; part of the history of political liberty. I do not speak with any fondness, but the language of coldest history, when I say that Boston commands attention as the town which was appointed in the destiny of nations to lead the civilization of North America.

A capital fact distinguishing this colony from

all other colonies was that the persons composing it consented to come on the one condition that the charter should be transferred from the company in England to themselves; and so they brought the government with them.

On the 3d of November, 1620, King James incorporated forty of his subjects, Sir F. Gorges and others, the council established at Plymouth in the county of Devon for the planting, ruling, ordering and governing of New England in America. The territory — conferred on the patentees in absolute property, with unlimited jurisdiction, the sole power of legislation, the appointment of all officers and all forms of government — extended from the 40th to the 48th degree of north latitude, and in length from the Atlantic to the Pacific.

John Smith writes (1624): "Of all the four parts of the world that I have yet seen not inhabited, could I but have means to transplant a colony, I would rather live here than anywhere; and if it did not maintain itself, were we but once indifferently well fitted, let us starve. Here are many isles planted with corn, groves, mulberries, salvage gardens and good harbours. The seacoast, as you pass, shows you all along large cornfields and great troops of well-proportioned people." Massachusetts in particular, he calls "the paradise of these parts," notices its high mountain, and its river, "which doth pierce many days' journey into the entrails of that country." Morton arrived in 1622, in June, beheld the country, and "the more he looked, the more he liked it."

In sixty-eight years after the foundation of Boston, Dr. Mather writes of it, "The town hath indeed three elder Sisters in this colony, but it hath wonderfully outgrown them all, and her mother, Old Boston in England, also; yea, within a few years after the first settlement it grew to be the metropolis of the whole English America."

How easy it is, after the city is built, to see where it ought to stand. In our beautiful bay, with its broad and deep waters covered with sails from every port; with its islands hospitably shining in the sun; with its waters bounded and marked by lighthouses, buoys and sea-marks; every foot sounded and charted; with its shores trending steadily from the two arms which the capes of Massachusetts stretch out to sea, down to the bottom of the bay where the city domes and spires sparkle through the haze, — a good boatman can easily find his way for the first time to the State House, and wonder that Governor Carver had not better eyes than to stop on the Plymouth Sands.

But it took ten years to find this out. The colony of 1620 had landed at Plymouth. It was December, and the ground was covered with snow. Snow and moonlight make all places alike; and the weariness of the sea, the shrinking from cold weather and the pangs of hunger must justify them.

But the next colony planted itself at Salem, and the next at Weymouth; another at Medford; before these men, instead of jumping on to the first land that offered, wisely judged that the best point for a city was at the bottom of a deep and islanded bay, where a copious river entered it, and where a bold shore was bounded by a country of rich undulating woodland.

The planters of Massachusetts do not appear to have been hardy men, rather, comfortable citizens, not at all accustomed to the rough task of discoverers; and they exaggerated their troubles. Bears and wolves were many; but early, they believed there were lions; Monadnoc was burned over to kill them. John Smith was stung near to death by the most poisonous tail of a fish, called a sting-ray. In the journey of Rev. Peter Bulkeley and his company through the forest from Boston to Concord they fainted from the powerful odor of the sweetfern in the sun; — like what befell, still earlier, Biorn and Thorfinn, Northmen, in their expedition to the same coast; who ate so many grapes from the wild vines that they were reeling drunk. The lions have never appeared since, — nor before. Their crops suffered from pigeons and mice. Nature has never again indulged in these exasperations. It seems to have been the last outrage ever committed by the sting-rays or by the sweetfern or by the fox-grapes; they have been of peaceable behavior ever since.

Any geologist or engineer is accustomed to face more serious dangers than any enumerated, excepting the hostile Indians. But the awe was real and overpowering in the superstition with which every new object was magnified. The superstition which hung over the new ocean had not yet been scattered; the powers of the savage were not known; the dangers of the wilderness were unexplored; and in that time terrors of witchcraft, terrors of evil spirits, and a certain degree of terror still clouded the idea of God in the mind of the purest.

The divine will descends into the barbarous mind in some strange disguise; its pure truth not to be guessed from the rude vizard under which it goes masquerading. The common eye cannot tell what the bird will be, from the egg, nor the pure truth from the grotesque tenet which sheathes it. But by some secret tie it holds the poor savage to it, and he goes muttering his rude ritual or mythology, which yet conceals some grand commandment; as courage, veracity, honesty, or chastity and generosity.

So these Englishmen, with the Middle Ages still obscuring their reason, were filled with Christian thought. They had a culture of their own. They read Milton, Thomas à Kempis, Bunyan and Flavel with religious awe and delight, not for entertainment. They were precisely the idealists of England; the most religious in a religious era. An old lady who remembered these pious people said of them that "they had to hold on hard to the huckleberry bushes to hinder themselves from being translated."

In our own age we are learning to look, as on chivalry, at the sweetness of that ancient piety which makes the genius of St. Bernard, Latimer,

Scougal, Jeremy Taylor, Herbert and Leighton. Who can read the fiery ejaculations of Saint Augustine, a man of as clear a sight as almost any other; of Thomas à Kempis, of Milton, of Bunyan even, without feeling how rich and expansive a culture — not so much a culture as a higher life — they owed to the promptings of this sentiment; without contrasting their immortal heat with the cold complexion of our recent wits? Who can read the pious diaries of the Englishmen in the time of the Commonwealth and later, without a sigh that we write no diaries to-day? Who shall restore to us the odoriferous Sabbaths which made the earth and the humble roof a sanctity?

This spirit, of course, involved that of Stoicism, as, in its turn, Stoicism did this. Yet how much more attractive and true that this piety should be the central trait and the stern virtues follow than that Stoicism should face the gods and put Jove on his defence. That piety is a refutation of every skeptical doubt. These men are a bridge to us between the unparalleled piety of the Hebrew epoch and our own. These ancient men, like great gardens with great banks of flowers, send out their perfumed breath across the great tracts of time. How needful is David,

Paul, Leighton, Fénelon, to our devotion. Of these writers, of this spirit which deified them, I will say with Confucius, "If in the morning I hear of the right way, and in the evening die, I can be happy."

I trace to this deep religious sentiment and to its culture great and salutary results to the people of New England; first, namely, the culture of the intellect, which has always been found in the Calvinistic Church. The colony was planted in 1620; in 1638 Harvard College was founded. The General Court of Massachusetts, in 1647, "To the end that learning may not be buried in the graves of the forefathers, ordered, that every township, after the Lord has increased them to the number of fifty householders, shall appoint one to teach all children to write and read; and where any town shall increase to the number of a hundred families, they shall set up a Grammar School, the Masters thereof being able to instruct youth so far as they may be fitted for the University."

Many and rich are the fruits of that simple statute. The universality of an elementary education in New England is her praise and her power in the whole world. To the schools succeeds the village lyceum, — now very general throughout all the country towns of New England, — where every week through the winter, lectures are read and debates sustained which prove a college for the young rustic. Hence it happens that the young farmers and mechanics, who work all summer in the field or shop, in the winter often go into a neighboring town to teach the district school arithmetic and grammar. As you know, too, New England supplies annually a large detachment of preachers and schoolmasters and private tutors to the interior of the South and West.

New England lies in the cold and hostile latitude, which by shutting men up in houses and tight and heated rooms a large part of the year, and then again shutting up the body in flannel and leather, defrauds the human being in some degree of his relations to external nature; takes from the muscles their suppleness, from the skin its exposure to the air; and the New Englander, like every other Northerner, lacks that beauty and grace which the habit of living much in the air, and the activity of the limbs not in labor but in graceful exercise, tend to produce in climates nearer to the sun. Then the necessity, which always presses the Northerner, of providing fuel and many clothes and tight houses and much food against the long winter, makes him anxiously frugal, and generates in him that spirit of detail which is not grand and enlarging, but goes rather to pinch the features and degrade the character.

As an antidote to the spirit of commerce and of economy, the religious spirit — always enlarging, firing man, prompting the pursuit of the vast, the beautiful, the unattainable — was especially necessary to the culture of New England. In the midst of her laborious and economical and rude and awkward population, where is little elegance and no facility; with great accuracy in details, little spirit of society or knowledge of the world, you shall not unfrequently meet that refinement which no education and no habit of society can bestow; which makes the elegance of wealth look stupid, and unites itself by natural affinity to the highest minds of the world; nourishes itself on Plato and Dante, Michael Angelo and Milton; on whatever is pure and sublime in art, — and I may say, gave a hospitality in this country to the spirit of Coleridge and Wordsworth, and to the music of Beethoven, before yet their genius had found a hearty welcome in Great Britain.[1]

I do not look to find in England better manners than the best manners here. We can show native examples, and I may almost say (travellers as we are) natives who never crossed the sea, who possess all the elements of noble behavior.

It is the property of the religious sentiment to be the most refining of all influences. No external advantages, no good birth or breeding, no culture of the taste, no habit of command, no association with the elegant, — even no depth of affection that does not rise to a religious sentiment, can bestow that delicacy and grandeur of bearing which belong only to a mind accustomed to celestial conversation. All else is coarse and external; all else is tailoring and cosmetics beside this;[1] for thoughts are expressed in every look or gesture, and these thoughts are as if angels had talked with the child.

By this instinct we are lifted to higher ground. The religious sentiment gave the iron purpose and arm. That colonizing was a great and generous scheme, manly meant and manly done. When one thinks of the enterprises that are attempted in the heats of youth, the Zoars, New Harmonies and Brook Farms, Oakdales and Phalansteries, which have been so profoundly ventilated, but end in a protracted picnic which after a few weeks or months dismisses the partakers to their old homes, we see with new increased respect the solid, well-calculated scheme of these emigrants, sitting down hard and fast where they came, and building their empire by due degrees.

John Smith says, "Thirty, forty, or fifty sail went yearly in America only to trade and fish, but nothing would be done for a plantation, till about some hundred of your Brownists of England, Amsterdam and Leyden went to New Plymouth; whose humorous ignorances caused them for more than a year to endure a wonderful deal of misery, with an infinite patience."

What should hinder that this America, so long kept in reserve from the intellectual races until they should grow to it, glimpses being afforded which spoke to the imagination, yet the firm shore hid until science and art should be ripe to propose it as a fixed aim, and a man should be found who should sail steadily west sixty-eight days from the port of Palos to find it, — what should hinder that this New Atlantis should have its happy ports, its mountains of security, its gardens fit for human abode where ll elements were right for the health, power and virtue of man?

America is growing like a cloud, towns on towns, states on states; and wealth (always interesting, since from wealth power cannot be divorced) is piled in every form invented for comfort or pride.

If John Bull interest you at home, come and see him under new conditions, come and see the Jonathanization of John.[1]

There are always men ready for adventures, — more in an over-governed, over-peopled country, where all the professions are crowded and all character suppressed, than elsewhere. This thirst for adventure is the vent which Destiny offers; a war, a crusade, a gold-mine, a new country, speak to the imagination and offer swing and play to the confined powers.

The American idea, Emancipation, appears in our freedom of intellection, in our reforms and in our bad politics; it has, of course, its sinister side, which is most felt by the drilled and scholastic, but if followed it leads to heavenly places.

European and American are each ridiculous out of his sphere. There is a Columbia of thought and art and character, which is the last and endless sequel of Columbus's adventure.

European critics regret the detachment of the Puritans to this country without aristocracy; which a little reminds one of the pity of the Swiss mountaineers when shown a handsome Englishman: "What a pity he has no goitre!" The future historian will regard the detachment of the Puritans without aristocracy the supreme fortune of the colony; as great a gain to mankind as the opening of this continent.

There is a little formula, couched in pure Saxon, which you may hear in the corners of streets and in the yard of the dame's school, from very little republicans: "I 'm as good as you be," which contains the essence of the Massachusetts Bill of Rights and of the American Declaration of Independence. And this was at the bottom of Plymouth Rock and of Boston Stone; and this could be heard (by an acute ear) in the Petitions to the King, and the platforms of churches, and was said and rung in every tone of the psalmody of the Puritans; in every note of Old Hundred and Hallelujah and Short Particular Metre.

What is very conspicuous is the saucy independence which shines in all their eyes. They could say to themselves, Well, at least this yoke of man, of bishops, of courtiers, of dukes, is off my neck. We are a little too close to wolf and famine than that anybody should give himself airs here in the swamp.

London is a long way off, with beadles and pursuivants and horse-guards. Here in the clam-banks and the beech and chestnut forest, I shall take leave to breathe and think freely. If you do not like it, if you molest me, I can cross the brook and plant a new state out of reach of anything but squirrels and wild pigeons.

Bonaparte sighed for his republicans of 1789. The soul of a political party is by no means usually the officers and pets of the party, who wear the honors and fill the high seats and spend the salaries. No, but the theorists and extremists, the men who are never contented and never to be contented with the work actually accomplished, but who from conscience are engaged to what that party professes,— these men will work and watch and rally and never tire in carrying their point. The theology and the instinct of freedom that grew here in the dark in serious men furnished a certain rancor which consumed all opposition, fed the party and carried it, over every rampart and obstacle, to victory.

Boston never wanted a good principle of rebellion in it, from the planting until now; there is always a minority unconvinced, always a heresiarch, whom the governor and deputies labor with but cannot silence. Some new light, some new doctrinaire who makes an unnecessary ado to establish his dogma; some Wheelwright or defender of Wheelwright; some protester against the cruelty of the magistrates to the Quakers; some tender minister hospitable to Whitfield against the counsel of all the ministers; some John Adams and Josiah Quincy and Governor Andrew to undertake and carry the defence of patriots in the courts against the uproar of all the province; some defender of the slave against the politician and the merchant; some champion of first principles of humanity against the rich and luxurious; some adversary of the death penalty; some pleader for peace; some noble protestant, who will not stoop to infamy when all are gone mad, but will stand for liberty and justice, if alone, until all come back to him.[1]

I confess I do not find in our people, with all

their education, a fair share of originality of thought; — not any remarkable book of wisdom; not any broad generalization, any equal power of imagination. No Novum Organon; no Mécanique Céleste; no Principia; no Paradise Lost; no Hamlet; no Wealth of Nations; no National Anthem have we yet contributed.

Nature is a frugal mother and never gives without measure. When she has work to do, she qualifies men for that and sends them equipped for that. In Massachusetts she did not want epic poems and dramas yet, but first, planters of towns, fellers of the forest, builders of mills and forges, builders of roads, and farmers to till and harvest corn for the world. Corn, yes, but honest corn; corn with thanks to the Giver of corn; and the best thanks, namely, obedience to his law; this was the office imposed on our Founders and people; liberty, clean and wise. It was to be built on Religion, the Emancipator; Religion which teaches equality of all men in view of the spirit which created man.

The seed of prosperity was planted. The people did not gather where they had not sown. They did not try to unlock the treasure of the world except by honest keys of labor and skill.

They knew, as God knew, that command of Nature comes by obedience to Nature; that reward comes by faithful service; that the most noble motto was that of the Prince of Wales,—"I serve,"—and that he is greatest who serves best. There was no secret of labor which they disdained.

They accepted the divine ordination that man is for use; that intelligent being exists to the utmost use; and that his ruin is to live for pleasure and for show. And when within our memory some flippant senator wished to taunt the people of this country by calling them "the mudsills of society," he paid them ignorantly a true praise; for good men are as the green plain of the earth is, as the rocks, and the beds of rivers are, the foundation and flooring and sills of the state.

The power of labor which belongs to the English race fell here into a climate which befriended it, and into a maritime country made for trade, where was no rival and no envious lawgiver. The sailor and the merchant made the law to suit themselves, so that there was never, I suppose, a more rapid expansion in population, wealth and all the elements of power, and in the citizens' consciousness of power and sustained assertion of it, than was exhibited here.

Moral values become also money values. When men saw that these people, besides their industry and thrift, had a heart and soul, and would stand by each other at all hazards, they desired to come and live here. A house in Boston was worth as much again as a house just as good in a town of timorous people, because here the neighbors would defend each other against bad governors and against troops; quite naturally house-rents rose in Boston.

Besides, youth and health like a stirring town, above a torpid place where nothing is doing. In Boston they were sure to see something going forward before the year was out. For here was the moving principle itself, the *primum mobile*, a living mind agitating the mass and always afflicting the conservative class with some odious novelty or other; a new religious sect, a political point, a point of honor, a reform in education, a philanthropy.

From Roger Williams and Eliot and Robinson and the Quaker women who for a testimony walked naked into the streets, and as the record tells us "were arrested and publicly whipped, — the baggages that they were;"[1] from Wheelwright the Antinomian, and Ann Hutchinson, and Whitfield, and Mother Ann the first Shaker, down to Abner Kneeland, and Father Lamson, and William Garrison, there never was wanting some thorn of dissent and innovation and heresy to prick the sides of conservatism.

With all their love of his person, they took immense pleasure in turning out the governor and deputy and assistants, and contravening the counsel of the clergy; as they had come so far for the sweet satisfaction of resisting the Bishops and the King.

The Massachusetts colony grew and filled its own borders with a denser population than any other American State (Kossuth called it the City State), all the while sending out colonies to every part of New England; then South and West, until it has infused all the Union with its blood.

We are willing to see our sons emigrate, as to see our hives swarm. That is what they were made to do, and what the land wants and invites. The towns or countries in which the man lives and dies where he was born, and his son and son's son live and die where he did, are of no great account.

I know that this history contains many black lines of cruel injustice; murder, persecution, and execution of women for witchcraft.

I am afraid there are anecdotes of poverty and disease in Broad Street that match the dismal statistics of New York and London. No doubt all manner of vices can be found in this, as in every city; infinite meanness, scarlet crime. Granted. But there is yet in every city a certain permanent tone; a tendency to be in the right or in the wrong; audacity or slowness; labor or luxury; giving or parsimony; which side is it on? And I hold that a community, as a man, is entitled to be judged by his best.

We are often praised for what is least ours. Boston too is sometimes pushed into a theatrical attitude of virtue, to which she is not entitled and which she cannot keep. But the genius of Boston is seen in her real independence, productive power and northern acuteness of mind, — which is in nature hostile to oppression. It is a good city as cities go; Nature is good. The climate is electric, good for wit and good for character. What public souls have lived here, what social benefactors, what eloquent preachers, skilful workmen, stout captains, wise merchants; what fine artists, what gifted conversers, what mathematicians, what lawyers, what wits; and where is the middle class so able, virtuous and instructed?

And thus our little city thrives and enlarges, striking deep roots, and sending out boughs and buds, and propagating itself like a banyan over the continent. Greater cities there are that sprung from it, full of its blood and name and traditions. It is very willing to be outnumbered and outgrown, so long as they carry forward its life of civil and religious freedom, of education, of social order, and of loyalty to law.[1] It is very willing to be outrun in numbers, and in wealth; but it is very jealous of any superiority in these, its natural instinct and privilege. You cannot conquer it by numbers, or by square miles, or by counted millions of wealth. For it owes its existence and its power to principles not of yesterday, and the deeper principle will always prevail over whatever material accumulations.

As long as she cleaves to her liberty, her education and to her spiritual faith as the foundation of these, she will teach the teachers and rule the rulers of America. Her mechanics, her farmers will toil better; she will repair mischief; she will furnish what is wanted in the hour of need; her sailors will man the Constitution; her mechanics repair the broken rail; her troops will be the first in the field to vindicate the majesty of a free nation, and remain last on the field to secure it. Her genius will write the laws and her historians record the fate of nations.

In an age of trade and material prosperity, we have stood a little stupefied by the elevation of our ancestors. We praised the Puritans because we did not find in ourselves the spirit to do the like. We praised with a certain adulation the invariable valor of the old war-gods and war-councillors of the Revolution. Washington has seemed an exceptional virtue. This praise was a concession of unworthiness in those who had so much to say of it. The heroes only shared this power of a sentiment, which, if it now breathes into us, will make it easy to us to understand them, and we shall not longer flatter them. Let us shame the fathers, by superior virtue in the sons.

It is almost a proverb that a great man has not a great son. Bacon, Newton and Washington were childless. But, in Boston, Nature is more indulgent, and has given good sons to good sires, or at least continued merit in the same blood. The elder President Adams has to divide voices of fame with the younger President Adams. The elder Otis could hardly excel the popular eloquence of the younger Otis; and the Quincy of the Revolution seems compensated for the shortness of his bright career in the son who so long lingers among the last of those bright clouds,

> "That on the steady breeze of honor sail
> In long succession calm and beautiful."[1]

Here stands to-day, as of yore, our little city of the rocks; here let it stand forever, on the man-bearing granite of the North! Let her stand fast by herself! She has grown great. She is filled with strangers, but she can only prosper by adhering to her faith. Let every child that is born of her and every child of her adoption see to it to keep the name of Boston as clean as the sun; and in distant ages her motto shall be the prayer of millions on all the hills that gird the town, "As with our Fathers, so God be with us!" SICUT PATRIBUS, SIT DEUS NOBIS!

divide voices of fame with the younger President Adams. The elder Otis could hardly excel the popular eloquence of the younger Otis; and the Quincy of the Revolution seems compensated for the shortness of his bright career in the son who so long lingers among the last of those bright clouds,

> "That on the steady breeze of honor sail
> In long succession calm and beautiful."

Here stands to-day, as of yore, our little city of the rocks; here let it stand forever, on the man-bearing granite of the North! Let her stand fast by herself! She has grown great. She is filled with strangers, but she can only prosper by adhering to her faith. Let every child that is born of her and every child of her adoption see to it to keep the name of Boston as clean as the sails; and in distant ages her motto shall be the prayer of millions on all the hills that gird the town, "As with our Fathers, so God be with us!" SICUT PATRIBUS, SIT DEUS NOBIS!

VI

MICHAEL ANGELO

"NEVER did sculptor's dream unfold
A form which marble doth not hold
In its white block; yet it therein shall find
Only the hand secure and bold
Which still obeys the mind."

MICHAEL ANGELO'S *Sonnets*.

"Non ha l' ottimo artista alcun concetto,
Ch' un marmo solo in sè non circoscriva
Col suo soverchio, e solo a quello arriva
La man che obbedisce all' intelletto."

M. Angelo, *Sonnetto primo*.

MICHAEL ANGELO

FEW lives of eminent men are harmonious; few that furnish, in all the facts, an image corresponding with their fame. But all things recorded of Michael Angelo Buonarotti agree together. He lived one life; he pursued one career. He accomplished extraordinary works; he uttered extraordinary words; and in this greatness was so little eccentricity, so true was he to the laws of the human mind, that his character and his works, like Sir Isaac Newton's, seem rather a part of Nature than arbitrary productions of the human will. Especially we venerate his moral fame. Whilst his name belongs to the highest class of genius, his life contains in it no injurious influence. Every line in his biography might be read to the human race with wholesome effect. The means, the materials of his activity, were coarse enough to be appreciated, being addressed for the most part to the eye; the results, sublime and all innocent. A purity severe and even terrible goes out from the lofty productions of his pencil and his chisel, and again from the more perfect sculpture of his own life, which heals and exalts. "He nothing common did, or mean,"[1] and, dying at the end of near ninety years, had not yet become old, but was engaged in executing his grand conceptions in the ineffaceable architecture of Saint Peter's.

Above all men whose history we know, Michael Angelo presents us with the perfect image of the artist. He is an eminent master in the four fine arts, Painting, Sculpture, Architecture and Poetry. In three of them by visible means, and in poetry by words, he strove to express the Idea of Beauty. This idea possessed him and determined all his activity. Beauty in the largest sense, beauty inward and outward, comprehending grandeur as a part, and reaching to goodness as its soul, — this to receive and this to impart, was his genius.

It is a happiness to find, amid the falsehood and griefs of the human race, a soul at intervals born to behold and create only Beauty. So shall not the indescribable charm of the natural world, the great spectacle of morn and evening which shut and open the most disastrous day, want observers. The ancient Greeks called the world κόσμος, *Beauty*; a name which, in our artificial state of society, sounds fanciful and impertinent. Yet, in proportion as man rises above the servitude to wealth and a pursuit of mean pleasures, he perceives that what is most real is most beautiful, and that, by the contemplation of such objects, he is taught and exalted. This truth, that perfect beauty and perfect goodness are one, was made known to Michael Angelo; and we shall endeavor by sketches from his life to show the direction and limitations of his search after this element.

In considering a life dedicated to the study of Beauty, it is natural to inquire, what is Beauty? Can this charming element be so abstracted by the human mind as to become a distinct and permanent object? Beauty cannot be defined. Like Truth, it is an ultimate aim of the human being. It does not lie within the limits of the understanding. "The nature of the beautiful" — we gladly borrow the language of Moritz, a German critic — "consists herein, that because the understanding in the presence of the beautiful cannot ask, 'Why is it beautiful?' for that reason is it so. There is no standard whereby the understanding can determine whether objects are beautiful or otherwise. What other standard of the beautiful exists than the entire circuit of all harmonious proportions of the great system of Nature? All particular beauties scattered up and down in Nature are only so far beautiful as they suggest more or less in themselves this entire circuit of harmonious proportions." This great Whole the understanding cannot embrace. Beauty may be felt. It may be produced. But it cannot be defined.

The Italian artists sanction this view of Beauty by describing it as *il più nell' uno*, "the many in one," or multitude in unity, intimating that what is truly beautiful seems related to all Nature. A beautiful person has a kind of universality, and appears to have truer conformity to all pleasing objects in external Nature than another. Every great work of art seems to take up into itself the excellencies of all works, and to present, as it were, a miniature of Nature.

In relation to this element of Beauty, the minds of men divide themselves into two classes. In the first place, all men have an organization corresponding more or less to the entire system of Nature, and therefore a power of deriving pleasure from Beauty. This is Taste. In the second place, certain minds, more closely harmonized with Nature, possess the power of abstracting Beauty from things, and reproducing it in new forms, on any object to which accident may determine their activity; as stone, canvas, song, history. This is Art.

Since Beauty is thus an abstraction of the harmony and proportion that reigns in all Nature, it is therefore studied in Nature, and not in what does not exist. Hence the celebrated French maxim of Rhetoric, *Rien de beau que le vrai;* "Nothing is beautiful but what is true." It has a much wider application than to Rhetoric; as wide, namely, as the terms of the proposition admit. In art, Michael Angelo is himself but a document or verification of this maxim. He labored to express the beautiful, in the entire conviction that it was only to be attained unto by knowledge of the true. The common eye is satisfied with the surface on which it rests. The wise eye knows that it is surface, and, if beautiful, only the result of interior harmonies, which, to him who knows them, compose the image of higher beauty. Moreover, he knew well that only by an understanding of the internal mechanism can the outside be faithfully delineated. The walls of houses are transparent to the architect. The symptoms disclose the constitution to the physician; and to the artist it belongs by a better knowledge of anatomy, and, within anatomy, of life and thought, to acquire the power of true drawing. "The human form," says Goethe, "cannot be comprehended through seeing its surface. It must be stripped of the muscles, its parts separated, its joints observed, its divisions marked, its action and counteraction learned; the hidden, the reposing, the foundation of the apparent, must be searched, if one would really see and imitate what moves as a beautiful, inseparable whole in living waves before the eye." Michael Angelo dedicated himself, from his childhood to his death, to a toilsome observation of Nature. The first anecdote recorded of him shows him to be already on the right road. Granacci, a painter's apprentice, having lent him, when a boy, a print of Saint Antony beaten by devils, together with some colors and pencils, he went to the fish-market to observe the form and color of fins and of the eyes of fish. Cardinal Farnese one day found him, when an old man, walking alone in the Coliseum, and expressed his surprise at finding him solitary amidst the ruins; to which he replied, "I go yet to school that I may continue to learn." And one of the last drawings in his portfolio is a sublime hint of his own feeling; for it is a sketch of an old man with a long beard, in a go-cart, with an hour-glass before him; and the motto, *Ancora imparo*, "I still learn."

In this spirit he devoted himself to the study of anatomy for twelve years; we ought to say, rather, as long as he lived. The depth of his knowledge in anatomy has no parallel among the artists of modern times. Most of his designs, his contemporaries inform us, were made with a pen, and in the style of an engraving on copper or wood; a manner more expressive but not admitting of correction. When Michael Angelo would begin a statue, he made first on paper the *skeleton*; afterwards, upon another paper, the same figure clothed with muscles. The studies of the statue of Christ in the Church of Minerva at Rome, made in this manner, were long preserved.

Those who have never given attention to the arts of design are surprised that the artist should find so much to study in a fabric of such limited parts and dimensions as the human body. But reflection discloses evermore a closer analogy between the finite form and the infinite inhabitant. Man is the highest, and indeed the only proper object of plastic art. There needs no better proof of our instinctive feeling of the immense expression of which the human figure is capable than the uniform tendency which the religion of every country has betrayed towards Anthropomorphism, or attributing to the Deity the human form. And behold the effect of this familiar object every day! No acquaintance with the secrets of its mechanism, no degrading views of human nature, not the most swinish compost of mud and blood that was ever misnamed philosophy, can avail to hinder us from doing involuntary reverence to any exhibition of majesty or surpassing beauty in human clay.

Our knowledge of its highest expression we owe to the Fine Arts. Not easily in this age will any man acquire by himself such perceptions of the dignity or grace of the human frame as the student of art owes to the remains of Phidias, to the Apollo, the Jove, the paintings and statues of Michael Angelo, and the works of Canova. There are now in Italy, both on canvas and in marble, forms and faces which the imagination is enriched by contemplating. Goethe says that he is but half himself who has never seen the Juno in the Rondanini Palace at Rome. Seeing these works true to human nature and yet superhuman, "we feel that we are greater than we know." Seeing these works, we appreciate the taste which led Michael Angelo, against the taste and against the admonition of his patrons, to cover the walls of churches with unclothed figures, "improper," says his biographer, "for the place, but proper for the exhibition of all the pomp of his profound knowledge."

The love of beauty which never passes beyond outline and color was too slight an object to occupy the powers of his genius. There is a closer relation than is commonly thought between the fine arts and the useful arts; and it is an essential fact in the history of Michael Angelo that his love of beauty is made solid and perfect by his deep understanding of the mechanic arts. Architecture is the bond that unites the elegant and the economical arts, and his skill in this is a pledge of his capacity in both kinds. His Titanic handwriting in marble and travertine is to be found in every part of Rome and Florence; and even at Venice, on defective evidence, he is said to have given the plan of the bridge of the Rialto. Nor was his a skill in ornament, or confined to the outline and designs of towers and façades, but a thorough acquaintance with all the secrets of the art, with all the details of economy and strength.

When the Florentines united themselves with

Venice, England and France, to oppose the power of the Emperor Charles V., Michael Angelo was appointed Military Architect and Engineer, to superintend the erection of the necessary works. He visited Bologna to inspect its celebrated fortifications, and, on his return, constructed a fortification on the heights of San Miniato, which commands the city and environs of Florence. On the 24th of October, 1529, the Prince of Orange, general of Charles V., encamped on the hills surrounding the city, and his first operation was to throw up a rampart to storm the bastion of San Miniato. His design was frustrated by the providence of Michael Angelo. Michael made such good resistance that the Prince directed the artillery to demolish the tower. The artist hung mattresses of wool on the side exposed to the attack, and by means of a bold projecting cornice, from which they were suspended, a considerable space was left between them and the wall. This simple expedient was sufficient, and the Prince was obliged to turn his siege into a blockade.

After an active and successful service to the city for six months, Michael Angelo was informed of a treachery that was ripening within the walls. He communicated it to the government with his advice upon it; but was mortified by receiving from the government reproaches at his credulity and fear. He replied that "it was useless for him to take care of the walls, if they were determined not to take care of themselves," and he withdrew privately from the city to Ferrara, and thence to Venice. The news of his departure occasioned a general concern in Florence, and he was instantly followed with apologies and importunities to return. He did so, and resumed his office. On the 21st of March, 1530, the Prince of Orange assaulted the city by storm. Michael Angelo is represented as having ordered his defence so vigorously that the Prince was compelled to retire. By the treachery, however, of the general of the Republic, Malatesta Baglioni, all his skill was rendered unavailing, and the city capitulated on the 9th of August. The excellence of the works constructed by our artist has been approved by Vauban, who visited them and took a plan of them.

In Rome, Michael Angelo was consulted by Pope Paul III. in building the fortifications of San Borgo. He built the stairs of Ara Celi leading to the church once the temple of Jupiter Capitolinus; he arranged the piazza of the

Capitol, and built its porticos. He was charged with rebuilding the Pons Palatinus over the Tiber. He prepared, accordingly, a large quantity of blocks of travertine, and was proceeding with the work, when, through the intervention of his rivals, this work was taken from him and intrusted to Nanni di Bacio Bigio, who plays but a pitiful part in Michael's history. Nanni sold the travertine, and filled up the piers with gravel at a small expense. Michael Angelo made known his opinion that the bridge could not resist the force of the current; and one day riding over it on horseback, with his friend Vasari, he cried, "George, this bridge trembles under us; let us ride faster lest it fall whilst we are upon it." It fell, five years after it was built, in 1557, and is still called the "Broken Bridge."

Versatility of talent in men of undoubted ability always awakens the liveliest interest; and we observe with delight that, besides the sublimity and even extravagance of Michael Angelo, he possessed an unexpected dexterity in minute mechanical contrivances. When the Sistine Chapel was prepared for him, that he might paint the ceiling, he found the platform on which he was to work suspended by ropes which passed through the ceiling. Michael demanded of San Gallo, the pope's architect, how these holes were to be repaired in the picture. San Gallo replied: "That was for him to consider, for the platform could be constructed in no other way." Michael removed the whole, and constructed a movable platform to rest and roll upon the floor, which is believed to be the same simple contrivance which is used in Rome, at this day, to repair the walls of churches. He gave this model to a carpenter, who made it so profitable as to furnish a dowry for his two daughters. He was so nice in tools that he made with his own hand the wimbles, the files, the rasps, the chisels and all other irons and instruments which he needed in sculpture; and in painting, he not only mixed but ground his colors himself, trusting no one.

And not only was this discoverer of Beauty, and its teacher among men, rooted and grounded in those severe laws of practical skill, which genius can never teach, and which must be learned by practice alone, but he was one of the most industrious men that ever lived. His diligence was so great that it is wonderful how he endured its fatigues. The midnight battles, the forced marches, the winter campaigns of Julius Cæsar or Charles XII. do not indicate greater strength of body or of mind. He finished the gigantic painting of the ceiling of the Sistine Chapel in twenty months, a fact which enlarges, it has been said, the known powers of man. Indeed he toiled so assiduously at this painful work, that, for a long time after, he was unable to see any picture but by holding it over his head. A little bread and wine was all his nourishment; and he told Vasari that he often slept in his clothes, both because he was too weary to undress, and because he would rise in the night and go immediately to work. "I have found," says his friend, "some of his designs in Florence, where, whilst may be seen the greatness of his genius, it may also be known that when he wished to take Minerva from the head of Jove, there needed the hammer of Vulcan." He used to make to a single figure nine, ten, or twelve heads before he could satisfy himself, seeking that there should be in the composition a certain universal grace such as Nature makes, saying that "he needed to have his compasses in his eye, and not in his hand, because the hands work whilst the eye judges." He was accustomed to say, "Those figures alone are good from which the labor is scraped off when the scaffolding is taken away."

At near eighty years, he began in marble a group of four figures for a dead Christ, because, he said, to exercise himself with the mallet was good for his health.

And what did he accomplish? It does not fall within our design to give an account of his works, yet for the sake of the completeness of our sketch we will name the principal ones. Sculpture, he called *his* art, and to it he regretted he had not singly given himself. The style of his paintings is monumental; and even his poetry partakes of that character. In sculpture, his greatest work is the statue of Moses in the Church of Pietro in Vincolo, in Rome. It is a sitting statue of colossal size, and is designed to embody the Hebrew Law. The lawgiver is supposed to gaze upon the worshippers of the golden calf. The majestic wrath of the figure daunts the beholder. In the Piazza del Gran Duca at Florence, stands, in the open air, his David, about to hurl the stone at Goliath. In the church called the Minerva, at Rome, is his Christ; an object of so much devotion to the people that the right foot has been shod with a brazen sandal to prevent it from being kissed away. In Saint Peter's, is his Pietà, or dead Christ in the arms of his mother. In the mausoleum of the Medici at Florence are the tombs of Lorenzo and Cosmo, with the grand statues of Night and Day, and Aurora and Twilight. Several statues of less fame, and bas-reliefs, are in Rome and Florence and Paris.

His paintings are in the Sistine Chapel, of which he first covered the ceiling with the story of the Creation, in successive compartments, with the great series of the Prophets and Sibyls in alternate tablets, and a series of greater and smaller fancy pieces in the lunettes. This is his capital work painted in fresco. Every one of these pieces, every figure, every hand and foot and finger, is a study of anatomy and design. Slighting the secondary arts of coloring, and all the aids of graceful finish, he aimed exclusively, as a stern designer, to express the vigor and magnificence of his conceptions. Upon the wall, over the altar, is painted the Last Judgment.

Of his designs, the most celebrated is the cartoon representing soldiers coming out of the bath and arming themselves; an incident of the war of Pisa. The wonderful merit of this drawing, which contrasts the extremes of relaxation and vigor, is conspicuous even in the coarsest prints.

Of his genius for architecture it is sufficient to say that he built Saint Peter's, an ornament of the earth. He said he would hang the Pantheon in the air; and he redeemed his pledge by suspending that vast cupola, without offence to grace or to stability, over the astonished beholder. He did not live to complete the work; but is there not something affecting in the spectacle of an old man, on the verge of ninety years, carrying steadily onward, with the heat and determination of manhood, his poetic conceptions into progressive execution, surmounting by the dignity of his purposes all obstacles and all enmities, and only hindered by the limits of life from fulfilling his designs? Very slowly came he, after months and years, to the dome. At last he began to model it very small in wax. When it was finished, he had it copied larger in wood, and by this model it was built. Long after it was completed, and often since, to this day, rumors are occasionally spread that it is giving way, and it is said to have been injured by unskilful attempts to repair it. Benedict XIV., during one of these panics, sent for the architect Marchese Polini, to come to Rome and examine it. Polini put an end to all the various projects of repairs, by the satisfying sentence: "The cupola does not start, and if it should start, nothing can be done but to pull it down."[1]

The impulse of his grand style was instantaneous upon his contemporaries. Every stroke of his pencil moved the pencil in Raphael's hand. Raphael said, "I bless God I live in the times of Michael Angelo." Sir Joshua Reynolds, two centuries later, declared to the British Institution, "I feel a self-congratulation in knowing myself capable of such sensations as he intended to excite."

A man of such habits and such deeds made good his pretensions to a perception and to delineation of external beauty. But inimitable as his works are, his whole life confessed that his hand was all inadequate to express his thought. "He alone," he said, "is an artist whose hands can perfectly execute what his mind has conceived;" and such was his own mastery that men said, "the marble was flexible in his hands." Yet, contemplating ever with love the idea of absolute beauty, he was still dissatisfied with his own work. The things proposed to him in his imagination were such that, for not being able with his hands to express so grand and terrible conceptions, he often abandoned his work. For this reason he often only blocked his statue. A little before he died, he burned a great number of designs, sketches and cartoons made by him, being impatient of their defects. Grace in living forms, except in very rare instances, did not satisfy him. He never made but one portrait (a cartoon of Messer Tommaso di Cavalieri), because he abhorred to draw a likeness unless it were of infinite beauty.[1]

Such was his devotion to art. But let no man suppose that the images which his spirit worshipped were mere transcripts of external grace, or that this profound soul was taken or holden in the chains of superficial beauty. To him, of all men, it was transparent. Through it he beheld the eternal spiritual beauty which ever clothes itself with grand and graceful outlines, as its appropriate form. He called external grace "the frail and weary weed, in which God dresses the soul which he has called into Time." "As from the fire, heat cannot be divided, no more can beauty from the eternal." He was conscious in his efforts of higher aims than to address the eye. He sought, through the eye, to reach the soul. Therefore, as, in the first place, he sought to approach the Beautiful by the study of the True, so he failed not to make the next step of progress, and to seek Beauty in its highest form, that of Goodness. The sublimity of his art is in his life. He did not only build a divine temple, and paint and carve saints and prophets. He lived out the same inspiration. There is no spot upon his fame. The fire and sanctity of his pencil breathe in his words. When he was informed that Paul IV. desired he should paint again the side of the chapel where the Last Judgment was painted, because of the indecorous nudity of the figures, he replied, "Tell the Pope that this is easily done. Let him reform the world and he will find the pictures will reform themselves." He saw clearly that if the corrupt and vulgar eyes that could see nothing but indecorum in his terrific prophets and angels could be purified as his own were pure, they would only find occasion for devotion in the same figures. As he refused to undo his work, Daniel di Volterra was employed to clothe the figures; hence ludicrously called *Il Braghettone*. When the Pope suggested to him that the chapel would be enriched if the figures were ornamented with gold, Michael Angelo replied, "In those days, gold was not worn; and the characters I have painted were neither rich nor desirous of wealth, but holy men, with whom gold was an object of contempt."

Not until he was in the seventy-third year of his age, he undertook the building of Saint Peter's. On the death of San Gallo, the architect of the church, Paul III. first entreated, then commanded the aged artist to assume the charge of this great work, which, though commenced forty years before, was only commenced by Bramante, and ill continued by San Gallo. Michael Angelo, who believed in his own ability as a sculptor, but distrusted his capacity as an architect, at first refused and then reluctantly complied. His heroic stipulation with the Pope was worthy of the man and the work. He required that he should be permitted to accept this work without any fee or reward, because he undertook it as a religious act; and, furthermore, that he should be absolute master of the whole design, free to depart from the plans of San Gallo and to alter what had been already done.

This disinterestedness and spirit — no fee and no interference — reminds one of the reward named by the ancient Persian. When importuned to claim some compensation of the empire for the important services he had rendered it, he demanded " that he and his should neither command nor obey, but should be free." However, as it was undertaken, so was it performed. When the Pope, delighted with one of his chapels, sent him one hundred crowns of gold, as one month's wages, Michael sent them back. The Pope was angry, but the artist was immovable. Amidst endless annoyances from the envy and interest of the office-holders and agents in the work whom he had displaced, he steadily ripened and executed his vast ideas. The combined desire to fulfil, in everlasting stone, the conceptions of his mind, and to complete his worthy offering to Almighty God, sustained him through numberless vexations with unbroken spirit. In answer to the importunate solicitations of the Duke of Tuscany that he would come to Florence, he replies that "to leave Saint Peter's in the state in which it now was would be to ruin the structure, and thereby be guilty of a great sin;" that he hoped he should shortly see the execution of his plans brought to such a point that they could no longer be interfered with, and this was the capital object of his wishes, "if," he adds, "I do not commit a great crime by disappointing the cormorants who are daily hoping to get rid of me."

A natural fruit of the nobility of his spirit is

his admiration of Dante, to whom two of his sonnets are addressed. He shared Dante's "deep contempt of the vulgar, not of the simple inhabitants of lowly streets or humble cottages, but of that sordid and abject crowd of all classes and all places who obscure, as much as in them lies, every beam of beauty in the universe." In like manner, he possessed an intense love of solitude. He lived alone, and never or very rarely took his meals with any person. As will be supposed, he had a passion for the country, and in old age speaks with extreme pleasure of his residence with the hermits in the mountains of Spoleto; so much so that he says he is "only half in Rome, since, truly, peace is only to be found in the woods." Traits of an almost savage independence mark all his history. Although he was rich, he lived like a poor man, and never would receive a present from any person; because it seemed to him that if a man gave him anything, he was always obligated to that individual. His friend Vasari mentions one occasion on which his scruples were overcome. It seems that Michael was accustomed to work at night with a pasteboard cap or helmet on his head, into which he stuck a candle, that his work might be lighted and his hands at liberty. Vasari observed that he did not use wax candles, but a better sort made of the tallow of goats. He therefore sent him four bundles of them, containing forty pounds. His servant brought them after nightfall, and presented them to him. Michael Angelo refused to receive them. "Look you, Messer Michael Angelo," replied the man, "these candles have well-nigh broken my arm, and I will not carry them back; but just here, before your door, is a spot of soft mud, and they will stand upright in it very well, and there I will light them all." "Put them down, then," returned Michael, "since you shall not make a bonfire at my gate." Meantime he was liberal to profusion to his old domestic Urbino, to whom he gave at one time two thousand crowns, and made him rich in his service.

Michael Angelo was of that class of men who are too superior to the multitude around them to command a full and perfect sympathy. They stand in the attitude rather of appeal from their contemporaries to their race. It has been the defect of some great men that they did not duly appreciate or did not confess the talents and virtues of others, and so lacked one of the richest sources of happiness and one of the best elements of humanity. This apathy perhaps happens as often from preoccupied attention as from jealousy. It has been supposed that artists more than others are liable to this defect. But Michael Angelo's praise on many works is to this day the stamp of fame. Michael Angelo said of Masaccio's pictures that when they were first painted they must have been alive. He said of his predecessor, the architect Bramante, that he laid the first stone of Saint Peter's, clear, insulated, luminous, with fit design for a vast structure. He often expressed his admiration of Cellini's bust of Altoviti. He loved to express admiration of Titian, of Donatello, of Ghiberti, of Brunelleschi. And it is said that when he left Florence to go to Rome, to build Saint Peter's, he turned his horse's head on the last hill from which the noble dome of the cathedral (built by Brunelleschi) is visible, and said, "Like you, I will not build; better than you I cannot." Indeed, as we have said, the reputation of many works of art now in Italy derives a sanction from the tradition of his praise. It is more commendation to say, "This was Michael Angelo's favorite," than to say, "This was carried to Paris by Napoleon." Michael, however, had the philosophy to say, "Only an inventor can use the inventions of others."

There is yet one more trait in Michael Angelo's history, which humanizes his character without lessening its loftiness; this is his platonic love. He was deeply enamoured of the most accomplished lady of the time, Vittoria Colonna, the widow of the Marquis di Pescara, who, after the death of her husband, devoted herself to letters, and to the writing of religious poetry. She was also an admirer of his genius, and came to Rome repeatedly to see him. To her his sonnets are addressed; and they all breathe a chaste and divine regard, unparalleled in any amatory poetry except that of Dante and Petrarch. They are founded on the thought that beauty is the virtue of the body, as virtue is the beauty of the soul; that a beautiful person is sent into the world as an image of the divine beauty, not to provoke but to purify the sensual into an intellectual and divine love. He enthrones his mistress as a benignant angel, who is to refine and perfect his own character. Condivi, his friend, has left this testimony: "I have often heard Michael Angelo reason and discourse upon love, but never heard him speak otherwise than upon platonic love. As for me, I am ignorant what Plato has said upon this subject; but this I know very well, that, in a long intimacy, I never heard from his mouth a single word that was not perfectly decorous and having for its object to extinguish in youth every improper desire, and that his own nature is a stranger to depravity." The poems themselves cannot be read without awakening sentiments of virtue. An eloquent vindication of their philosophy may be found in a paper by Signor Radici in the London Retrospective Review, and, by the Italian scholar, in the Discourse of Benedetto Varchi upon one sonnet of Michael Angelo, contained in the volume of his poems published by Biagioli, from which, in substance, the views of Radici are taken.

Towards his end, there seems to have grown in him an invincible appetite of dying, for he knew that his spirit could only enjoy contentment after death. So vehement was this desire that, he says, "my soul can no longer be appeased by the wonted seductions of painting and sculpture." A fine melancholy, not unrelieved by his habitual heroism, pervades his thoughts on this subject. At the age of eighty years, he wrote to Vasari, sending him various spiritual sonnets he had written, and tells him he "is at the end of his life, that he is careful where he bends his thoughts, that he sees it is already twenty-four o'clock, and no fancy arose in his mind but DEATH was sculptured on it." In conversing upon this subject with one of his friends, that person remarked that Michael might well grieve that one who was incessant in his creative labors should have no restoration. "No," replied Michael, "it is nothing; for if life pleases us, death, being a work of the same master, ought not to displease us." But a nobler sentiment, uttered by him, is contained in his reply to a letter of Vasari, who had informed him of the rejoicings made at the house of his nephew Lionardo, at Florence, over the birth of another Buonarotti. Michael admonishes him that "a man ought not to smile, when all those around him weep; and that we ought not to show that joy when a child is born, which should be reserved for the death of one who has lived well."

Amidst all these witnesses to his independence, his generosity, his purity and his devotion, are we not authorized to say that this man was penetrated with the love of the highest beauty, that is, goodness; that his was a soul so enamoured of grace that it could not stoop to meanness or depravity; that art was to him no means of livelihood or road to fame, but the end of living, as it was the organ through which he sought to suggest lessons of an unutterable wisdom; that here was a man who lived to demonstrate that to the human faculties, on every hand, worlds of grandeur and grace are opened, which no profane eye and no indolent eye can behold, but which, to see and to enjoy, demands the severest discipline of all the physical, intellectual and moral faculties of the individual?

The city of Florence, on the river Arno, still treasures the fame of this man. There, his picture hangs in every window; there, the tradition of his opinions meets the traveller in every spot. "Do you see that statue of Saint George? Michael Angelo asked it why it did not speak."[1] — "Do you see this fine church of Santa Maria Novella? It is that which Michael Angelo called 'his bride.'" — "Look at these bronze gates of the Baptistery, with their high reliefs, cast by Ghiberti five hundred years ago. Michael Angelo said, 'they were fit to be the gates of Paradise.'" Here is the church, the palace, the Laurentian library, he built. Here is his own house. In the church of Santa Croce are his mortal remains. Whilst he was yet alive, he asked that he might be buried in that church, in such a spot that the dome of the cathedral might be visible from his tomb when the doors of the church stood open. And there and so is he laid. The innumerable pilgrims whom the genius of Italy draws to the city duly visit this church, which is to Florence what Westminster Abbey is to England. There, near the tomb of Nicholas Macchiavelli, the historian and philosopher; of Galileo, the great-hearted astronomer; of Boccaccio, and of Alfieri, stands the monument of Michael Angelo Buonarotti. Three significant garlands are sculptured on the tomb; they should be four, but that his countrymen feared their own partiality. The forehead of the bust, esteemed a faithful likeness, is furrowed with eight deep wrinkles one above another.[1] The traveller from a distant continent, who gazes on that marble brow, feels that he is not a stranger in the foreign church; for the great name of Michael Angelo sounds hospitably in his ear. He was not a citizen of any country; he belonged to the human race; he was a brother and a friend to all who acknowledge the beauty that beams in universal Nature, and who seek by labor and self-denial to approach its source in perfect goodness.[2]

VII

MILTON

I FRAMED his tongue to music,
  I armed his hand with skill,
I moulded his face to beauty,
  And his heart the throne of will.

MILTON

THE discovery of the lost work of Milton, the treatise Of the Christian Doctrine, in 1823, drew a sudden attention to his name. For a short time the literary journals were filled with disquisitions on his genius; new editions of his works, and new compilations of his life, were published. But the new-found book having in itself less attraction than any other work of Milton, the curiosity of the public as quickly subsided, and left the poet to the enjoyment of his permanent fame, or to such increase or abatement of it only as is incidental to a sublime genius, quite independent of the momentary challenge of universal attention to his claims.

But if the new and temporary renown of the poet is silent again, it is nevertheless true that he has gained, in this age, some increase of permanent praise. The fame of a great man is not rigid and stony like his bust. It changes with time. It needs time to give it due perspective. It was very easy to remark an altered tone in the criticism when Milton reappeared as an author, fifteen years ago, from any that had been bestowed on the same subject before. It implied merit indisputable and illustrious; yet so near to the modern mind as to be still alive and life-giving. The aspect of Milton, to this generation, will be part of the history of the nineteenth century. There is no name in English literature between his age and ours that rises into any approach to his own. And as a man's fame, of course, characterizes those who give it, as much as him who receives it, the new criticism indicated a change in the public taste, and a change which the poet himself might claim to have wrought.

The reputation of Milton had already undergone one or two revolutions long anterior to its recent aspects. In his lifetime, he was little or not at all known as a poet, but obtained great respect from his contemporaries as an accomplished scholar and a formidable pamphleteer. His poem fell unregarded among his countrymen.[1] His prose writings, especially the Defence of the English People, seem to have been read with avidity. These tracts are remarkable compositions. They are earnest, spiritual, rich with allusion, sparkling with innumerable ornaments; but as writings designed to gain a practical point, they fail. They are not effective, like similar productions of Swift and Burke; or, like what became also controversial tracts, several masterly speeches in the history of the American Congress. Milton seldom deigns a glance at the obstacles that are to be overcome before that which he proposes can be done. There is no attempt to conciliate, — no mediate, no preparatory course suggested, — but, peremptory and impassioned, he demands, on the instant, an ideal justice. Therein they are discriminated from modern writings, in which a regard to the actual is all but universal.

Their rhetorical excellence must also suffer some deduction. They have no perfectness. These writings are wonderful for the truth, the learning, the subtility and pomp of the language; but the whole is sacrificed to the particular. Eager to do fit justice to each thought, he does not subordinate it so as to project the main argument. He writes whilst he is heated; the piece shows all the rambles and resources of indignation, but he has never *integrated* the parts of the argument in his mind. The reader is fatigued with admiration, but is not yet master of the subject.

Two of his pieces may be excepted from this description, one for its faults, the other for its excellence. The Defence of the People of

England, on which his contemporary fame was founded, is, when divested of its pure Latinity, the worst of his works. Only its general aim, and a few elevated passages, can save it. We could be well content if the flames to which it was condemned at Paris, at Toulouse, and at London, had utterly consumed it. The lover of his genius will always regret that he should not have taken counsel of his own lofty heart at this, as at other times, and have written from the deep convictions of love and right, which are the foundations of civil liberty. There is little poetry or prophecy in this mean and ribald scolding. To insult Salmasius, not to acquit England, is the main design. What under heaven had Madame de Saumaise, or the manner of living of Saumaise, or Salmasius, or his blunders of grammar, or his niceties of diction, to do with the solemn question whether Charles Stuart had been rightly slain?[1] Though it evinces learning and critical skill, yet, as an historical argument, it cannot be valued with similar disquisitions of Robertson and Hallam, and even less celebrated scholars. But when he comes to speak of the reason of the thing, then he always recovers himself. The voice of the mob is silent, and Milton speaks. And the peroration, in which he implores his countrymen to refute this adversary by their great deeds, is in a just spirit. The other piece is his Areopagitica, the discourse, addressed to the Parliament, in favor of removing the censorship of the press; the most splendid of his prose works. It is, as Luther said of one of Melancthon's writings, "alive, hath hands and feet, — and not like Erasmus's sentences, which were made, not grown." The weight of the thought is equalled by the vivacity of the expression, and it cheers as well as teaches. This tract is far the best known and the most read of all, and is still a magazine of reasons for the freedom of the press. It is valuable in history as an argument addressed to a government to produce a practical end, and plainly presupposes a very peculiar state of society.

But deeply as that peculiar state of society, in which and for which Milton wrote, has engraved itself in the remembrance of the world, it shares the destiny which overtakes everything local and personal in Nature; and the accidental facts on which a battle of principles was fought have already passed, or are fast passing, into oblivion. We have lost all interest in Milton as the redoubted disputant of a sect;

but by his own innate worth this man has steadily risen in the world's reverence, and occupies a more imposing place in the mind of men at this hour than ever before.

It is the aspect which he presents to this generation, that alone concerns us. Milton the polemic has lost his popularity long ago; and if we skip the pages of Paradise Lost where "God the Father argues like a school divine," so did the next age to his own. But, we are persuaded, he kindles a love and emulation in us which he did not in foregoing generations. We think we have seen and heard criticism upon the poems, which the bard himself would have more valued than the recorded praise of Dryden, Addison and Johnson, because it came nearer to the mark; was finer and closer appreciation; the praise of intimate knowledge and delight; and, of course, more welcome to the poet than the general and vague acknowledgment of his genius by those able but unsympathizing critics. We think we have heard the recitation of his verses by genius which found in them that which itself would say; recitation which told, in the diamond sharpness of every articulation, that now first was such perception and enjoyment possible; the perception and enjoyment of all his varied rhythm, and his perfect fusion of the classic and the English styles. This is a poet's right; for every masterpiece of art goes on for some ages reconciling the world unto itself, and despotically fashioning the public ear. The opposition to it, always greatest at first, continually decreases and at last ends; and a new race grows up in the taste and spirit of the work, with the utmost advantage for seeing intimately its power and beauty.[1]

But it would be great injustice to Milton to consider him as enjoying merely a critical reputation. It is the prerogative of this great man to stand at this hour foremost of all men in literary history, and so (shall we not say?) of all men, in the power *to inspire*. Virtue goes out of him into others. Leaving out of view the pretensions of our contemporaries (always an incalculable influence), we think no man can be named whose mind still acts on the cultivated intellect of England and America with an energy comparable to that of Milton. As a poet, Shakspeare undoubtedly transcends, and far surpasses him in his popularity with foreign nations; but Shakspeare is a voice merely; who and what he was that sang, that sings, we know not. Milton stands erect, commanding, still visible as a man among men, and reads the laws of the moral sentiment to the new-born race. There is something pleasing in the affection with which we can regard a man who died a hundred and sixty years ago in the other hemisphere, who, in respect to personal relations, is to us as the wind, yet by an influence purely spiritual makes us jealous for his fame as for that of a near friend. He is identified in the mind with all select and holy images, with the supreme interests of the human race. If hereby we attain any more precision, we proceed to say that we think no man in these later ages, and few men ever, possessed so great a conception of the manly character. Better than any other he has discharged the office of every great man, namely, to raise the idea of Man in the minds of his contemporaries and of posterity, — to draw after Nature a life of man, exhibiting such a composition of grace, of strength and of virtue, as poet had not described nor hero lived. Human nature in these ages is indebted to him for its best portrait. Many philosophers in England, France and Germany have formally dedicated their study to this problem; and we think it impossible to recall one in those countries who communicates the same vibration of hope, of self-reverence, of piety, of delight in beauty, which the name of Milton awakens. Lord Bacon, who has written much and with prodigious ability on this science, shrinks and falters before the absolute and uncourtly Puritan. Bacon's Essays are the portrait of an ambitious and profound calculator, — a great man of the vulgar sort. Of the upper world of man's being they speak few and faint words. The man of Locke is virtuous without enthusiasm, and intelligent without poetry. Addison, Pope, Hume and Johnson, students, with very unlike temper and success, of the same subject, cannot, taken together, make any pretension to the amount or the quality of Milton's inspirations. The man of Lord Chesterfield is unworthy to touch his garment's hem. Franklin's man is a frugal, inoffensive, thrifty citizen, but savors of nothing heroic. The genius of France has not, even in her best days, yet culminated in any one head — not in Rousseau, not in Pascal, not in Fénelon — into such perception of all the attributes of humanity as to entitle it to any rivalry in these lists. In Germany, the greatest writers are still too recent to institute a comparison; and yet we are tempted to say that art and not life seems to be the end of their effort. But the idea of a purer existence than any he saw around him, to be realized in the life and conversation of men, inspired every act and every writing of John Milton. He defined the object of education to be, "to fit a man to perform justly, skilfully and magnanimously all the offices, both private and public, of peace and war." He declared that "he who would aspire to write well hereafter in laudable things, ought himself to be a true poem; that is, a composition and pattern of the best and honorablest things, not presuming to sing high praises of heroic men or famous cities, unless he have in himself the experience and the practice of all that which is praiseworthy." Nor is there in literature a more noble outline of a wise external education than that which he drew up, at the age of thirty-six, in his Letter to Samuel Hartlib.[1] The muscles, the nerves and the flesh with which this skeleton is to be filled up and covered exist in his works and must be sought there.

For the delineation of this heroic image of man, Milton enjoyed singular advantages. Perfections of body and of mind are attributed to him by his biographers, that, if the anecdotes had come down from a greater distance of time, or had not been in part furnished or corroborated by political enemies, would lead us to suspect the portraits were ideal, like the Cyrus of Xenophon, the Telemachus of Fénelon, or the popular traditions of Alfred the Great.

Handsome to a proverb, he was called the lady of his college. Aubrey says, "This harmonical and ingenuous soul dwelt in a beautiful, well-proportioned body." His manners and his carriage did him no injustice. Wood, his political opponent, relates that "his deportment was affable, his gait erect and manly, bespeaking courage and undauntedness." Aubrey adds a sharp trait, that "he pronounced the letter R very hard, a certain sign of satirical genius." He had the senses of a Greek. His eye was quick, and he was accounted an excellent master of his rapier. His ear for music was so acute that he was not only enthusiastic in his love, but a skilful performer himself; and his voice, we are told, was delicately sweet and harmonious. He insists that music shall make a part of a generous education.

With these keen perceptions, he naturally received a love of Nature and a rare susceptibility to impressions from external beauty. In the midst of London, he seems, like the creatures of the field and the forest, to have been tuned in concord with the order of the world; for, he believed, his poetic vein only flowed from the autumnal to the vernal equinox; and in his essay on Education, he doubts whether, in the fine days of spring, any study can be accomplished by young men. "In those vernal seasons of the year, when the air is calm and pleasant, it were an injury and sullenness against Nature not to go out and see her riches and partake in her rejoicing with heaven and earth." His sensibility to impressions from beauty needs no proof from his history; it shines through every page. The form and the voice of Leonora Baroni seemed to have captivated him in Rome, and to her he addressed his Italian sonnets and Latin epigrams.

To these endowments it must be added that his address and his conversation were worthy of his fame. His house was resorted to by men of wit, and foreigners came to England, we are told, "to see the Lord Protector and Mr. Milton." In a letter to one of his foreign correspondents, Emeric Bigot, and in reply apparently to some compliment on his powers of conversation, he writes: "Many have been celebrated for their compositions, whose common conversation and intercourse have betrayed no marks of sublimity or genius. But as far as possible, I aim to show myself equal in thought and speech to what I have written, if I have written anything well."

These endowments received the benefit of a careful and happy discipline. His father's care, seconded by his own endeavor, introduced him to a profound skill in all the treasures of Latin, Greek, Hebrew and Italian tongues; and, to enlarge and enliven his elegant learning, he was sent into Italy, where he beheld the remains of ancient art, and the rival works of Raphael, Michael Angelo and Correggio; where, also, he received social and academical honors from the learned and the great. In Paris, he became acquainted with Grotius; in Florence or Rome, with Galileo; and probably no traveller ever entered that country of history with better right to its hospitality, none upon whom its influences could have fallen more congenially.

Among the advantages of his foreign travel, Milton certainly did not count it the least that it contributed to forge and polish that great weapon of which he acquired such extraordinary mastery, — his power of language. His lore of foreign tongues added daily to his consummate skill in the use of his own. He was a benefactor of the English tongue by showing its capabilities.[1] Very early in life he became conscious that he had more to say to his fellow men than they had fit words to embody. At nineteen years, in a college exercise, he addresses his native language, saying to it that it would be his choice to leave trifles for a grave argument,—

> "Such as may make thee search thy coffers round,
> Before thou clothe my fancy in fit sound;
> Such where the deep transported mind may soar
> Above the wheeling poles, and at Heaven's door
> Look in, and see each blissful deity,
> How he before the thunderous throne doth lie."[2]

Michael Angelo calls "him alone an artist, whose hands can execute what his mind has conceived." The world, no doubt, contains many of that class of men whom Wordsworth denominates *silent poets*, whose minds teem with images which they want words to clothe. But Milton's mind seems to have no thought or emotion which refused to be recorded. His mastery of his native tongue was more than to use it as well as any other; he cast it into new forms. He uttered in it things unheard before. Not imitating but rivalling Shakspeare, he scattered, in tones of prolonged and delicate melody, his pastoral and romantic fancies; then, soaring into unattempted strains, he made it capable of an unknown majesty, and bent it to express every trait of beauty, every shade of thought; and searched the kennel and jakes as well as the palaces of sound for the harsh discords of his polemic wrath. We may even apply to his performance on the instrument of language, his own description of music:—

> "Notes, with many a winding bout
> Of linkèd sweetness long drawn out,
> With wanton heed and giddy cunning,
> The melting voice through mazes running,
> Untwisting all the chains that tie
> The hidden soul of harmony." [1]

But whilst Milton was conscious of possessing this intellectual voice, penetrating through ages and propelling its melodious undulations forward through the coming world, he knew that this mastery of language was a secondary power, and he respected the mysterious source whence it had its spring; namely, clear conceptions and a devoted heart. "For me," he said, in his Apology for Smectymnuus, "although I cannot say that I am utterly untrained in those rules which best rhetoricians have given, or unacquainted with those examples which the prime authors of eloquence have written in any learned tongue, yet true eloquence I find to be none but the serious and hearty love of truth; and that whose mind soever is fully possessed with a fervent desire to know good things, and with the dearest charity to infuse the knowledge of them into others, when such a man would speak, his words, by what I can express, like so many nimble and airy servitors, trip about him at command, and in well-ordered files, as he would wish, fall aptly into their own places."

But as basis or fountain of his rare physical and intellectual accomplishments, the man Milton was just and devout. He is rightly dear to mankind, because in him, among so many perverse and partial men of genius, — in him humanity rights itself; the old eternal goodness finds a home in his breast, and for once shows itself beautiful. His gifts are subordinated to his moral sentiments; and his virtues are so graceful that they seem rather talents than labors. Among so many contrivances as the world has seen to make holiness ugly, in Milton at least it was so pure a flame that the foremost impression his character makes is that of elegance. The victories of the conscience in him are gained by the commanding charm which all the severe and restrictive virtues have for him. His virtues remind us of what Plutarch said of Timoleon's victories, that they resembled Homer's verses, they ran so easy and natural. His habits of living were austere. He was abstemious in diet, chaste, an early riser, and industrious. He tells us, in a Latin poem, that the lyrist may indulge in wine and in a freer life; but that he who would write an epic to the nations must eat beans and drink water. Yet in his severity is no grimace or effort. He serves from love, not from fear. He is innocent and exact, because his taste was so pure and delicate. He acknowledges to his friend Diodati, at the age of twenty-one, that he is enamoured, if ever any was, of moral perfection: "For whatever the Deity may have bestowed upon me in other respects, he has certainly inspired me, if any ever were inspired, with a passion for the good and fair. Nor did Ceres, according to the fable, ever seek her daughter Proserpine with such unceasing solicitude as I have sought this *τοῦ καλοῦ ἰδέαν*, this perfect model of the beautiful in all forms and appearances of things." [1]

When he was charged with loose habits of living, he declares that "a certain niceness of nature, an honest haughtiness and self-esteem either of what I was or what I might be, and a modesty, kept me still above those low descents of mind beneath which he must deject and plunge himself that can agree" to such degradation. "His mind gave him," he said, "that every free and gentle spirit, without that oath of chastity, ought to be born a knight; nor needed to expect the gilt spur, or the laying of a sword upon his shoulder, to stir him up, by his counsel and his arm, to secure and protect" attempted innocence.

He states these things, he says, "to show that though Christianity had been but slightly taught him, yet a certain reservedness of natural disposition and moral discipline, learned out of the noblest philosophy, was enough to keep him in disdain of far less incontinences than these" that had been charged on him. In like spirit, he replies to the suspicious calumny respecting his morning haunts. "Those morning haunts are where they should be, at home; not sleeping, or concocting the surfeits of an irregular feast, but up and stirring, in winter, often ere the sound of any bell awake men to labor or devotion; in summer, as oft with the bird that first rouses, or not much tardier, to read good authors, or cause them to be read, till the attention be weary, or memory have its perfect fraught; then with useful and generous labors preserving the body's health and hardiness, to render lightsome, clear and not lumpish obedience to the mind, to the cause of religion and our country's liberty, when it shall require firm hearts in sound bodies to stand and cover their stations. These are the morning practices."[1] This native honor never forsook him. It is the spirit of Comus, the loftiest song in the praise of chastity that is in any language. It always sparkles in his eyes. It breathed itself over his decent form. It refined his amusements, which consisted in gardening, in exercise with the sword and in playing on the organ. It engaged his interest in chivalry, in courtesy, in whatsoever savored of generosity and nobleness. This magnanimity shines in all his life. He accepts a high impulse at every risk, and deliberately undertakes the defence of the English people, when advised by his physicians that he does it at the cost of sight. There is a forbearance even in his polemics. He opens the war and strikes the first blow. When he had cut down his opponents, he left the details of death and plunder to meaner partisans. He said, "he had learned the prudence of the Roman soldier, not to stand breaking of legs, when the breath was quite out of the body."

To this antique heroism, Milton added the genius of the Christian sanctity. Few men could be cited who have so well understood what is peculiar in the Christian ethics, and the precise aid it has brought to men, in being an emphatic affirmation of the omnipotence of spiritual laws, and, by way of marking the contrast to vulgar opinions, laying its chief stress on humility. The indifferency of a wise mind to what is called high and low, and the fact that true greatness is a perfect humility, are revelations of Christianity which Milton well understood. They give an inexhaustible truth to all his compositions. His firm grasp of this truth is his weapon against the prelates. He celebrates in the martyrs "the unresistible might of weakness." He told the bishops that "instead of showing the reason of their lowly condition from divine example and command, they seek to prove their high preëminence from human consent and authority." He advises that in country places, rather than to trudge many miles to a church, public worship be maintained nearer home, as in a house or barn. "For notwithstanding the gaudy superstition of some still devoted ignorantly to temples, we may be well assured that he who disdained not to be born in a manger disdains not to be preached in a barn." And the following passage, in the Reason of Church Government, indicates his own perception of the doctrine of humility. "Albeit I must confess to be half in doubt whether I should bring it forth or no, it being so contrary to the eye of the world, that I shall endanger either not to be regarded, or not to be understood. For who is there, almost, that measures wisdom by simplicity, strength by suffering, dignity by lowliness?" Obeying this sentiment, Milton deserved the apostrophe of Wordsworth: —

> "Pure as the naked heavens, majestic, free,
> So didst thou travel on life's common way
> In cheerful godliness; and yet thy heart
> The lowliest duties on itself did lay." [1]

He laid on himself the lowliest duties. Johnson petulantly taunts Milton with "great promise and small performance," in returning from Italy because his country was in danger, and then opening a private school. Milton, wiser, felt no absurdity in this conduct. He returned into his revolutionized country, and assumed an honest and useful task, by which he might serve the state daily, whilst he launched from time to time his formidable bolts against the enemies of liberty. He felt the heats of that "love" which "esteems no office mean." He compiled a logic for boys; he wrote a grammar; and devoted much of his time to the preparing of a Latin dictionary. But the religious sentiment warmed his writings and conduct with the highest affection of faith. The memorable covenant, which in his youth, in the second book of the Reason of Church Government, he makes with God and his reader, expressed the faith of his old age. For the first time since many ages, the invocations of the Eternal Spirit in the commencement of his books are not poetic forms, but are thoughts, and so are still read with delight. His views of choice of profession, and choice in marriage, equally expect a divine leading.[1]

Thus chosen, by the felicity of his nature and of his breeding, for the clear perception of all that is graceful and all that is great in man, Milton was not less happy in his times. His birth fell upon the agitated years when the discontents of the English Puritans were fast drawing to a head against the tyranny of the Stuarts. No period has surpassed that in the general activity of mind. It is said that no opinion, no civil, religious, moral dogma can be produced that was not broached in the fertile brain of that age. Questions that involve all social and personal rights were hasting to be decided by the sword, and were searched by eyes to which the love of freedom, civil and religious, lent new illumination. Milton, gentle, learned, delicately bred in all the elegancy of art and learning, was set down in England in the stern, almost fanatic society of the Puritans. The part he took, the zeal of his fellowship, make us acquainted with the greatness of his spirit as in tranquil times we could not have known it. Susceptible as Burke to the attractions of historical prescription, of royalty, of chivalry, of an ancient church illustrated by old martyrdoms and installed in cathedrals, — he threw himself, the flower of elegancy, on the side of the reeking conventicle; the side of humanity, but unlearned and unadorned. His muse was brave and humane, as well as sweet.[1] He felt the dear love of native land and native language. The humanity which warms his pages begins, as it should, at home. He preferred his own English, so manlike he was, to the Latin, which contained all the treasures of his memory.

"My mother bore me," he said, "a speaker of what God made mine own, and not a translator." He told the Parliament that "the imprimaturs of Lambeth House had been writ in Latin; for that our English, the language of men ever famous and foremost in the achievements of liberty, will not easily find servile letters enow to spell such a dictatory presumption." At one time he meditated writing a poem on the settlement of Britain, and a history of England was one of the three main tasks which he proposed to himself. He proceeded in it no further than to the Conquest. He studied with care the character of his countrymen, and once in the History, and once again in the Reason of Church Government, he has recorded his judgment of the English genius.

Thus drawn into the great controversies of the times, in them he is never lost in a party. His private opinions and private conscience always distinguish him. That which drew him to the party was his love of liberty, ideal liberty; this therefore he could not sacrifice to any party. Toland tells us, "As he looked upon true and absolute freedom to be the greatest happiness of this life, whether to societies or single persons, so he thought constraint of any sort to be the utmost misery; for which reason he used to tell those about him the entire satisfaction of his mind that he had constantly employed his strength and faculties in the defence of liberty, and in direct opposition to slavery." Truly he was an apostle of freedom; of freedom in the house, in the state, in the church; freedom of speech, freedom of the press; yet in his own mind discriminated from savage license, because that which he desired was the liberty of the wise man, containing itself in the limits of virtue. He pushed, as far as any in that democratic age, his ideas of *civil* liberty. He proposed to establish a republic, of which the federal power was weak and loosely defined, and the substantial power should remain with primary assemblies. He maintained that a nation may try, judge and slay their king, if he be a tyrant. He pushed as far his views of *ecclesiastical* liberty. He taught the doctrine of unlimited toleration. One of his tracts is writ to prove that no power on earth can compel in matters of religion. He maintained the doctrine of *literary* liberty, denouncing the censorship of the press, and insisting that a book shall come into the world as freely as a man, so only it bear the name of author or printer, and be responsible for itself like a man. He maintained the doctrine of *domestic* liberty, or the liberty of divorce, on the ground that unfit disposition of mind was a better reason for the act of divorce than infirmity of body, which was good ground in law. The tracts he wrote on these topics are, for the most part, as fresh and pertinent to-day as they were then. The events which produced them, the practical issues to which they tend, are mere occasions for this philanthropist to blow his trumpet for human rights. They are all varied applications of one principle, the liberty of the wise man. He sought absolute truth, not accommodating truth. His opinions on all subjects are formed for man as he ought to be, for a nation of Miltons. He would be divorced when he finds in his consort unfit disposition; knowing that he should not abuse that liberty, because with his whole heart he abhors licentiousness and loves chastity. He defends the slaying of the king, because a king is a king no longer than he governs by the laws; "it would be right to kill Philip of Spain making an inroad into England, and what right the king of Spain hath to govern us at all, the same hath the king Charles to govern tyrannically." He would remove hirelings out of the church, and support preachers by voluntary contributions; requiring that such only should preach as have faith enough to accept so self-denying and precarious a mode of life, scorning to take thought for the aspects of prudence and expediency. The most devout man of his time, he frequented no church;[1] probably from a disgust at the fierce spirit of the pulpits. And so, throughout all his actions and opinions, is he a consistent spiritualist, or believer in the omnipotence of spiritual laws. He wished that his writings should be communicated only to those who desired to see them. He thought nothing honest was low. He thought he could be famous only in proportion as he enjoyed the approbation of the good. He admonished his friend "not to admire military prowess, or things in which force is of most avail. For it would not be matter of rational wonder, if the wethers of our country should be born with horns that could batter down cities and towns. Learn to estimate great characters, not by the amount of animal strength, but by the habitual justice and temperance of their conduct."

Was there not a fitness in the undertaking of such a person to write a poem on the subject of Adam, the first man? By his sympathy with all Nature; by the proportion of his powers; by great knowledge, and by religion, he would reascend to the height from which our nature is supposed to have descended. From a just knowledge of what man should be, he described what he was. He beholds him as he walked in Eden:—

> "His fair large front and eye sublime declared
> Absolute rule; and hyacinthine locks
> Round from his parted forelock manly hung
> Clustering, but not beneath his shoulders broad." [1]

And the soul of this divine creature is excellent as his form. The tone of his thought and passion is as healthful, as even and as vigorous as befits the new and perfect model of a race of gods.

The perception we have attributed to Milton, of a purer ideal of humanity, modifies his poetic genius. The man is paramount to the poet. His fancy is never transcendent, extravagant; but as Bacon's imagination was said to be "the noblest that ever contented itself to minister to the understanding," so Milton's ministers to the character. Milton's sublimest song, bursting into heaven with its peals of melodious thunder, is the voice of Milton still. Indeed, throughout his poems, one may see, under a thin veil, the opinions, the feelings, even the incidents of the poet's life, still reappearing. The sonnets are all occasional poems. L' Allegro and Il Penseroso are but a finer autobiography of his youthful fancies at Harefield; the Comus a transcript, in charming numbers, of that philosophy of chastity, which, in the Apology for Smectymnuus, and in the Reason of Church Government, he declares to be his defence and religion. The Samson Agonistes is too broad an expression of his private griefs to be mistaken, and is a version of the Doctrine and Discipline of Divorce. The most affecting passages in Paradise Lost are personal allusions; and when we are fairly in Eden, Adam and Milton are often difficult to be separated. Again, in Paradise Regained, we have the most distinct marks of the progress of the poet's mind, in the revision and enlargement of his religious opinions. This may be thought to abridge his praise as a poet. It is true of Homer and Shakspeare that they do not appear in their poems; that those prodigious geniuses did cast themselves so totally into their song that their individuality vanishes, and the poet towers to the sky, whilst the man quite disappears. The fact is memorable. Shall we say that in our admiration and joy in these wonderful poems we have even a feeling of regret that the men knew not what they did; that they were too passive in their great service; were channels through which streams of thought flowed from a higher source, which they did not appropriate, did not blend with their own being? Like prophets, they seem but imperfectly aware of the import of their own utterances. We hesitate to say such things, and say them only to the unpleasing dualism, when the man and the poet show like a double consciousness. Perhaps we speak to no fact, but to mere fables, of an idle mendicant Homer, and of a Shakspeare content with a mean and jocular way of life. Be it how it may, the genius and office of Milton were different, namely, to ascend by the aids of his learning and his religion — by an equal perception, that is, of the past and the future — to a higher insight and more lively delineation of the heroic life of man. This was his poem; whereof all his indignant pamphlets and all his soaring verses are only single cantos or detached stanzas. It was plainly needful that his poetry should be a version of his own life, in order to give weight and solemnity to his thoughts; by which they might penetrate and possess the imagination and the will of mankind. The creations of Shakspeare are cast into the world of thought to no further end than to delight. Their intrinsic beauty is their excuse for being. Milton, fired "with dearest charity to infuse the knowledge of good things into others," tasked his giant imagination and exhausted the stores of his intellect for an end beyond, namely, to teach. His own conviction it is which gives such authority to his strain. Its reality is its force. If out of the heart it came, to the heart it must go. What schools and epochs of common rhymers would it need to make a counterbalance to the severe oracles of his muse:—

> "In them is plainest taught and easiest learnt,
> What makes a nation happy, and keeps it so." [1]

The lover of Milton reads one sense in his prose and in his metrical compositions; and sometimes the muse soars highest in the former, because the thought is more sincere. Of his prose in general, not the style alone but the argument also is poetic; according to Lord Bacon's definition of poetry, following that of

Aristotle, "Poetry, not finding the actual world exactly conformed to its idea of good and fair, seeks to accommodate the shows of things to the desires of the mind, and to create an ideal world better than the world of experience." Such certainly is the explanation of Milton's tracts. Such is the apology to be entered for the plea for freedom of divorce; an essay, which, from the first, until now, has brought a degree of obloquy on his name. It was a sally of the extravagant spirit of the time, overjoyed, as in the French Revolution, with the sudden victories it had gained, and eager to carry on the standard of truth to new heights. It is to be regarded as a poem on one of the griefs of man's condition, namely, unfit marriage. And as many poems have been written upon unfit society, commending solitude, yet have not been proceeded against, though their end was hostile to the state; so should this receive that charity which an angelic soul, suffering more keenly than others from the unavoidable evils of human life, is entitled to.

We have offered no apology for expanding to such length our commentary on the character of John Milton; who, in old age, in solitude, in neglect, and blind, wrote the Paradise Lost; a man whom labor or danger never deterred from whatever efforts a love of the supreme interests of man prompted. For are we not the better; are not all men fortified by the remembrance of the bravery, the purity, the temperance, the toil, the independence and the angelic devotion of this man, who, in a revolutionary age, taking counsel only of himself, endeavored, in his writings and in his life, to carry out the life of man to new heights of spiritual grace and dignity, without any abatement of its strength?

man when labor or danger were encountered from whatever efforts a love of the [illegible] interest or merit prompted. How are we not the better, are not all men fortified by the remembrance of [illegible] between the [illegible], the [illegible], the and the independence, and the heroic devotion of the man who, in a revolutionary age, taking counsel only of himself and nature, in his writings and in his life, to carry out the life of man to new heights of spiritual grace and dignity without any abatement of its strength?

VIII

ART AND CRITICISM

To clothe the fiery thought
   In simple words succeeds,
For still the craft of genius is
   To mask a king in weeds.

ART AND CRITICISM

LITERATURE is but a poor trick, you will say, when it busies itself to make words pass for things; and yet I am far from thinking this subordinate service unimportant. The secondary services of literature may be classed under the name of Rhetoric, and are quite as important in letters as iron is in war. An enumeration of the few principal weapons of the poet or writer will at once suggest their value.

Writing is the greatest of arts, the subtilest, and of most miraculous effect; and to it the education is costliest. On the writer the choicest influences are concentrated, — nothing that does not go to his costly equipment: a war, an earthquake, revival of letters, the new dispensation by Jesus, or by Angels; Heaven, Hell, power, science, the *Néant*,[1] exist to him as colors for his brush.

In this art modern society has introduced a new element, by introducing a new audience. The decline of the privileged orders, all over the world; the advance of the Third Estate; the transformation of the laborer into reader and writer has compelled the learned and the thinkers to address them. Chiefly in this country, the common school has added two or three audiences: once, we had only the boxes; now, the galleries and the pit.[1]

There is, in every nation, a style which never becomes obsolete, a certain mode of phraseology so consonant and congenial to the analogy and principles of its respective language as to remain settled and unaltered. This style is probably to be sought in the common intercourse of life, among those who speak only to be understood, without ambition of elegance. The polite are always catching modish innovations, and the learned depart from established forms of speech, in hope of finding or making better; those who wish for distinction forsake the vulgar, when the vulgar is right; but there is a conversation above grossness and below refinement where prosperity resides, and where Shakspeare seems to have gathered his comic dialogue. Goethe valued himself not on his learning or eccentric flights, but that he knew how to write German. And many of his poems are so idiomatic, so strongly rooted in the German soil, that they are the terror of translators, who say they cannot be rendered into any other language without loss of vigor, as we say of any darling passage of our own masters. "Le style c'est l'homme," said Buffon; and Goethe said, "Poetry here, poetry there, I have learned to speak German." And when I read of various extraordinary polyglots, self-made or college-made, who can understand fifty languages, I answer that I shall be glad and surprised to find that they know one. For if I were asked how many masters of English idiom I know, I shall be perplexed to count five.

Ought not the scholar to convey his meaning in terms as short and strong as the smith and the drover use to convey theirs? You know the history of the eminent English writer on gypsies, George Borrow; he had one clear perception, that the key to every country was command of the language of the common people. He therefore mastered the *patois* of the gypsies, called Romany, which is spoken by them in all countries where they wander, in Europe, Asia, Africa. Yet much of the raw material of the street-talk is absolutely untranslatable into print, and one must learn from Burke how to be severe without being unparliamentary. Rabelais and Montaigne are masters of this Romany, but cannot be read aloud, and so far fall short. Whitman is our American master, but has not got out of the Fire-Club and gained the *entrée* of the sitting-rooms. Bacon, if "he could out-cant a London chirurgeon," must have possessed the Romany under his brocade robes. Luther said, "I preach coarsely; that giveth content to all. Hebrew, Greek and Latin I spare, until we learned ones come together, and then we make it so curled and finical that God himself wondereth at us." He who would be powerful must have the terrible gift of familiarity,— Mirabeau, Chatham, Fox, Burke, O'Connell, Patrick Henry; and among writers, Swift, De Foe and Carlyle.

Look at this forlorn caravan of travellers who wander over Europe dumb, — never exchange a word, in the mother tongue of either, with prince or peasant; but condemned to the company of a courier and of the padrone when they cannot take refuge in the society of countrymen. A well-chosen series of stereoscopic views would have served a better purpose, which they can explore at home, sauced with joyful discourse and with reference to all the books in your library.

Speak with the vulgar, think with the wise. See how Plato managed it, with an imagination so gorgeous, and a taste so patrician, that Jove, if he descended, was to speak in his style. Into the exquisite refinement of his Academy, he introduces the low-born Socrates, relieving the purple diction by his perverse talk, his gallipots, and cook, and trencher, and cart-wheels — and steadily kept this coarseness to flavor a dish else too luscious. Everybody knows the points in which the mob has the advantage of the Academy, and all able men have known how to import the petulance of the street into correct discourse. I heard, when a great bank president was expounding the virtues of his party and of the government to a silent circle of bank pensioners, a grave Methodist exclaimed "Fiddlesticks!" The whole party were surprised and cheered, except the bank president, though it would be difficult to explain the propriety of the expression, as no music or fiddle was so much as thought of.

Not only low style, but the lowest classifying words outvalue arguments; as, upstart, dab, cockney, prig, granny, lubber, puppy, peacock — "A cocktail House of Commons." I remember when a venerable divine [Dr. Osgood] called the young preacher's sermon "patty cake." The *sans-culottes* at Versailles cried out, "Let our little Mother Mirabeau speak!" Who has not heard in the street how forcible is bosh, gammon and gas. The short Saxon words with which the people help themselves are better than Latin. The language of the street is always strong. I envy the boys the force of the double negative (no shoes, no money, no nothing), though clean contrary to our grammar rules, and I confess to some titillation of my ears from a rattling oath.[1]

In the infinite variety of talents, 't is certain that some men swear with genius. I knew a poet in whose talent Nature carried this freak so far that his only graceful verses were pretty blasphemies. "The better the worse," you will say; and I own it reminds one of Vathek's collection of monstrous men with humps of a picturesque peak, and horns of exquisite polish.[2] What traveller has not listened to the vigor of the *Sacre!* of the French postilion, the *Sia ammazato!* of the Italian contadino, or the deep stomach of an English drayman's execration. I remember an occasion when a proficient in this style came from North Street to Cambridge and drew a crowd of young critics in the college yard, who found his wrath so æsthetic and fertilizing that they took notes, and even overstayed the hour of the mathematical professor.

'T is odd what revolutions occur. We were educated in horror of Satan, but Goethe remarked that all men like to hear him named. Burns took him into compassion and expressed a blind wish for his reformation.

> "Ye aiblins might, I dinna ken,
> Still have a stake." [1]

And George Sand finds a whole nation who regard him as a personage who has been greatly wronged, and in which he is really the subject of a covert worship. As a study in language, the use of this word is curious, to see how words help us and must be philosophical. The Devil in philosophy is absolute negation, falsehood, nothing; and in the popular mind, the Devil is a malignant person. Yet all our speech expresses the first sense. "The Devil a monk was he," means, *he was no monk*, and "The Devil you did!" means *you did not*. Natural science gives us the inks, the shades; ink of Erebus — night of Chaos.[2] . . . Goethe, who had collected all the diabolical hints in men and nature for traits for his *Walpurgis Nacht*, continued the humor of collecting such horrors after this first occasion had passed, and professed to point his guest to his Walpurgis Sack, or Acherontian Bag, in which, he said, he put all his dire hints and images, and into which, he said, he should be afraid to fall himself, lest he should be burnt up. Dante is the professor that shall teach both the noble low style, the power of working up all his experience into heaven and hell ; also the sculpture of compression.

The next virtue of rhetoric is compression, the science of omitting, which makes good the old verse of Hesiod, "Fools, they did not know that half was better than the whole." The French have a neat phrase, that the secret of boring you is that of telling all, — "Le secret d'ennuyer est celui de tout dire ;" which we translate short, "Touch and go." The silences, pauses, of an orator are as telling as his words.[1] What the poet omits exalts every syllable that he writes. In good hands it will never become sterility. A good writer must convey the feeling of a flamboyant witness, and at the same time of chemic selection, — as if in his densest period was no cramp, but room to turn a chariot and horses between his valid words. There is hardly danger in America of excess of condensation ; there must be no cramp insufficiency, but the superfluous must be omitted. In the Hindoo mythology, "Viswaharmán" placed the sun on his lathe to grind off some of his effulgence, and in this manner reduced it to an eighth, — more was inseparable. . . .

In architecture the beauty is increased in the degree in which the material is safely diminished; as when you break up a prose wall, and leave all the strength in the poetry of columns. As soon as you read aloud, you will find what sentences drag. Blot them out, and read again, you will find the words that drag. 'T is like a pebble inserted in a mosaic. Resolute blotting rids you of all those phrases that sound like something and mean nothing, with which scriptural forms play a large part. Never say, "I beg not to be misunderstood." It is only graceful in the case when you are afraid that what is called a better meaning will be taken, and you wish to insist on a worse; a man has a right to pass, like Dean Swift, for a worse man than he is, but not for a better.

And I sometimes wish that the Board of Education might carry out the project of a college for graduates of our universities, to which editors and members of Congress and writers of books might repair, and learn to sink what we could best spare of our words; to gazette those Americanisms which offend us in all journals. Some of these are odious. *Some* as an adverb

— "reeled some;" *considerable* as an adverb for *much;* "quite a number;" *slim* for *bad;* the adjective *graphic*, which means *what is written*, — graphic arts and oral arts, arts of writing, and arts of speech and song, — but is used as if it meant *descriptive:* "Minerva's graphic thread." A Mr. Randall, M. C., who appeared before the committee of the House of Commons on the subject of the American mode of closing a debate, said, "that the one-hour rule worked well; made the debate short and graphic." 'T is the worst praise you can give a speech that it is as if written.

Never use the word *development*, and be wary of the whole family of Fero.[1] Dangerous words in like kind are *display*, *improvement*, *peruse*, *circumstances*, *commence* for *begin.* Vulgarisms to be gazetted, *moiety* used for *a small part;* — "nothing would answer but;" "there is none but what" — "there being scarce a person of any note in England but what some time or other paid a visit or sent a present to our Lady of Walsingham" (Bishop Parcy); "might have to go;" "I have been to Europe;" "in our midst;" *considerable* — "it is considerable of a compliment," "under considerable of a cloud;" *balance* for *remainder*

— "spent the balance of his life;" "*as a general thing;*" "*after all.*" Confusions of *lie* and *lay*, *sit* and *set*, *shall* and *will*.

Persons have been named from their abuse of certain phrases, as "Pyramid" Lambert, "Finality" Russell, "Humanity" Martin, "Horizon" Turner.

Every age gazettes a quantity of words which it has used up. We are now offended with "Standpoint,"[1] "Myth," "Subjective," "the Good and the True" and "the Cause."

A list might be made of showy words that tempt young writers: *asphodel*, *harbinger*, *chalice*, *flamboyant*,[2] *golden*, *diamond*, *amethyst*, *opal* and the rest of the precious stones, *carcanet*, *diadem*.

But these cardinal rules of rhetoric find best examples in the great masters, and are main sources of the delight they give. Shakspeare might be studied for his dexterity in the use of these weapons, if it were not for his heroic strength. There is no such master of low style as he, and therefore none can securely soar so high. I do not mean that he delights in comedy, exults in bringing the street itself, uproarious with laughter and animal joy, on to the scene, with Falstaff and Touchstone and Trinculo and the fools; but that in the conduct of the play, and the speech of the heroes, he keeps the level tone which is the tone of high and low alike, and most widely understood. A man of experience altogether, his very sonnets are as solid and close to facts as the Banker's Gazette; and the only check on the detail of each of his portraits is his own universality, which made bias or fixed ideas impossible — his impartiality is like a sunbeam.

His fun is as wise as his earnest, its foundations are below the frost.[1] His muse is moral simply from its depth, and I value the intermixture of the common and the transcendental as in Nature. One would say Shakspeare must have been a thousand years old when he wrote his first piece; so thoroughly is his thought familiar to him, so solidly worded, as if it were already a proverb, and not only hereafter to become one. Well, that millennium is really only a little acceleration in his process of thought; his loom is better toothed, cranked and pedalled than other people's, and he can turn off a hundred yards to their one. Shakspeare is nothing but a large utterance. We cannot find that anything in his age was more worth expression than anything in ours; nor give any account of his existence, but only the fact that there was a wonderful symbolizer and expressor, who has no rival in all ages and who has thrown an accidental lustre over his time and subject.

My friend thinks the reason why the French mind is so shallow, and still to seek, running into vagaries and blind alleys, is because they do not read Shakspeare; whilst the English and Germans, who read Shakspeare and the Bible, have a great onward march. Shakspeare would have sufficed for the culture of a nation for vast periods. The Chinese have got on so long with their solitary Confucius and Mencius; the Arabs with their Mahomet; the Scandinavians with their Snorre Sturleson; and if the English island had been larger and the Straits of Dover wider, to keep it at pleasure a little out of the imbroglio of Europe, they might have managed to feed on Shakspeare for some ages yet; as the camel in the desert is fed by his humps, in long absence from food.

Montaigne must have the credit of giving to literature that which we listen for in barrooms, the low speech, — words and phrases that no scholar coined; street-cries and warcries; words of the boatman, the farmer and the lord; that have neatness and necessity, through their use in the vocabulary of work and appetite, like the pebbles which the incessant attrition of the sea has rounded. Every historic autobiographic trait authenticating the man adds to the value of the book. We can't afford to take the horse out of the Essays; it would take the rider too.

Herrick is a remarkable example of the low style. He is, therefore, a good example of the modernness of an old English writer. So Latimer, so Chaucer, so the Bible. He found his subject where he stood, between his feet, in his house, pantry, barn, poultry-yard, in his village, neighbors' gossip and scandal. Like Montaigne in this, that his subject cost him nothing, and he knew what he spake of, and did not write up to it, but could write down (a main secret),[1] and took his level, so that he had all his strength, the easiness of strength; he took what he knew, and "took it easy," as we say. The Germans praise in Goethe the comfortable stoutness. Herrick's merit is the simplicity and manliness of his utterance, and, rarely, the weight of his sentence. He has, and knows that he has, a noble, idiomatic English, a perfect, plain style, from which he can soar to a fine, lyric delicacy, or descend to coarsest sarcasm, without losing his firm footing. This flower of speech is accompanied with an assurance of fame. We have an artist who in this merit of which I speak will easily cope with these celebrities.

In Carlyle as in Byron one is more struck with the rhetoric than with the matter. He has manly superiority rather than intellectuality, and so makes hard hits all the time. There 's more character than intellect in every sentence — herein strongly resembling Samuel Johnson. The best service Carlyle has rendered is to rhetoric, or art of writing. In his books the vicious conventions of writing are all dropped. You have no board interposed between you and the writer's mind, but he talks flexibly, now high, now low, in loud emphasis, in undertones, then laughs till the walls ring, then calmly moderates, then hints, or raises an eyebrow. He has gone nigher to the wind than any other craft.

Carlyle, with his inimitable ways of saying the thing, is next best to the inventor of the thing, and I think of him when I read the famous inscription on the pyramid, "I King Saib built this pyramid. I, when I had built it, covered it with satin. Let him who cometh after me, and says he is equal to me, cover it with mats." What he has said shall be proverb, nobody shall be able to say it otherwise. No book can any longer be tolerable in the old husky Neal-on-the-Puritans model. In short, I think the revolution wrought by Carlyle is precisely parallel to that going forward in picture, by the stereoscope. Until history is interesting, it is not yet written.

Here has come into the country, three months ago, a History of Friedrich, infinitely the wittiest book that ever was written; a book that, one would think, the English people would rise up in a mass to thank him for, by cordial acclamation, and signify, by crowning him with chaplet of oak-leaves, their joy that such a head existed among them, and sympathizing and much-reading America would make a new treaty or send a minister extraordinary to offer congratulations of honoring delight to England in acknowledgment of such a donation; a book holding so many memorable and heroic facts, working directly on practice; with new heroes, things unvoiced before — the German Plutarch, now that we have exhausted the Greek and Roman and British biography — with a range, too, of thought and wisdom, so large, so colloquially elastic, that we not so much read a stereotype page as we see the eyes of the writer looking into ours, whilst he is humming and chuckling, with undertones, and trumpet-tones, and shrugs, and long commanding glances, stereoscoping every figure that passes, and every hill, river, wood, hummock and pebble in the long perspective, with its wonderful mnemonics, whereby great and insignificant men are ineffaceably marked and medalled in the memory by what they were, had and did; and withal a book that is a judgment-day for its moral verdict on the men and nations and manners of modern times. And this book makes no noise. I have hardly seen a notice of it in any newspaper or journal, and you would think there was no such book. I am not aware that Mr. Buchanan has sent a special messenger to Great Cheyne Row, Chelsea; but the secret interior wits and hearts of men take note of it, not the less surely. They have said nothing lately in praise of the air, or of fire, or of the blessing of love, and yet, I suppose, they are sensible of these, and not less of this Book, which is like these.

After Low Style and Compression what the books call *Metonomy* is a principal power of rhetoric. It means, using one word or image for another. It is a low idealism. Idealism regards the world as symbolic, and all these symbols or forms as fugitive and convertible expressions. The power of the poet is in controlling these symbols; in using every fact in Nature, however great and stable, as a fluent symbol, and in measuring his strength by the facility with which he makes the mood of mind give its color to things. The world, history, the powers of Nature,—he can make them speak what sense he will.

All conversation, as all literature, appears to me the pleasure of rhetoric, or, I may say, of *metonomy*. "To make of motes mountains, and of mountains motes," Isocrates said, "was the orator's office." Well, that is what poetry and thinking do. Whatever new object we see, we perceive to be only a new version of our familiar experience, and we set about translating it at once into our parallel facts. We have hereby our vocabulary.

Everything has two handles. Pindar when the victor in a race by mules offered him a trifling present, pretended to be hurt at thought of writing on demi-asses. When, however, he offered a sufficient present, he composed the poem:—

"Hail, daughters of the tempest-footed horse,
That skims like wind along the course."

That was the other handle. I passed at one time through a place called New City, then supposed, like each of a hundred others, to be destined to greatness. I fell in with one of the founders who showed its advantages and its river and port and the capabilities: "Sixty houses, sir, were built in a night, like tents." After Chicago had secured the confluence of the railroads to itself, I chanced to meet my founder again, but now removed to Chicago. He had transferred to that city the magnificent dreams which he had once communicated to me, and no longer remembered his first emporium. "Where is the town? Was there not," I asked, "a river and a harbor there?" "Oh yes, there was a guzzle out of a sand-bank." "And the town?" "There are still the sixty houses, but when I passed it, one owl was the only inhabitant." When Samuel Dexter, long since, argued the claims of South Boston Bridge, he had to meet loud complaints of the shutting out of the coasting-trade by the proposed improvements. "Now," said he, "I come to the grand charge that we have obstructed the commerce and navigation of Roxbury Ditch." 'T is very easy to call the gracious spring "poor goody herb-wife," or to represent the farm, which stands for the organization of the gravest needs, as a poor trifle of pea-vines, turnips and hen-roosts. Everything has two handles. Shakspeare says, "A plague of opinion; a man can wear it on both sides, like a leather jerkin."

Here is my friend E.,[1] the model of opinionists. He is the April day incarnated and walking, soft sunshine and hailstones, sour east wind and flowery southwest — alternating, and each sovereign, and painting all things its own color. He has it all his own way. He complains of Nature,— too many leaves, too windy and grassy, and I suppose the birds are too feathery and the horses too leggy. He thinks Egypt a humbug, and Palestine used up, and England a flash in the pan; and that the only art is landscape-painting. But when we came, in the woods, to a clump of goldenrod,— "Ah!" he says, "here they are! these things consume a great deal of time. I don't know but they are of more importance than any other of our investments." Well, this is the game that goes on every day in all companies; this is the ball that is tossed in every court of law, in every legislature and in literature, and in the history of every mind by sovereignty of thought to make facts and men obey our present humor or belief.

I designed to speak of one point more, the touching a principal question in criticism in recent times — the Classic and Romantic, or what is classic?

The art of writing is the highest of those permitted to man as drawing directly from the soul, and the means or material it uses are also of the soul. It brings man into alliance with what is great and eternal. It discloses to him the variety and splendor of his resources. And there is much in literature that draws us with a sublime charm — the superincumbent necessity by which each writer, an infirm, capricious, fragmentary soul, is made to utter his part in the chorus of humanity, is enriched by thoughts which flow from all past minds, shares the hopes of all existing minds; so that, whilst the world is made of youthful, helpless children of a day, literature resounds with the music of united vast ideas of affirmation and of moral truth.

What is the Classic? Classic art is the art of necessity; organic; modern or romantic bears the stamp of caprice or chance. One is the product of inclination, of caprice, of haphazard; the other carries its law and necessity within itself.

The politics of monarchy, when all hangs on the accidents of life and temper of a single person, may be called romantic politics. The democratic, when the power proceeds organically from the people and is responsible to them, are classic politics. The classic unfolds, the romantic adds. The classic *should*, the modern *would*. The classic is healthy, the romantic is sick. The classic draws its rule from the genius of that which it does, and not from by-ends. It does not make a novel to establish a principle of political economy.

Don't set out to please; you will displease. The Augsburg Allgemeine Zeitung deprecates an observatory founded for the benefit of navigation. Nor can we promise that our School of Design will secure a lucrative post to the pupils.

When I read Plutarch, or look at a Greek vase, I incline to accept the common opinion of scholars, that the Greeks had clearer wits than any other people. But there is anything but time in my idea of the antique. A clear or natural expression by word or deed is that which we mean when we love and praise the antique. In society I do not find it, in modern books, seldom; but when I come into the pastures, I find antiquity again. Once in the fields with the lowing cattle, the birds, trees and waters and satisfying curves of the landscape, and I cannot tell whether this is Thessaly and Enna, or whether Concord and Acton.

A man of genius or a work of love or beauty will not come to order, can't be compounded by the best rules, but is always a new and incalculable result, like health. Don't rattle your rules in our ears; we must behave as we can. Criticism is an art when it does not stop at the words of the poet, but looks at the order of his thoughts and the essential quality of his mind. Then the critic is poet. 'T is a question not of talents but of tone; and not particular merits, but the mood of mind into which one and another can bring us.[1]

we mean when we love and praise the antique. In short, I do not find it in modern books seldom; but when I come into the pasture, I find antiquity again. Once in the fields with the lowing cattle, the birds, trees and waters and satisfying curves of the landscape, and I cannot tell whether this is Thessaly and Enna, or whether Concord and Acton.

A man of genius or a work of love or beauty will not come to order, can't be compounded by the best rules, but is always a new and incalculable result, like health. Don't carry your rules in our ears; we must behave as we can. Criticism is an art when it does not stop at the words of the poet, but looks at the order of his thoughts and the essential quality of his mind. Then the critic is poet. 'Tis a question not of talents but of tone; and not particular merits but the mood of mind into which one and another can bring us.

IX

PAPERS FROM THE DIAL

THE tongue is prone to lose the way;
Not so the pen, for in a letter
We have not better things to say,
But surely say them better.

PAPERS FROM THE DIAL

I

THOUGHTS ON MODERN LITERATURE

IN our fidelity to the higher truth we need not disown our debt, in our actual state of culture, in the twilights of experience, to these rude helpers. They keep alive the memory and the hope of a better day. When we flout all particular books as initial merely, we truly express the privilege of spiritual nature, but alas, not the fact and fortune of this low Massachusetts and Boston, of these humble Junes and Decembers of mortal life. Our souls are not self-fed, but do eat and drink of chemical water and wheat. Let us not forget the genial miraculous force we have known to proceed from a book. We go musing into the vault of day and night; no constellation shines, no muse descends, the stars are white points, the roses, brick-colored leaves, and frogs pipe, mice cheep, and wagons creak along the road. We return to the house and take up Plutarch or Augustine, and read a few sentences or pages, and lo! the air swims with life, secrets of magnanimity and grandeur invite us on every hand, life is made up of them. Such is our debt to a book. Observe moreover that we ought to credit literature with much more than the bare word it gives us. I have just been reading poems which now in memory shine with a certain steady, warm, autumnal light. That is not in their grammatical construction which they give me. If I analyze the sentences, it eludes me, but is the genius and suggestion of the whole. Over every true poem lingers a certain wild beauty, immeasurable; a happiness lightsome and delicious fills the heart and brain, as they say every man walks environed by his proper atmosphere, extending to some distance around him. This beautiful result must be credited to literature also in casting its account.

In looking at the library of the Present Age, we are first struck with the fact of the immense miscellany. It can hardly be characterized by any species of book, for every opinion, old and new, every hope and fear, every whim and folly, has an organ. It exhibits a vast carcass of tradition every year with as much solemnity as a new revelation. Along with these it vents books that breathe of new morning, that seem to heave with the life of millions, books for which men and women peak and pine; books which take the rose out of the cheek of him that wrote them, and give him to the midnight a sad, solitary, diseased man; which leave no man where they found him, but make him better or worse; and which work dubiously on society and seem to inoculate it with a venom before any healthy result appears.

In order to any complete view of the literature of the present age, an inquiry should include what it quotes, what it writes and what it wishes to write. In our present attempt to enumerate some traits of the recent literature, we shall have somewhat to offer on each of these topics, but we cannot promise to set in very exact order what we have to say.

In the first place it has all books. It reprints the wisdom of the world. How can the age be a bad one which gives me Plato and Paul and Plutarch, Saint Augustine, Spinoza, Chapman, Beaumont and Fletcher, Donne and Sir Thomas Browne, beside its own riches? Our presses groan every year with new editions of all the select pieces of the first of mankind, — meditations, history, classifications, opinions, epics, lyrics, which the age adopts by quoting them. If we should designate favorite studies in which the age delights more than in the rest of this great mass of the permanent literature of the human race, one or two instances would be conspicuous. First; the prodigious growth and influence of the genius of Shakspeare, in the last one hundred and fifty years, is itself a fact of the first importance. It almost alone has called out the genius of the German nation into an activity which, spreading from the poetic into the scientific, religious and philosophical domains, has made theirs now at last the paramount intellectual influence of the world, reacting with great energy on England and America. And thus, and not by mechanical diffusion, does an original genius work and spread himself.[1]

The poetry and speculation of the age are marked by a certain philosophic turn, which discriminates them from the works of earlier times. The poet is not content to see how "Fair hangs the apple from the rock," "What music a sunbeam awoke in the groves," nor of Hardiknute, how

> "Stately stept he east the wa,
> And stately stept he west,"

but he now revolves, What is the apple to me? and what the birds to me? and what is Hardiknute to me? and what am I? And this is called subjectiveness, as the eye is withdrawn from the object and fixed on the subject or mind.

We can easily concede that a steadfast tendency of this sort appears in modern literature. It is the new consciousness of the one mind, which predominates in criticism. It is the uprise of the soul, and not the decline. It is founded on that insatiable demand for unity, the need to recognize one nature in all the variety of objects, which always characterizes a genius of the first order. Accustomed always to behold the presence of the universe in every part, the soul will not condescend to look at any new part as a stranger, but saith, — "I know all already, and what art thou? Show me thy relations to me, to all, and I will entertain thee also."

There is a pernicious ambiguity in the use of the term *subjective.* We say, in accordance with the general view I have stated, that the single soul feels its right to be no longer confounded with numbers, but itself to sit in judgment on history and literature, and to summon all facts and parties before its tribunal. And in this sense the age is subjective.

But, in all ages, and now more, the narrow-minded have no interest in anything but in its relation to their personality. What will help them to be delivered from some burden, eased in some circumstance, flattered or pardoned or enriched; what will help to marry or to divorce them, to prolong or to sweeten life, is sure of their interest; and nothing else. Every form under the whole heaven they behold in this most partial light or darkness of intense selfishness, until we hate their being. And this habit of intellectual selfishness has acquired in our day the fine name of subjectiveness.

Nor is the distinction between these two habits to be found in the circumstance of using the first person singular, or reciting facts and feelings of personal history. A man may say I, and never refer to himself as an individual; and a man may recite passages of his life with no feeling of egotism. Nor need a man have a vicious subjectiveness because he deals in abstract propositions.[1]

But the criterion which discriminates these two habits in the poet's mind is the tendency of his composition; namely, whether it leads us to Nature, or to the person of the writer. The great always introduce us to facts; small men introduce us always to themselves. The great man, even whilst he relates a private fact personal to him, is really leading us away from him to an universal experience. His own affection is in Nature, in *what is*, and, of course, all his communication leads outward to it, starting from whatsoever point. The great never with their own consent become a load on the minds they instruct. The more they draw us to them, the farther from them or more independent of them we are, because they have brought us to the knowledge of somewhat deeper than both them and us. The great never hinder us; for their activity is coincident with the sun and moon, with the course of the rivers and of the winds, with the stream of laborers in the street and with all the activity and well-being of the race. The great lead us to Nature, and in our age to metaphysical Nature, to the invisible awful facts, to moral abstractions, which are not less Nature than is a river, or a coal-mine, — nay, they are far more Nature, — but its essence and soul.

But the weak and wicked, led also to analyze, saw nothing in thought but luxury. Thought for the selfish became selfish. They invited us to contemplate Nature, and showed us an abominable self. Would you know the genius of the writer? Do not enumerate his talents or his feats, but ask thyself, What spirit is he of? Do gladness and hope and fortitude flow from his page into thy heart? Has he led thee to Nature because his own soul was too happy in beholding her power and love? Or is his passion for the wilderness only the sensibility of the sick, the exhibition of a talent which only shines whilst you praise it; which has no root in the character, and can thus minister to the vanity but not to the happiness of the possessor; and which derives all its *éclat* from our conventional education, but would not make itself intelligible to the wise man of another age or country? The water we wash with never speaks of itself, nor does fire or wind or tree. Neither does the noble natural man: he yields himself to your occasion and use, but his act expresses a reference to universal good.

Another element of the modern poetry akin to this subjective tendency, or rather the direction of that same on the question of resources, is the Feeling of the Infinite. Of the perception now fast becoming a conscious fact, — that there is One Mind, and that all the powers and privileges which lie in any, lie in all; that I, as a man, may claim and appropriate whatever of true or fair or good or strong has anywhere been exhibited; that Moses and Confucius, Montaigne and Leibnitz, are not so much individuals as they are parts of man and parts of me, and my intelligence proves them my own, — literature is far the best expression. It is true, this is not the only nor the obvious lesson it teaches. A selfish commerce and government have caught the eye and usurped the hand of the masses. It is not to be contested that selfishness and the senses write the laws under which we live, and that the street seems to be built, and the men and women in it moving, not in reference to pure and grand ends, but rather to very short and sordid ones. Perhaps no considerable minority, no one man, leads a quite clean and lofty life. What then? We concede in sadness the fact. But we say that these low customary ways are not all that survives in human beings. There is that in us which mutters, and that which groans, and that which triumphs, and that which aspires. There are facts on which men of the world superciliously smile, which are worth all their trade and politics; which drive young men into gardens and solitary places, and cause extravagant gestures, starts, distortions of the countenance and passionate exclamations; sentiments, which find no aliment or language for themselves on the wharves, in court, or market, but which are soothed by silence, by darkness, by the pale stars, and the presence of Nature. All over the modern world the educated and susceptible have betrayed their discontent with the limits of our municipal life, and with the poverty of our dogmas of religion and philosophy. They betray this impatience by fleeing for resource to a conversation with Nature, which is courted in a certain moody and exploring spirit, as if they anticipated a more intimate union of man with the world than has been known in recent ages. Those who cannot tell what they desire or expect still sigh and struggle with indefinite thoughts and vast wishes. The very child in the nursery prattles mysticism, and doubts and philosophizes. A wild striving to express a more inward and infinite sense characterizes the works of every art. The music of Beethoven is said, by those who understand it, to labor with vaster conceptions and aspirations than music has attempted before. This feeling of the Infinite has deeply colored the poetry of the period. This new love of the vast, always native in Germany, was imported into France by De Staël, appeared in England in Coleridge, Wordsworth, Byron, Shelley, Felicia Hemans, and finds a most genial climate in the American mind. Scott and Crabbe, who formed themselves on the past, had none of this tendency; their poetry is objective. In Byron, on the other hand, it predominates; but in Byron it is blind, it sees not its true end — an infinite good, alive and beautiful, a life nourished on absolute beatitudes, descending into Nature to behold itself reflected there. His will is perverted, he worships the accidents of society, and his praise of Nature is thieving and selfish.[1]

Nothing certifies the prevalence of this taste in the people more than the circulation of the poems — one would say most incongruously united by some bookseller — of Coleridge, Shelley and Keats. The only unity is in the subjectiveness and the aspiration common to the three writers. Shelley, though a poetic mind, is never a poet. His muse is uniformly imitative; all his poems composite. A good English scholar he is, with ear, taste and memory; much more, he is a character full of noble and prophetic traits; but imagination, the original, authentic fire of the bard, he has not. He is clearly modern, and shares with Richter, Châteaubriand, Manzoni and Wordsworth the feeling of the Infinite, which so labors for expression in their different genius. But all his lines are arbitrary, not necessary. When we read poetry, the mind asks, — Was this verse one of twenty which the author might have written as well; or is this what that man was created to say? But whilst every line of the true poet will be genuine, he is in a boundless power and freedom to say a million things. And the reason why he can say one thing well is because his vision extends to the sight of all things, and so he describes each as one who knows many and all.

The fame of Wordsworth is a leading fact in modern literature, when it is considered how hostile his genius at first seemed to the reigning taste, and with what limited poetic talents his great and steadily growing dominion has been established. More than any poet his success has been not his own but that of the idea which he shared with his coevals, and which he has rarely succeeded in adequately expressing. The Excursion awakened in every lover of Nature the right feeling. We saw stars shine, we felt the awe of mountains, we heard the rustle of the wind in the grass, and knew again the ineffable secret of solitude. It was a great joy. It was nearer to Nature than anything we had before. But the interest of the poem ended almost with the narrative of the influences of

Nature on the mind of the Boy, in the First Book. Obviously for that passage the poem was written, and with the exception of this and of a few strains of the like character in the sequel, the whole poem was dull. Here was no poem, but here was poetry, and a sure index where the subtle muse was about to pitch her tent and find the argument of her song. It was the human soul in these last ages striving for a just publication of itself. Add to this, however, the great praise of Wordsworth, that more than any other contemporary bard he is pervaded with a reverence of somewhat higher than (conscious) thought. There is in him that property common to all great poets, a wisdom of humanity, which is superior to any talents which they exert. It is the wisest part of Shakspeare and of Milton. For they are poets by the free course which they allow to the informing soul, which through their eyes beholdeth again and blesseth the things which it hath made. The soul is superior to its knowledge, wiser than any of its works.[1]

With the name of Wordsworth rises to our recollection the name of his contemporary and friend, Walter Savage Landor — a man working in a very different and peculiar spirit, yet one whose genius and accomplishments deserve a wiser criticism than we have yet seen applied to them, and the rather that his name does not readily associate itself with any school of writers. Of Thomas Carlyle, also, we shall say nothing at this time, since the quality and energy of his influence on the youth of this country will require at our hands, ere long, a distinct and faithful acknowledgment.[1]

But of all men he who has united in himself, and that in the most extraordinary degree, the tendencies of the era, is the German poet, naturalist and philosopher, Goethe. Whatever the age inherited or invented, he made his own. He has owed to Commerce and to the victories of the Understanding, all their spoils. Such was his capacity that the magazines of the world's ancient or modern wealth, which arts and intercourse and skepticism could command, — he wanted them all. Had there been twice so much, he could have used it as well. Geologist, mechanic, merchant, chemist, king, radical, painter, composer, — all worked for him, and a thousand men seemed to look through his eyes. He learned as readily as other men breathe. Of all the men of this time, not one has seemed so much at home in it as he. He was not afraid to live. And in him this encyclopædia of facts, which it has been the boast of the age to compile, wrought an equal effect. He was knowing; he was brave; he was clean from all narrowness; he has a perfect propriety and taste, — a quality by no means common to the German writers. Nay, since the earth as we said had become a reading-room, the new opportunities seem to have aided him to be that resolute realist he is, and seconded his sturdy determination to see things for what they are. To look at him one would say there was never an observer before. What sagacity, what industry of observation. To read his record is a frugality of time, for you shall find no word that does not stand for a thing, and he is of that comprehension which can see the value of truth. His love of Nature has seemed to give a new meaning to that word. There was never man more domesticated in this world than he. And he is an apology for the analytic spirit of the period, because, of his analysis, always wholes were the result.[1] All conventions, all traditions he rejected. And yet he felt his entire right and duty to stand before and try and judge every fact in Nature. He thought it necessary to dot round with his own pen the entire sphere of knowables; and for many of his stories, this seems the only reason: Here is a piece of humanity I had hitherto omitted to sketch; — take this. He does not say so in syllables, yet a sort of conscientious feeling he had to be *up* to the universe is the best account and apology for many of them. He shared also the subjectiveness of the age, and that too in both the senses I have discriminated. With the sharpest eye for form, color, botany, engraving, medals, persons and manners, he never stopped at surface, but pierced the purpose of a thing and studied to reconcile that purpose with his own being. What he could so reconcile was good; what he could not, was false. Hence a certain greatness encircles every fact he treats; for to him it has a soul, an eternal reason why it was so, and not otherwise. This is the secret of that deep realism, which went about among all objects he beheld, to find the cause why they must be what they are. It was with him a favorite task to find a theory of every institution, custom, art, work of art, which he observed. Witness his explanation of the Italian mode of reckoning the hours of the day, as growing out of the Italian climate; of the obelisk of Egypt, as growing out of a common natural fracture in the granite parallelopiped in Upper Egypt; of the Doric architecture, and the Gothic; of the Venetian music of the gondolier, originating in the habit of the fishers' wives of the Lido singing on shore to their husbands on the sea; of the amphitheatre, which is the enclosure of the natural cup of heads that arranges itself round every spectacle in the street; of the coloring of Titian and Paul Veronese, which one may verify in common daylight in Venice every afternoon; of the Carnival at Rome; of the domestic rural architecture in Italy; and many the like examples.

But also that other vicious subjectiveness, that vice of the time, infected him also. We are provoked with his Olympian self-complacency, the patronizing air with which he vouchsafes to tolerate the genius and performances of other mortals, "the good Hiller," "our excellent Kant," "the friendly Wieland," etc. There is a good letter from Wieland to Merck, in which Wieland relates that Goethe read to a select party his journal of a tour in Switzerland with the Grand Duke, and their passage through the Vallais and over the St. Gothard. "It was," says Wieland, "as good as Xenophon's Anabasis. The piece is one of the most masterly productions, and is thought and written with the greatness peculiar to him. The fair hearers were enthusiastic at the nature in this piece; I liked the sly art in the composition, whereof they saw nothing, still better. It is a true poem, so concealed is the art too. But what most remarkably in this, as in all his other works, distinguishes him from Homer and Shakspeare is that the Me, the *Ille ego*, everywhere glimmers through, although without any boasting and with an infinite fineness." This subtle element of egotism in Goethe certainly does not seem to deform his compositions, but to lower the moral influence of the man. He differs from all the great in the total want of frankness. Who saw Milton, who saw Shakspeare, saw them do their best, and utter their whole heart manlike among their brethren. No man was permitted to call Goethe brother. He hid himself, and worked always to astonish, which is egotism, and therefore little.

If we try Goethe by the ordinary canons of criticism, we should say that his thinking is of great altitude, and all level; not a succession of summits, but a high Asiatic table-land. Dramatic power, the rarest talent in literature, he has very little. He has an eye constant to the fact of life and that never pauses in its advance. But the great felicities, the miracles of poetry, he has never. It is all design with him, just thought and instructed expression, analogies, allusion, illustration, which knowledge and correct thinking supply; but of Shakspeare and the transcendent muse, no syllable. Yet in the court and law to which we ordinarily speak, and without adverting to absolute standards, we claim for him the praise of truth, of fidelity to his intellectual nature. He is the king of all scholars. In these days and in this country, where the scholars are few and idle, where men read easy books and sleep after dinner, it seems as if no book could so safely be put in the hands of young men as the letters of Goethe, which attest the incessant activity of this man, to eighty years, in an endless variety of studies, with uniform cheerfulness and greatness of mind. They cannot be read without shaming us into an emulating industry. Let him have the praise of the love of truth. We think, when we contemplate the stupendous glory of the world, that it were life enough for one man merely to lift his hands and cry with Saint Augustine, "Wrangle who pleases, I will wonder." Well, this he did. Here was a man who, in the feeling that the thing itself was so admirable as to leave all comment behind, went up and down, from object to object, lifting the veil from every one, and did no more. What he said of Lavater, may truelier be said of him, that "it was fearful to stand in the presence of one before whom all the boundaries within which Nature has circumscribed our being were laid flat." His are the bright and terrible eyes which meet the modern student in every sacred chapel of thought, in every public enclosure.

But now, that we may not seem to dodge the question which all men ask, nor pay a great man so ill a compliment as to praise him only in the conventional and comparative speech, let us honestly record our thought upon the total worth and influence of this genius. Does he represent, not only the achievement of that age in which he lived, but that which it would be and is now becoming? And what shall we think of that absence of the moral sentiment, that singular equivalence to him of good and evil in action, which discredit his compositions to the pure? The spirit of his biography, of his poems, of his tales, is identical, and we may here set down by way of comment of his genius the impressions recently awakened in us by the story of Wilhelm Meister.

All great men have written proudly, nor cared to explain. They knew that the intelligent reader would come at last, and would thank them. So did Dante, so did Macchiavel. Goethe has done this in Meister. We can fancy him saying to himself: 'There are poets enough of the Ideal; let me paint the Actual, as, after years of dreams, it will still appear and reappear to wise men. That all shall right itself in the long Morrow, I may well allow, and my novel may wait for the same regeneration. The age, that can damn it as false and falsifying, will see that it is deeply one with the genius and history of all the centuries. I have given my characters a bias to error. Men have the same. I have let mischance befall instead of good fortune. They do so daily. And out of many vices and misfortunes, I have let a great success grow, as I had known in my own and many other examples. Fierce churchmen and effeminate aspirants will chide and hate my name, but every keen beholder of life will justify my truth, and will acquit me of prejudging the cause of humanity by painting it with this morose fidelity. To a profound soul is not austere truth the sweetest flattery?'

Yes, O Goethe! but the ideal is truer than

the actual. That is ephemeral, but this changes not. Moreover, because Nature is moral, that mind only can see, in which the same order entirely obtains. An interchangeable Truth, Beauty and Goodness, each wholly interfused in the other, must make the humors of that eye which would see causes reaching to their last effect and reproducing the world forever. The least inequality of mixture, the excess of one element over the other, in that degree diminishes the transparency of things, makes the world opaque to the observer, and destroys so far the value of his experience. No particular gifts can countervail this defect. In reading Meister, I am charmed with the insight; to use a phrase of Ben Jonson's, "it is rammed with life." I find there actual men and women even too faithfully painted. I am moreover instructed in the possibility of a highly accomplished society, and taught to look for great talent and culture under a gray coat. But this is all. The limits of artificial society are never quite out of sight. The vicious conventions, which hem us in like prison walls and which the poet should explode at his touch, stand for all they are worth in the newspaper. We are never lifted above ourselves, we are not transported out of the dominion of the senses, or cheered with an infinite tenderness, or armed with a grand trust.

Goethe, then, must be set down as the poet of the Actual, not of the Ideal; the poet of limitation, not of possibility; of this world, and not of religion and hope; in short, if we may say so, the poet of prose, and not of poetry. He accepts the base doctrine of Fate, and gleans what straggling joys may yet remain out of its ban. He is like a banker or a weaver with a passion for the country; he steals out of the hot streets before sunrise, or after sunset, or on a rare holiday, to get a draft of sweet air and a gaze at the magnificence of summer, but dares not break from his slavery and lead a man's life in a man's relation to Nature. In that which should be his own place, he feels like a truant, and is scourged back presently to his task and his cell. Poetry is with Goethe thus external, the gilding of the chain, the mitigation of his fate; but the Muse never assays those thunder-tones which cause to vibrate the sun and the moon, which dissipate by dreadful melody all this iron network of circumstance, and abolish the old heavens and the old earth before the free will or Godhead of man. That Goethe had not a moral perception proportionate to his other powers is not, then, merely a circumstance, as we might relate of a man that he had or had not the sense of tune or an eye for colors, but it is the cardinal fact of health or disease; since, lacking this, he failed in the high sense to be a creator, and, with divine endowments, drops by irreversible decree into the common history of genius. He was content to fall into the track of vulgar poets and spend on common aims his splendid endowments, and has declined the office proffered to now and then a man in many centuries in the power of his genius, of a Redeemer of the human mind. He has written better than other poets only as his talent was subtler, but the ambition of creation he refused. Life for him is prettier, easier, wiser, decenter, has a gem or two more on its robe, but its old eternal burden is not relieved; no drop of healthier blood flows yet in its veins. Let him pass. Humanity must wait for its physician still at the side of the road, and confess as this man goes out that they have served it better, who assured it out of the innocent hope in their hearts that a Physician will come, than this majestic Artist, with all the treasuries of wit, of science, and of power at his command.[1]

The criticism, which is not so much spoken as felt in reference to Goethe, instructs us directly in the hope of literature. We feel that a man gifted like him should not leave the world as he found it. It is true, though somewhat sad, that every fine genius teaches us how to blame himself. Being so much, we cannot forgive him for not being more. When one of these grand monads is incarnated whom Nature seems to design for eternal men and draw to her bosom, we think that the old weariness of Europe and Asia, the trivial forms of daily life will now end, and a new morning break on us all. What is Austria? What is England? What is our graduated and petrified social scale of ranks and employments? Shall not a poet redeem us from these idolatries, and pale their legendary lustre before the fires of the Divine Wisdom which burn in his heart? All that in our sovereign moments each of us has divined of the powers of thought, all the hints of omnipresence and energy which we have caught, this man should unfold, and constitute facts.

And this is the insatiable craving which alternately saddens and gladdens men at this day. The Doctrine of the Life of Man established after the truth through all his faculties; — this is the thought which the literature of this hour meditates and labors to say. This is that which tunes the tongue and fires the eye and sits in the silence of the youth. Verily it will not long want articulate and melodious expression. There is nothing in the heart but comes presently to the lips. The very depth of the sentiment, which is the author of all the cutaneous life we see, is guarantee for the riches of science and of song in the age to come. He who doubts whether this age or this country can yield any contribution to the literature of the world only betrays his own blindness to the necessities of the human soul. Has the power of poetry ceased, or the need? Have the eyes ceased to see that which they would have, and which they have not? Have they ceased to see other eyes? Are there no lonely, anxious, wondering children, who must tell their tale? Are we not evermore whipped by thoughts?

> "In sorrow steeped, and steeped in love
> Of thoughts not yet incarnated." [1]

The heart beats in this age as of old, and the passions are busy as ever. Nature has not lost one ringlet of her beauty, one impulse of resistance and valor. From the necessity of loving none are exempt, and he that loves must utter his desires. A charm as radiant as beauty ever beamed, a love that fainteth at the sight of its object, is new to-day.

> "The world does not run smoother than of old,
> There are sad haps that must be told."

Man is not so far lost but that he suffers ever the great Discontent which is the elegy of his loss and the prediction of his recovery. In the gay saloon he laments that these figures are not what Raphael and Guercino painted. Withered though he stand, and trifler though he be, the august spirit of the world looks out from his eyes. In his heart he knows the ache of spiritual pain, and his thought can animate the sea and land. What, then, shall hinder the Genius of the time from speaking its thought? It cannot be silent, if it would. It will write in a higher spirit and a wider knowledge and with a grander practical aim than ever yet guided the pen of poet. It will write the annals of a changed world, and record the descent of principles into practice, of love into Government, of love into Trade. It will describe the new heroic life of man, the now unbelieved possibility of simple living and of clean and noble relations with men. Religion will bind again these that were sometime frivolous, customary, enemies, skeptics, self-seekers, into a joyful reverence for the circumambient Whole, and that which was ecstasy shall become daily bread.

II

WALTER SAVAGE LANDOR

WE sometimes meet in a stage-coach in New England an erect, muscular man, with fresh complexion and a smooth hat, whose nervous speech instantly betrays the English traveller; — a man nowise cautious to conceal his name or that of his native country, or his very slight esteem for the persons and the country that surround him. When Mr. Bull rides in an American coach, he speaks quick and strong; he is very ready to confess his ignorance of everything about him, — persons, manners, customs, politics, geography. He wonders that the Americans should build with wood, whilst all this stone is lying in the road-side; and is astonished to learn that a wooden house may last a hundred years; nor will he remember the fact as many minutes after it has been told him: he wonders that they do not make elder-wine and cherry-bounce, since here are cherries, and every mile is crammed with elder-bushes. He has never seen a good horse in America, nor a good coach, nor a good inn. Here is very good earth and water and plenty of them; that he is free to allow; to all other gifts of Nature or man his eyes are sealed by the inexorable demand for the precise conveniences to which he is accustomed in England. Add to this proud blindness the better quality of great downrightness in speaking the truth, and the love of fair play, on all occasions, and moreover the peculiarity which is alleged of the Englishman, that his virtues do not come out until he quarrels.

Transfer these traits to a very elegant and accomplished mind, and we shall have no bad picture of Walter Savage Landor, who may stand as a favorable impersonation of the genius of his countrymen at the present day. A sharp, dogmatic man, with a great deal of knowledge, a great deal of worth, and a great deal of pride; with a profound contempt for all that he does not understand; a master of all elegant learning, and capable of the utmost delicacy of sentiment, and yet prone to indulge a sort of ostentation of coarse imagery and language. His partialities and dislikes are by no means culpable, but are often whimsical and amusing; yet they are quite sincere, and, like those of Johnson and Coleridge, are easily separable from the man. What he says of Wordsworth is true of himself, that he delights to throw a clod of dirt on the table, and cry, "Gentlemen, there is a better man than all of you." Bolivar, Mina and General Jackson will never be greater soldiers than Napoleon and Alexander, let Mr. Landor think as he will; nor will he persuade us to burn Plato and Xenophon, out of our admiration of Bishop Patrick, or Lucas on Happiness, or Lucas on Holiness, or even Barrow's Sermons. Yet a man may love a paradox without either losing his wit or his honesty. A less pardonable eccentricity is the cold and gratuitous obtrusion of licentious images, not so much the suggestion of merriment as of bitterness. Montaigne assigns as a reason for his license of speech that he is tired of seeing his Essays on the work-tables of ladies, and he is determined they shall for the future put them out of sight. In Mr. Landor's coarseness there is a certain air of defiance, and the rude word seems sometimes to arise from a disgust at niceness and over-refinement. Before a well-dressed company he plunges his fingers into a cesspool, as if to expose the whiteness of his hands and the jewels of his ring. Afterward, he washes them in water, he washes them in wine; but you are never secure from his freaks. A sort of Earl Peterborough in literature, his eccentricity is too decided not to have diminished his greatness. He has capital enough to have furnished the brain of fifty stock authors, yet has written no book.

But we have spoken all our discontent. Possibly his writings are open to harsher censure; but we love the man, from sympathy as well as for reasons to be assigned; and have no wish, if we were able, to put an argument in the mouth of his critics. Now for twenty years we have still found the Imaginary Conversations a sure resource in solitude, and it seems to us as original in its form as in its matter. Nay, when we remember his rich and ample page, wherein we are always sure to find free and sustained thought, a keen and precise understanding, an affluent and ready memory familiar with all chosen books, an industrious observation in every department of life, an experience to which nothing has occurred in vain, honor for every just and generous sentiment and a scourge like that of Furies for every oppressor, whether public or private, — we feel how dignified is this perpetual Censor in his curule chair, and we wish to thank a benefactor of the reading world.

Mr. Landor is one of the foremost of that small class who make good in the nineteenth century the claims of pure literature. In these busy days of avarice and ambition, when there is so little disposition to profound thought or to any but the most superficial intellectual entertainments, a faithful scholar, receiving from past ages the treasures of wit and enlarging them by his own love, is a friend and consoler of mankind. When we pronounce the names of Homer and Æschylus; Horace, Ovid and Plutarch; Erasmus, Scaliger and Montaigne; Ben Jonson and Isaak Walton; Dryden and Pope, — we pass at once out of trivial associations and enter into a region of the purest pleasure accessible to human nature. We have quitted all beneath the moon and entered that crystal sphere in which everything in the world of matter reappears, but transfigured and immortal. Literature is the effort of man to indemnify himself for the wrongs of his condition. The existence of the poorest playwright and the humblest scrivener is a good omen. A charm attaches to the most inferior names which have in any manner got themselves enrolled in the registers of the House of Fame, even as porters and grooms in the courts; to Creech and

Fenton, Theobald and Dennis, Aubrey and Spence. From the moment of entering a library and opening a desired book, we cease to be citizens, creditors, debtors, housekeepers and men of care and fear. What boundless leisure! what original jurisdiction! the old constellations have set, new and brighter have arisen; an Elysian light tinges all objects: —

> "In the afternoon we came unto a land
> In which it seemed always afternoon."[1]

And this sweet asylum of an intellectual life must appear to have the sanction of Nature, as long as so many men are born with so decided an aptitude for reading and writing. Let us thankfully allow every faculty and art which opens new scope to a life so confined as ours. There are vast spaces in a thought: a slave, to whom the religious sentiment is opened, has a freedom which makes his master's freedom a slavery.[2] Let us not be so illiberal with our schemes for the renovation of society and Nature as to disesteem or deny the literary spirit. Certainly there are heights in Nature which command this; there are many more which this commands. It is vain to call it a luxury, and as saints and reformers are apt to do, decry it as a species of day-dreaming. What else are sanctities, and reforms, and all other things? Whatever can make for itself an element, means, organs, servants and the most profound and permanent existence in the hearts and heads of millions of men, must have a reason for its being. Its excellency is reason and vindication enough. If rhyme rejoices us, there should be rhyme, as much as if fire cheers us, we should bring wood and coals. Each kind of excellence takes place for its hour and excludes everything else. Do not brag of your actions, as if they were better than Homer's verses or Raphael's pictures. Raphael and Homer feel that action is pitiful beside their enchantments. They could act too, if the stake was worthy of them: but now all that is good in the universe urges them to their task. Whoever writes for the love of truth and beauty, and not with ulterior ends, belongs to this sacred class; and among these, few men of the present age have a better claim to be numbered than Mr. Landor. Wherever genius or taste has existed, wherever freedom and justice are threatened, which he values as the element in which genius may work, his interest is sure to be commanded. His love of beauty is passionate, and betrays itself in all petulant and contemptuous expressions.

But beyond his delight in genius and his love of individual and civil liberty, Mr. Landor has a perception that is much more rare, the appreciation of character. This is the more remarkable considered with his intense nationality, to which we have already alluded. He is buttoned in English broadcloth to the chin. He hates the Austrians, the Italians, the French, the Scotch and the Irish. He has the common prejudices of an English landholder; values his pedigree, his acres and the syllables of his name; loves all his advantages, is not insensible to the beauty of his watch-seal, or the Turk's head on his umbrella; yet with all this miscellaneous pride there is a noble nature within him which instructs him that he is so rich that he can well spare all his trappings, and, leaving to others the painting of circumstance, aspire to the office of delineating character. He draws his own portrait in the costume of a village schoolmaster, and a sailor, and serenely enjoys the victory of Nature over fortune. Not only the elaborated story of Normanby, but the whimsical selection of his heads proves this taste. He draws with evident pleasure the portrait of a man who never said anything right and never did anything wrong. But in the character of Pericles he has found full play for beauty and greatness of behavior, where the circumstances are in harmony with the man. These portraits, though mere sketches, must be valued as attempts in the very highest kind of narrative, which not only has very few examples to exhibit of any success, but very few competitors in the attempt. The word Character is in all mouths; it is a force which we all feel; yet who has analyzed it? What is the nature of that subtle and majestic principle which attaches us to a few persons, not so much by personal as by the most spiritual ties? What is the quality of the persons who, without being public men, or literary men, or rich men, or active men, or (in the popular sense) religious men, have a certain salutary omnipresence in all our life's history, almost giving their own quality to the atmosphere and the landscape? A moral force, yet wholly unmindful of creed and catechism, intellectual, but scornful of books, it works directly and without means, and though it may be resisted at any time, yet resistance to it is a suicide. For the person who stands in this lofty relation to his fellow men is always the impersonation to them of their conscience. It is a sufficient proof of the extreme delicacy of this element, evanescing before any but the most sympathetic vision, that it has so seldom been employed in the drama and in novels. Mr. Landor, almost alone among living English writers, has indicated his perception of it.

These merits make Mr. Landor's position in the republic of letters one of great mark and dignity. He exercises with a grandeur of spirit the office of writer, and carries it with an air of old and unquestionable nobility. We do not recollect an example of more complete independence in literary history. He has no clanship, no friendships that warp him. He was one of the first to pronounce Wordsworth the great poet of the age, yet he discriminates his faults with the greater freedom. He loves Pindar, Æschylus, Euripides, Aristophanes, Demosthenes, Virgil, yet with open eyes. His position is by no means the highest in literature: he is not a poet or a philosopher. He is a man full of thoughts, but not, like Coleridge, a man of ideas. Only from a mind conversant with the First Philosophy can definitions be expected. Coleridge has contributed many valuable ones to modern literature. Mr. Landor's definitions are only enumerations of particulars; the generic law is not seized. But as it is not from the highest Alps or Andes but from less elevated summits that the most attractive landscape is commanded, so is Mr. Landor the most useful and agreeable of critics. He has commented on a wide variety of writers, with a closeness and extent of view which has enhanced the value of those authors to his readers. His Dialogue on the Epicurean philosophy is a theory of the genius of Epicurus. The Dialogue between Barrow and Newton is the best of all criticisms on the essays of Bacon. His picture of Demosthenes in three several Dialogues is new and adequate. He has illustrated the genius of Homer, Æschylus, Pindar, Euripides, Thucydides. Then he has examined before he has expatiated, and the minuteness of his verbal criticism gives a confidence in his fidelity when he speaks the language of meditation or of passion. His acquaintance with the English tongue is unsurpassed. He "hates false words, and seeks with care, difficulty and moroseness those that fit the thing." He knows the value of his own words. "They are not," he says, "written on slate." He never stoops to explanation, nor uses seven words where one will do. He is a master of condensation and suppression, and that in no vulgar way. He knows the wide difference between compression and an obscure elliptical style. The dense writer has yet ample room and choice of phrase, and even a gamesome mood often between his valid words. There is no inadequacy or disagreeable contraction in his sentence, any more than in a human face, where in a square space of a few inches is found room for every possible variety of expression.[1]

Yet it is not as an artist that Mr. Landor commends himself to us. He is not epic or dramatic, he has not the high, overpowering method by which the master gives unity and integrity to a work of many parts. He is too wilful, and never abandons himself to his genius. His books are a strange mixture of politics, etymology, allegory, sentiment, and personal history; and what skill of transition he may possess is superficial, not spiritual. His merit must rest, at last, not on the spirit of the dialogue or the symmetry of any of his historical portraits, but on the value of his sentences. Many of these will secure their own immortality in English literature; and this, rightly considered, is no mean merit. These are not plants and animals, but the genetical atoms of which both are composed. All our great debt to the Oriental world is of this kind, not utensils and statues of the precious metal, but bullion and gold-dust. Of many of Mr. Landor's sentences we are fain to remember what was said of those of Socrates; that they are cubes, which will stand firm, place them how or where you will.[1]

III

PRAYERS

> "NOT with fond shekels of the tested gold,
> Nor gems whose rates are either rich or poor
> As fancy values them: but with true prayers,
> That shall be up at heaven and enter there
> Ere sunrise; prayers from preservèd souls,
> From fasting maids, whose minds are delicate
> To nothing temporal."
>
> — SHAKSPEARE.

PYTHAGORAS said that the time when men are honestest is when they present themselves before the gods. If we can overhear the prayer we shall know the man. But prayers are not made to be overheard, or to be printed, so that we seldom have the prayer otherwise than it can be inferred from the man and his fortunes, which are the answer to the prayer, and always accord with it. Yet there are scattered about in the earth a few records of these devout hours, which it would edify us to read, could they be collected in a more catholic spirit than the wretched and repulsive volumes which usurp that name. Let us not have the prayers of one sect, nor of the Christian Church, but of men in all ages and religions who have prayed well.

The prayer of Jesus is (as it deserves) become a form for the human race. Many men have contributed a single expression, a single word to the language of devotion, which is immediately caught and stereotyped in the prayers of their church and nation. Among the remains of Euripides we have this prayer: "Thou God of all! infuse light into the souls of men, whereby they may be enabled to know what is the root from whence all their evils spring, and by what means they may avoid them." In the Phædrus of Plato, we find this petition in the mouth of Socrates: "O gracious Pan! and ye other gods who preside over this place! grant that I may be beautiful within; and that those external things which I have may be such as may best agree with a right internal disposition of mine; and that I may account him to be rich, who is wise and just." Wacic the Caliph, who died A. D. 845, ended his life, the Arabian historians tell us, with these words: "O thou whose kingdom never passes away, pity one whose dignity is so transient." But what led us to these remembrances was the happy accident which in this undevout age lately brought us acquainted with two or three diaries, which attest, if there be need of attestation, the eternity of the sentiment and its equality to itself through all the variety of expression. The first is the prayer of a deaf and dumb boy: —

"When my long-attached friend comes to me, I have pleasure to converse with him, and I rejoice to pass my eyes over his countenance; but soon I am weary of spending my time causelessly and unimproved, and I desire to leave him (but not in rudeness), because I wished to be engaged in my business. But thou, O my Father, knowest I always delight to commune with thee in my lone and silent heart; I am never full of thee; I am never weary of thee; I am always desiring thee. I hunger with strong hope and affection for thee, and I thirst for thy grace and spirit.

"When I go to visit my friends, I must put on my best garments, and I must think of my manner to please them. I am tired to stay long, because my mind is not free, and they sometimes talk gossip with me. But O my Father, thou visitest me in my work, and I can lift up my desires to thee, and my heart is cheered and at rest with thy presence, and I am always alone with thee, and thou dost not steal my time by foolishness. I always ask in my heart, where can I find thee?"

The next is a voice out of a solitude as strict and sacred as that in which Nature had isolated this eloquent mute: —

"My Father, when I cannot be cheerful or happy, I can be true and obedient, and I will not forget that joy has been, and may still be. If there is no hour of solitude granted me, still I will commune with thee. If I may not search out and pierce thy thought, so much the more may my living praise thee. At whatever price, I must be alone with thee; this must be the demand I make. These duties are not the life, but the means which enable us to show forth the life. So must I take up this cross, and bear it willingly. Why should I feel reproved when a busy one enters the room? I am not idle, though I sit with folded hands, but instantly I must seek some cover. For that shame I reprove myself. Are they only the valuable members of society who labor to dress and feed it? Shall we never ask the aim of all this hurry and foam, of this aimless activity? Let the purpose for which I live be always before me; let every thought and word go to confirm and illuminate that end; namely, that I must become near and dear to thee; that now I am beyond the reach of all but thee.

"How can we not be reconciled to thy will? I will know the joy of giving to my friend the dearest treasure I have. I know that sorrow comes not at once only. We cannot meet it and say, now it is overcome, but again, and yet again, its flood pours over us, and as full as at first.

"If but this tedious battle could be fought,
Like Sparta's heroes at one rocky pass,

'One day be spent in dying,' men had sought
The spot, and been cut down like mower's grass."

The next is in a metrical form. It is the aspiration of a different mind, in quite other regions of power and duty, yet they all accord at last.

"Great God, I ask thee for no meaner pelf
Than that I may not disappoint myself,
That in my action I may soar as high,
As I can now discern with this clear eye.

And next in value, which thy kindness lends,
That I may greatly disappoint my friends,
Howe'er they think or hope that it may be,
They may not dream how thou'st distinguished me.

That my weak hand may equal my firm faith,
And my life practise more than my tongue saith;
That my low conduct may not show,
Nor my relenting lines,
That I thy purpose did not know,
Or overrated thy designs."

The last of the four orisons is written in a singularly calm and healthful spirit, and contains this petition:—

"My Father: I now come to thee with a desire to thank thee for the continuance of our love, the one for the other. I feel that without thy love in me I should be alone here in the flesh. I cannot express my gratitude for what thou hast been and continuest to be to me. But thou knowest what my feelings are. When nought on earth seemeth pleasant to me, thou dost make thyself known to me, and teach that which is needful for me, and dost cheer my travels on. I know that thou hast not created me and placed me here on earth, amidst its toils and troubles and the follies of those around me, and told me to be like thyself when I see so little of thee here to profit by; thou hast not done this, and then left me here to myself, a poor, weak man, scarcely able to earn my bread. No; thou art my Father and I will love thee, for thou didst first love me, and lovest me still. We will ever be parent and child. Wilt thou give me strength to persevere in this great work of redemption. Wilt thou show me the true means of accomplishing it. . . . I thank thee for the knowledge that I have attained of thee by thy sons who have been before me, and especially for him who brought me so perfect a type of thy goodness and love to men. . . . I know that thou wilt deal with me as I deserve. I place myself therefore in thy hand, knowing that thou wilt keep me from harm so long as I consent to live under thy protecting care."

Let these few scattered leaves, which a chance (as men say, but which to us shall be holy) brought under our eye nearly at the same moment, stand as an example of innumerable similar expressions which no mortal witness has reported, and be a sign of the times. Might they be suggestion to many a heart of yet higher secret experiences which are ineffable! But we must not tie up the rosary on which we have strung these few white beads, without adding a pearl of great price from that book of prayer, the Confessions of Saint Augustine.

"And being admonished to reflect upon myself, I entered into the very inward parts of my soul, by thy conduct; and I was able to do it, because now thou wert become my helper. I entered and discerned with the eye of my soul (such as it was), even beyond my soul and mind itself, the Light unchangeable. Not this vulgar light which all flesh may look upon, nor as it were a greater of the same kind, as though the brightness of this should be manifold greater and with its greatness take up all space. Not such was this light, but other, yea, far other from all these. Neither was it so above my understanding, as oil swims above water, or as the heaven is above the earth. But it is above me, because it made me; and I am under it, because I was made by it. He that knows truth or verity knows what that light is, and he that knows it knows eternity, and it is known by charity. O eternal Verity! and true Charity! and dear Eternity! thou art my God, to thee do I sigh day and night. Thee when I first knew, thou liftedst me up that I might see, there was what I might see, and that I was not yet such as to see. And thou didst beat back my weak sight upon myself, shooting out beams upon me after a vehement manner; and I even trembled between love and horror, and I found myself to be far off, and even in the very region of dissimilitude from thee."

IV

AGRICULTURE OF MASSACHUSETTS

IN an afternoon in April, after a long walk, I traversed an orchard where boys were grafting apple-trees, and found the Farmer in his cornfield. He was holding the plough, and his son driving the oxen. This man always impresses me with respect, he is so manly, so sweet-tempered, so faithful, so disdainful of all appearances; excellent and reverable in his old weather-worn cap and blue frock bedaubed with the soil of the field; so honest withal that he always needs to be watched lest he should cheat himself. I still remember with some shame that in some dealing we had together a long time ago, I found that he had been looking to my interest in the affair, and I had been looking to my interest, and nobody had looked to his part. As I drew near this brave laborer in the midst of his own acres, I could not help feeling for him the highest respect. Here is the Cæsar, the Alexander of the soil, conquering and to conquer, after how many and many a hard-fought summer's day and winter's day; not like Napoleon, hero of sixty battles only, but of six thousand, and out of every one he has come victor; and here he stands, with Atlantic strength and cheer, invincible still. These slight and useless city limbs of ours will come to shame before this strong soldier, for his have done his own work and ours too. What good this man has or has had, he has earned. No rich father or father-in-law left him any inheritance of land or money. He borrowed the money with which he bought his farm, and has bred up a large family, given them a good education, and improved his land in every way year by year, and this without prejudice to himself the landlord, for here he is, a man every inch of him, and reminds us of the hero of the Robin Hood ballad, —

> "Much, the miller's son,
> There was no inch of his body
> But it was worth a groom."

Innocence and justice have written their names on his brow. Toil has not broken his spirit. His laugh rings with the sweetness and hilarity of a child; yet he is a man of a strongly intellectual taste, of much reading, and of an erect good sense and independent spirit which can neither brook usurpation nor falsehood in any shape. I walked up and down the field, as he ploughed his furrow, and we talked as we walked. Our conversation naturally turned on the season and its new labors. He had been reading the report of the Agricultural Survey of the Commonwealth, and had found good things in it; but it was easy to see that he felt toward the author much as soldiers do toward the historiographer who follows the camp, more good nature than reverence for the gownsman.

The First Report, he said, is better than the last, as I observe the first sermon of a minister is often his best, for every man has one thing which he specially wishes to say, and that comes out at first. But who is this book written for? Not for farmers; no pains are taken to send it to them; it was by accident that this volume came into my hands for a few days. And it is not for them. They could not afford to follow such advice as is given here; they have sterner teachers; their own business teaches them better. No; this was written for the literary men. But in that case, the state should not be taxed to pay for it. Let us see. The account of the maple sugar, — that is very good and entertaining, and, I suppose, true. The story of the farmer's daughter, whom education had spoiled for everything useful on a farm, — that is good, too, and we have much that is. like it in Thomas's Almanack. But why this recommendation of stone houses? They are not so cheap, not so dry, and not so fit for us. Our roads are always changing their direction, and after a man has built at great cost a stone house, a new road is opened, and he finds himself a mile or two from the highway. Then our people are not stationary, like those of old countries, but always alert to better themselves, and will remove from town to town as a new market opens or a better farm is to be had, and do not wish to spend too much on their buildings.

The Commissioner advises the farmers to sell their cattle and their hay in the fall, and buy again in the spring. But we farmers always know what our interest dictates, and do accordingly. We have no choice in this matter; our way is but too plain. Down below, where manure is cheap and hay dear, they will sell their oxen in November; but for me to sell my cattle and my produce in the fall would be to sell my farm, for I should have no manure to renew a crop in the spring. And thus Necessity farms it; necessity finds out when to go to Brighton, and when to feed in the stall, better than Mr. Colman can tell us.

But especially observe what is said throughout these Reports of the model farms and model farmers. One would think that Mr. D. and Major S. were the pillars of the Commonwealth. The good Commissioner takes off his hat when he approaches them, distrusts the value of "his feeble praise," and repeats his compliments as often as their names are introduced. And yet, in my opinion, Mr. D., with all his knowledge and present skill, would starve in two years on any one of fifty poor farms in this neighborhood on each of which now a farmer manages to get a good living. Mr. D. inherited a farm, and spends on it every year from other resources; otherwise his farm had ruined him long since; — and as for the Major, he never got rich by his skill in making land produce, but in making men produce. The truth is, a farm will not make an honest man rich in money. I do not know of a single instance in which a man has honestly got rich by farming alone. It cannot be done. The way in which men who have farms grow rich is either by other resources, or by trade, or by getting their labor for nothing, or by other methods of which I could tell you many sad anecdotes. What does the Agricultural Surveyor know of all this? What can he know? He is the victim of the Reports, that are sent him, of particular farms. He cannot go behind the estimates to know how the contracts were made, and how the sales were effected. The true men of skill, the poor farmers, who, by the sweat of their face, without an inheritance and without offence to their conscience have reared a family of valuable citizens and matrons to the state, reduced a stubborn soil to a good farm, although their buildings are many of them shabby, are the only right subjects of this Report; yet these make no figure in it. These should be holden up to imitation, and their methods detailed; yet their houses are very uninviting and inconspicuous to State Commissioners. So with these premiums to farms, and premiums at cattle-shows. The class that I describe must pay the premium which is awarded to the rich. Yet the premium obviously ought to be given for the good management of a poor farm.

In this strain the Farmer proceeded, adding many special criticisms. He had a good opinion of the Surveyor, and acquitted him of any blame in the matter, but was incorrigible in his skepticism concerning the benefits conferred by legislatures on the agriculture of Massachusetts.

I believe that my friend is a little stiff and inconvertible in his own opinions, and that there is another side to be heard; but so much wisdom seemed to lie under all his statement that it deserved a record.

V

EUROPE AND EUROPEAN BOOKS

IT was a brighter day than we have often known in our literary calendar, when within a twelvemonth a single London advertisement announced a new volume of poems by Wordsworth, poems by Tennyson, and a play by Henry Taylor. Wordsworth's nature or character has had all the time it needed in order to make its mark and supply the want of talent. We have learned how to read him. We have ceased to expect that which he cannot give. He has the merit of just moral perception, but not that of deft poetic execution. How would Milton curl his lip at such slipshod newspaper style. Many of his poems, as for example the Rylstone Doe, might be all improvised. Nothing of Milton, nothing of Marvell, of Herbert, of Dryden, could be. These are such verses as in a just state of culture should be *vers de société*, such as every gentleman could write but none would think of printing, or of claiming the poet's laurel on their merit. The Pindar, the Shakspeare, the Dante, whilst they have the just and open soul, have also the eye to see the dimmest star that glimmers in the Milky Way, the serratures of every leaf, the test-objects of the microscope, and then the tongue to utter the same things in words that engrave them on all the ears of mankind. The poet demands all gifts, and not one or two only.[1]

The poet, like the electric rod, must reach from a point nearer the sky than all surrounding objects, down to the earth, and into the dark wet soil, or neither is of use. The poet must not only converse with pure thought, but he must demonstrate it almost to the senses. His words must be pictures, his verses must be spheres and cubes, to be seen and smelled and handled. His fable must be a good story, and its meaning must hold as pure truth. In the debates on the Copyright Bill, in the English Parliament, Mr. Sergeant Wakley, the coroner, quoted Wordsworth's poetry in derision, and asked the roaring House of Commons what that meant, and whether a man should have public reward for writing such stuff. Homer, Horace, Milton and Chaucer would defy the coroner. Whilst they have wisdom to the wise, he would see that to the external they have external meaning. Coleridge excellently said of poetry, that poetry must first be good sense; as a palace might well be magnificent, but first it must be a house.

Wordsworth is open to ridicule of this kind. And yet Wordsworth, though satisfied if he can suggest to a sympathetic mind his own mood, and though setting a private and exaggerated value on his compositions; though confounding his accidental with the universal consciousness, and taking the public to task for not admiring his poetry, is really a master of the English language, and his poems evince a power of diction that is no more rivalled by his contemporaries than is his poetic insight.[1] But the capital merit of Wordsworth is that he has done more for the sanity of this generation than any other writer. Early in life, at a crisis it is said in his private affairs, he made his election between assuming and defending some legal rights, with the chances of wealth and a position in the world, and the inward promptings of his heavenly genius; he took his part; he accepted the call to be a poet, and sat down, far from cities, with coarse clothing and plain fare to obey the heavenly vision. The choice he had made in his will manifested itself in every line to be real. We have poets who write the poetry of society, of the patrician and conventional Europe, as Scott and Moore, and others who, like Byron or Bulwer, write the poetry of vice and disease. But Wordsworth threw himself into his place, made no reserves or stipulations; man and writer were not to be divided. He sat at the foot of Helvellyn and on the margin of Windermere, and took their lustrous mornings and their sublime midnights for his theme, and not Marlowe nor Massinger, not Horace nor Milton nor Dante. He once for all forsook the styles and standards and modes of thinking of London and Paris, and the books read there and the aims pursued, and wrote Helvellyn and Windermere and the dim spirits which these haunts harbored. There was not the least attempt to reconcile these with the spirit of fashion and selfishness, nor to show, with great deference to the superior judgment of dukes and earls, that although London was the home for men of great parts, yet Westmoreland had these consolations for such as fate had condemned to the country life, — but with a complete satisfaction he pitied and rebuked their false lives, and celebrated his own with the religion of a true priest. Hence the antagonism which was immediately felt between his poetry and the spirit of the age, that here not only criticism but conscience and will were parties; the spirit of literature and the modes of living and the conventional theories of the conduct of life were called in question on wholly new grounds, — not from Platonism, not from Christianity, but from the lessons which the country muse taught a stout pedestrian climbing a mountain and following a river from its parent rill down to the sea. The Cannings and Jeffreys of the capital, the Court Journals and Literary Gazettes were not well pleased, and voted the poet a bore. But that which rose in him so high as to the lips, rose in many others as high as to the heart. What he said, they were prepared to hear and confirm. The influence was in the air, and was wafted up and down into lone and into populous places, resisting the popular taste, modifying opinions which it did not change, and soon came to be felt in poetry, in criticism, in plans of life, and at last in legislation. In this country it very early found a stronghold, and its effect may be traced on all the poetry both of England and America.

But, notwithstanding all Wordsworth's grand merits, it was a great pleasure to know that

Alfred Tennyson's two volumes were coming out in the same ship; it was a great pleasure to receive them. The elegance, the wit and subtlety of this writer, his rich fancy, his power of language, his metrical skill, his independence of any living masters, his peculiar topics, his taste for the costly and gorgeous, discriminate the musky poet of gardens and conservatories, of parks and palaces.[1] Perhaps we felt the popular objection that he wants rude truth; he is too fine. In these boudoirs of damask and alabaster, one is farther off from stern Nature and human life than in Lalla Rookh and the Loves of the Angels. Amid swinging censers and perfumed lamps, amidst velvet and glory, we long for rain and frost. Otto-of-roses is good, but wild air is better. A critical friend of ours affirms that the vice which bereaved modern painters of their power is the ambition to begin where their fathers ended; to equal the masters in their exquisite finish, instead of their religious purpose. The painters are not willing to paint ill enough; they will not paint for their times, agitated by the spirit which agitates their country; so should their picture picture us, and draw all men after them; but they copy the technics of their predecessors, and paint for their predecessors' public. It seems as if the same vice had worked in poetry. Tennyson's compositions are not so much poems as studies in poetry, or sketches after the styles of sundry old masters. He is not the husband who builds the homestead after his own necessity, from foundation-stone to chimney-top and turret, but a tasteful bachelor who collects quaint staircases and groined ceilings. We have no right to such superfineness. We must not make our bread of pure sugar. These delicacies and splendors are then legitimate when they are the excess of substantial and necessary expenditure. The best songs in English poetry are by that heavy, hard, pedantic poet, Ben Jonson. Jonson is rude, and only on rare occasions gay. Tennyson is always fine, but Jonson's beauty is more grateful than Tennyson's. It is a natural manly grace of a robust workman. Ben's flowers are not in pots at a city florist's, arranged on a flower-stand, but he is a countryman at a harvest-home, attending his ox-cart from the fields, loaded with potatoes and apples, with grapes and plums, with nuts and berries, and stuck with boughs of hemlock and sweetbriar, with ferns and pond-lilies which the children have gathered. But let us not quarrel with our benefactors. Perhaps

Tennyson is too quaint and elegant. What then? It is long since we have had as good a lyrist; it will be long before we have his superior. Godiva is a noble poem that will tell the legend a thousand years. The poem of all the poetry of the present age for which we predict the longest term is Abou ben Adhem, of Leigh Hunt.[1] Fortune will still have her part in every victory, and it is strange that one of the best poems should be written by a man who has hardly written any other. And Godiva is a parable which belongs to the same gospel. Locksley Hall and The Two Voices are meditative poems, which were slowly written to be slowly read. The Talking Oak, though a little hurt by its wit and ingenuity, is beautiful, and the most poetic of the volume. Ulysses belongs to a high class of poetry, destined to be the highest, and to be more cultivated in the next generation. Œnone was a sketch of the same kind. One of the best specimens we have of the class is Wordsworth's Laodamia, of which no special merit it can possess equals the total merit of having selected such a subject in such a spirit.[2]

Next to the poetry, the novels, which come to us in every ship from England, have an importance increased by the immense extension of their circulation through the new cheap press, which sends them to so many willing thousands. We have heard it alleged with some evidence that the prominence given to intellectual power in Bulwer's romances has proved a main stimulus to mental culture in thousands of young men in England and America. The effect on manners cannot be less sensible, and we can easily believe that the behavior of the ballroom and of the hotel has not failed to draw some addition of dignity and grace from the fair ideals with which the imagination of a novelist has filled the heads of the most imitative class.

We are not very well versed in these books, yet we have read Mr. Bulwer enough to see that the story is rapid and interesting; he has really seen London society, and does not draw ignorant caricatures. He is not a genius, but his novels are marked with great energy and with a courage of experiment which in each instance had its degree of success. The story of Zanoni was one of those world-fables which is so agreeable to the human imagination that it is found in some form in the language of every country, and is always reappearing in literature. Many of the details of this novel preserve a poetic truth. We read Zanoni with pleasure, because magic is natural. It is implied in all superior culture that a complete man would need no auxiliaries to his personal presence. The eye and the word are certainly far subtler and stronger weapons than either money or knives. Whoever looked on the hero would consent to his will, being certified that his aims were universal, not selfish; and he would be obeyed as naturally as the rain and the sunshine are. For this reason, children delight in fairy tales. Nature is described in them as the servant of man, which they feel ought to be true. But Zanoni pains us and the author loses our respect, because he speedily betrays that he does not see the true limitations of the charm; because the power with which his hero is armed is a toy, inasmuch as the power does not flow from its legitimate fountains in the mind, is a power for London; a divine power converted into a burglar's false key or a highwayman's pistol to rob and kill with.[1]

But Mr. Bulwer's recent stories have given us who do not read novels occasion to think of this department of literature, supposed to be the natural fruit and expression of the age. We conceive that the obvious division of modern romance is into two kinds: first, the novels of costume or of circumstance, which is the old style, and vastly the most numerous. In this class, the hero, without any particular character, is in a very particular circumstance; he is greatly in want of a fortune or of a wife, and usually of both, and the business of the piece is to provide him suitably. This is the problem to be solved in thousands of English romances, including the Porter novels and the more splendid examples of the Edgeworth and Scott romances.

It is curious how sleepy and foolish we are, that these tales will so take us. Again and again we have been caught in that old foolish trap. Had one noble thought, opening the chambers of the intellect, one sentiment from the heart of God been spoken by them, the reader had been made a participator of their triumph; he too had been an invited and eternal guest; but this reward granted them is property, all-excluding property, a little cake baked for them to eat and for none other, nay, a preference and cosseting which is rude and insulting to all but the minion.

Except in the stories of Edgeworth and Scott, whose talent knew how to give to the book a thousand adventitious graces, the novels of costume are all one, and there is but one standard English novel, like the one orthodox sermon, which with slight variation is repeated every Sunday from so many pulpits.

But the other novel, of which Wilhelm Meister is the best specimen, the novel of *character*, treats the reader with more respect; the development of character being the problem, the reader is made a partaker of the whole prosperity. Everything good in such a story remains with the reader when the book is closed. A noble book was Wilhelm Meister. It gave the hint of a cultivated society which we found nowhere else. It was founded on power to do what was necessary, each person finding it an indispensable qualification of membership that he could do something useful, as in mechanics or agriculture or other indispensable art; then a probity, a justice was to be its element, symbolized by the insisting that each property should be cleared of privilege, and should pay its full tax to the state. Then a perception of beauty was the equally indispensable element of the association, by which each was dignified and all were dignified; then each was to obey his genius to the length of abandonment. They watched each candidate vigilantly, without his knowing that he was observed, and when he had given proof that he was a faithful man, then all doors, all houses, all relations were open to him; high behavior fraternized with high behavior, without question of heraldry, and the only power recognized is the force of character.[1]

The novels of Fashion, of Disraeli, Mrs. Gore, Mr. Ward, belong to the class of novels of costume, because the aim is purely external success. Of the tales of fashionable life, by far the most agreeable and the most efficient was Vivian Grey. Young men were and still are the readers and victims. Byron ruled for a time, but Vivian, with no tithe of Byron's genius, rules longer.[2] One can distinguish the Vivians in all companies. They would quiz their father and mother and lover and friend. They discuss sun and planets, liberty and fate, love and death, over the soup. They never sleep, go nowhere, stay nowhere, eat nothing, and know nobody, but are up to anything, though it were the genesis of Nature, or the last cataclysm, — Festus-like, Faust-like, Jove-like, and could write an Iliad any rainy morning, if fame were not such a bore. Men, women, though the greatest and fairest, are stupid things; but a rifle, and a mild pleasant gunpowder, a spaniel, and a cheroot, are themes for Olympus. I fear it was in part the influence of such pictures on living society which made the style of manners of which we have so many pictures, as, for example, in the following account of the English fashionist. "His highest triumph is to appear with the most wooden manners, as little polished as will suffice to avoid castigation, nay, to contrive even his civilities so that they may appear as near as may be to affronts; instead of a noble high-bred ease, to have the courage to offend against every restraint of decorum, to invert the relation in which our sex stand to women, so that they appear the attacking, and he the passive or defensive party."

We must here check our gossip in mid-volley and adjourn the rest of our critical chapter to a more convenient season.

VI

PAST AND PRESENT

HERE is Carlyle's new poem, his Iliad of English woes, to follow his poem on France, entitled the History of the French Revolution. In its first aspect it is a political tract, and since Burke, since Milton, we have had nothing to compare with it. It grapples honestly with the facts lying before all men, groups and disposes them with a master's mind, and, with a heart full of manly tenderness, offers his best counsel to his brothers. Obviously, it is the book of a powerful and accomplished thinker, who has looked with naked eyes at the dreadful political signs in England for the last few years, has conversed much on these topics with such wise men of all ranks and parties as are drawn to a scholar's house, until such daily and nightly meditation has grown into a great connection, if not a system of thoughts; and the topic of English politics becomes the best vehicle for the expression of his recent thinking, recommended to him by the desire to give some timely counsels, and to strip the worst mischiefs of their plausibility. It is a brave and just book, and not a semblance. "No new truth," say the critics on all sides. Is it so? Truth is very old, but the merit of seers is not to invent but to dispose objects in their right places, and he is the commander who is always in the mount, whose eye not only sees details, but throws crowds of details into their right arrangement and a larger and juster totality than any other. The book makes great approaches to true contemporary history, a very rare success, and firmly holds up to daylight the absurdities still tolerated in the English and European system. It is such an appeal to the conscience and honor of England as cannot be forgotten, or be feigned to be forgotten. It has the merit which belongs to every honest book, that it was self-examining before it was eloquent, and so hits all other men, and, as the country people say of good preaching, "comes bounce down into every pew." Every reader shall carry away something. The scholar shall read and write, the farmer and mechanic shall toil, with new resolution, nor forget the book when they resume their labor.

Though no theocrat, and more than most philosophers a believer in political systems, Mr. Carlyle very fairly finds the calamity of the times, not in bad bills of Parliament, nor the

Thomas Carlyle

remedy in good bills, but the vice in false and superficial aims of the people, and the remedy in honesty and insight. Like every work of genius, its great value is in telling such simple truths. As we recall the topics, we are struck with the force given to the plain truths; the picture of the English nation all sitting enchanted,— the poor, enchanted so that they cannot work, the rich, enchanted so that they cannot enjoy, and are rich in vain; the exposure of the progress of fraud into all parts and social activities; the proposition that the laborer must have a greater share in his earnings; that the principle of permanence shall be admitted into all contracts of mutual service; that the state shall provide at least schoolmaster's education for all the citizens; the exhortation to the workman that he shall respect the work and not the wages;[1] to the scholar, that he shall be there for light; to the idle, that no man shall sit idle; the picture of Abbot Samson, the true governor, who "is not there to expect reason and nobleness of others, he is there to give them of his own reason and nobleness;" and the assumption throughout the book, that a new chivalry and nobility, namely, the dynasty of labor, is replacing the old nobilities.

These things strike us with a force which reminds us of the morals of the Oriental or early Greek masters, and of no modern book. Truly in these things is great reward. It is not by sitting still at a grand distance and calling the human race *larvæ*, that men are to be helped, nor by helping the depraved after their own foolish fashion, but by doing unweariedly the particular work we were born to do. Let no man think himself absolved because he does a generous action and befriends the poor, but let him see whether he so holds his property that a benefit goes from it to all. A man's diet should be what is simplest and readiest to be had, because it is so private a good. His house should be better, because that is for the use of hundreds, perhaps of thousands, and is the property of the traveller.[1] But his speech is a perpetual and public instrument; let that always side with the race and yield neither a lie nor a sneer. His manners,—let them be hospitable and civilizing, so that no Phidias or Raphael shall have taught anything better in canvas or stone; and his acts should be representative of the human race, as one who makes them rich in his having, and poor in his want.

It requires great courage in a man of letters to handle the contemporary practical questions; not because he then has all men for his rivals, but because of the infinite entanglements of the problem, and the waste of strength in gathering unripe fruits. The task is superhuman; and the poet knows well that a little time will do more than the most puissant genius. Time stills the loud noise of opinions, sinks the small, raises the great, so that the true emerges without effort and in perfect harmony to all eyes; but the truth of the present hour, except in particulars and single relations, is unattainable. Each man can very well know his own part of duty, if he will; but to bring out the truth for beauty, and as literature, surmounts the powers of art. The most elaborate history of to-day will have the oddest dislocated look in the next generation. The historian of to-day is yet three ages off. The poet cannot descend into the turbid present without injury to his rarest gifts. Hence that necessity of isolation which genius has always felt. He must stand on his glass tripod, if he would keep his electricity.

But when the political aspects are so calamitous that the sympathies of the man overpower the habits of the poet, a higher than literary inspiration may succor him. It is a costly proof of character that the most renowned scholar of England should take his reputation in his hand and should descend into the ring; and he has added to his love whatever honor his opinions may forfeit. To atone for this departure from the vows of the scholar and his eternal duties to this secular charity, we have at least this gain, that here is a message which those to whom it was addressed cannot choose but hear. Though they die, they must listen. It is plain that whether by hope or by fear, or were it only by delight in this panorama of brilliant images, all the great classes of English society must read, even those whose existence it proscribes. Poor Queen Victoria, — poor Sir Robert Peel, — poor Primate and Bishops, — poor Dukes and Lords! There is no help in place or pride, or in looking another way; a grain of wit is more penetrating than the lightning of the night-storm, which no curtains or shutters will keep out. Here is a book which will be read, no thanks to anybody but itself. What pains, what hopes, what vows, shall come of the reading! Here is a book as full of treason as an egg is full of meat, and every lordship and worship and high form and ceremony of English conservatism tossed like a football into the air, and kept in the air, with merciless kicks and rebounds, and yet not a word is punishable by statute. The wit has eluded all official zeal; and yet these dire jokes, these cunning thrusts, this flaming sword of Cherubim waved high in air, illuminates the whole horizon, and shows to the eyes of the universe every wound it inflicts. Worst of all for the party attacked, it bereaves them beforehand of all sympathy, by anticipating the plea of poetic and humane conservatism, and impressing the reader with the conviction that the satirist himself has the truest love for everything old and excellent in English land and institutions, and a genuine respect for the basis of truth in those whom he exposes.

We are at some loss how to state what strikes us as the fault of this remarkable book, for the variety and excellence of the talent displayed in it is pretty sure to leave all special criticism in the wrong. And we may easily fail in expressing the general objection which we feel. It appears to us as a certain disproportion in the picture, caused by the obtrusion of the whims of the painter. In this work, as in his former labors, Mr. Carlyle reminds us of a sick giant. His humors are expressed with so much force of constitution that his fancies are more attractive and more credible than the sanity of duller men. But the habitual exaggeration of the tone wearies whilst it stimulates. It is felt to be so much deduction from the universality of the picture.[1] It is not serene sunshine, but everything is seen in lurid storm-lights. Every object attitudinizes, to the very mountains and stars almost, under the refraction of this wonderful humorist; and instead of the common earth and sky, we have a Martin's Creation or Judgment Day. A crisis has always arrived which requires a *deus ex machinâ*. One can hardly credit, whilst under the spell of this magician, that the world always had the same bankrupt look, to foregoing ages as to us,—as of a failed world just re-collecting its old withered forces to begin again and try to do a little business. It was perhaps inseparable from the attempt to write a book of wit and imagination on English politics that a certain local emphasis and love of effect, such as is the vice of preaching, should appear,—producing on the reader a feeling of forlornness by the excess of value attributed to circumstances. But the splendor of wit cannot outdazzle the calm daylight, which always shows every individual man in balance with his age, and able to work out his own salvation from all the follies of that, and no such glaring contrasts or severalties in that or this.[1] Each age has its own follies, as its majority is made up of foolish young people; its superstitions appear no superstitions to itself; and if you should ask the contemporary, he would tell you, with pride or with regret (according as he was practical or poetic), that he had none. But after a short time, down go its follies and weakness and the memory of them; its virtues alone remain, and its limitation assumes the poetic form of a beautiful superstition, as the dimness of our sight clothes the objects in the horizon with mist and color. The revelation of Reason is this of the unchangeableness of the fact of humanity under all its subjective aspects; that to the cowering it always cowers, to the daring it opens great avenues. The ancients are only venerable to us because distance has destroyed what was trivial; as the sun and stars affect us only grandly, because we cannot reach to their smoke and surfaces and say, Is that all?

And yet the gravity of the times, the manifold and increasing dangers of the English State, may easily excuse some over-coloring of the picture; and we at this distance are not so far removed from any of the specific evils, and are deeply participant in too many, not to share the gloom and thank the love and the courage of the counsellor. This book is full of humanity, and nothing is more excellent in this as in all Mr. Carlyle's works than the attitude of the writer. He has the dignity of a man of letters, who knows what belongs to him, and never deviates from his sphere; a continuer of the great line of scholars, he sustains their office in the highest credit and honor. If the good heaven have any good word to impart to this unworthy generation, here is one scribe qualified and clothed for its occasion. One excellence he has in an age of Mammon and of criticism, that he never suffers the eye of his wonder to close. Let who will be the dupe of trifles, he cannot keep his eye off from that gracious Infinite which embosoms us.

As a literary artist he has great merits, beginning with the main one that he never wrote one dull line. How well-read, how adroit, that thousand arts in his one art of writing; with his expedient for expressing those unproven opinions which he entertains but will not endorse, by summoning one of his men of straw from the cell, — and the respectable Sauerteig, or

Teufelsdröckh, or Dryasdust, or Picturesque Traveller, says what is put into his mouth, and disappears. That morbid temperament has given his rhetoric a somewhat bloated character; a luxury to many imaginative and learned persons, like a showery south wind with its sunbursts and rapid chasing of lights and glooms over the landscape, and yet its offensiveness to multitudes of reluctant lovers makes us often wish some concession were possible on the part of the humorist.[1] Yet it must not be forgotten that in all his fun of castanets, or playing of tunes with a whiplash like some renowned charioteers, — in all this glad and needful venting of his redundant spirits, he does yet, ever and anon, as if catching the glance of one wise man in the crowd, quit his tempestuous key, and lance at him in clear level tone the very word, and then with new glee return to his game. He is like a lover or an outlaw who wraps up his message in a serenade, which is nonsense to the sentinel, but salvation to the ear for which it is meant. He does not dodge the question, but gives sincerity where it is due.

One word more respecting this remarkable style. We have in literature few specimens of magnificence. Plato is the purple ancient, and

Bacon and Milton the moderns of the richest strains. Burke sometimes reaches to that exuberant fulness, though deficient in depth. Carlyle, in his strange, half-mad way, has entered the Field of the Cloth of Gold, and shown a vigor and wealth of resource which has no rival in the tourney-play of these times; — the indubitable champion of England. Carlyle is the first domestication of the modern system, with its infinity of details, into style. We have been civilizing very fast, building London and Paris, and now planting New England and India, New Holland and Oregon, — and it has not appeared in literature; there has been no analogous expansion and recomposition in books. Carlyle's style is the first emergence of all this wealth and labor with which the world has gone with child so long. London and Europe, tunnelled, graded, corn-lawed, with trade-nobility, and East and West Indies for dependencies; and America, with the Rocky Hills in the horizon, have never before been conquered in literature. This is the first invasion and conquest. How like an air-balloon or bird of Jove does he seem to float over the continent, and, stooping here and there, pounce on a fact as a symbol which was never a symbol before. This is the first experiment, and something of rudeness and haste must be pardoned to so great an achievement. It will be done again and again, sharper, simpler; but fortunate is he who did it first, though never so giant-like and fabulous. This grandiose character pervades his wit and his imagination. We have never had anything in literature so like earthquakes as the laughter of Carlyle. He "shakes with his mountain mirth." It is like the laughter of the Genii in the horizon. These jokes shake down Parliament House and Windsor Castle, Temple and Tower, and the future shall echo the dangerous peals. The other particular of magnificence is in his rhymes. Carlyle is a poet who is altogether too burly in his frame and habit to submit to the limits of metre. Yet he is full of rhythm, not only in the perpetual melody of his periods, but in the burdens, refrains, and grand returns of his sense and music. Whatever thought or motto has once appeared to him fraught with meaning, becomes an omen to him henceforward, and is sure to return with deeper tones and weightier import, now as threat, now as confirmation, in gigantic reverberation, as if the hills, the horizon, and the next ages returned the sound.[1]

VII

A LETTER

AS we are very liable, in common with the letter-writing world, to fall behind-hand in our correspondence; and a little more liable because in consequence of our editorial function we receive more epistles than our individual share, we have thought that we might clear our account by writing a quarterly catholic letter to all and several who have honored us, in verse or prose, with their confidence, and expressed a curiosity to know our opinion. We shall be compelled to dispose very rapidly of quite miscellaneous topics.

And first, in regard to the writer who has given us his speculations on Railroads and Airroads, our correspondent shall have his own way. To the railway, we must say, — like the courageous lord mayor at his first hunting, when told the hare was coming, — "Let it come, in Heaven's name, I am not afraid on 't." Very unlooked-for political and social effects of the iron road are fast appearing. It will require an expansion of the police of the old world. When a railroad train shoots through Europe every

The Emerson House in Winter 1904

day from Brussels to Vienna, from Vienna to Constantinople, it cannot stop every twenty or thirty miles at a German custom-house, for examination of property and passports. But when our correspondent proceeds to flying-machines, we have no longer the smallest taper-light of credible information and experience left, and must speak on *a priori* grounds.

Shortly, then, we think the population is not yet quite fit for them, and therefore there will be none. Our friend suggests so many inconveniences from piracy out of the high air to orchards and lone houses, and also to other high fliers, and the total inadequacy of the present system of defence, that we have not the heart to break the sleep of the good public by the repetition of these details. When children come into the library, we put the inkstand and the watch on the high shelf until they be a little older; and Nature has set the sun and moon in plain sight and use, but laid them on the high shelf where her roystering boys may not in some mad Saturday afternoon pull them down or burn their fingers. The sea and the iron road are safer toys for such ungrown people; we are not yet ripe to be birds.

In the next place, to fifteen letters on Communities, and the Prospects of Culture, and the destinies of the cultivated class, — what answer? Excellent reasons have been shown us why the writers, obviously persons of sincerity and elegance, should be dissatisfied with the life they lead, and with their company. They have exhausted all its benefit, and will not bear it much longer. Excellent reasons they have shown why something better should be tried. They want a friend to whom they can speak and from whom they may hear now and then a reasonable word. They are willing to work, so it be with friends. They do not entertain anything absurd or even difficult. They do not wish to force society into hated reforms, nor to break with society. They do not wish a township or any large expenditure or incorporated association, but simply a concentration of chosen people. By the slightest possible concert, persevered in through four or five years, they think that a neighborhood might be formed of friends who would provoke each other to the best activity. They believe that this society would fill up the terrific chasm of ennui, and would give their genius that inspiration which it seems to wait in vain.

But, 'the selfishness!' One of the writers

relentingly says, "What shall my uncles and aunts do without me?" and desires distinctly to be understood not to propose the Indian mode of giving decrepit relatives as much of the mud of holy Ganges as they can swallow, and more, but to begin the enterprise of concentration by concentrating all uncles and aunts in one delightful village by themselves! — so heedless is our correspondent of putting all the dough into one pan, and all the leaven into another. Another objection seems to have occurred to a subtle but ardent advocate. Is it, he writes, a too great wilfulness and intermeddling with life, — which is better accepted than calculated? Perhaps so; but let us not be too curiously good. The Buddhist is a practical Necessitarian; the Yankee is not. We do a great many selfish things every day; among them all let us do one thing of enlightened selfishness. It were fit to forbid concert and calculation in this particular, if that were our system, if we were up to the mark of self-denial and faith in our general activity. But to be prudent in all the particulars of life, and in this one thing alone religiously forbearing; prudent to secure to ourselves an injurious society, temptations to folly and despair, degrading examples, and enemies; and only abstinent when it is proposed to provide ourselves with guides, examples, lovers!

We shall hardly trust ourselves to reply to arguments by which we would gladly be persuaded. The more discontent, the better we like it. It is not for nothing, we assure ourselves, that our people are busied with these projects of a better social state, and that sincere persons of all parties are demanding somewhat vital and poetic of our stagnant society. How fantastic and unpresentable soever the theory has hitherto seemed, how swiftly shrinking from the examination of practical men, let us not lose the warning of that most significant dream. How joyfully we have felt the admonition of larger natures which despised our aims and pursuits, conscious that a voice out of heaven spoke to us in that scorn. But it would be unjust not to remind our younger friends that whilst this aspiration has always made its mark in the lives of men of thought, in vigorous individuals it does not remain a detached object, but is satisfied along with the satisfaction of other aims. To live solitary and unexpressed is painful,—painful in proportion to one's consciousness of ripeness and equality to the offices of friendship. But herein we are never quite forsaken by the

Divine Providence. The loneliest man, after twenty years, discovers that he stood in a circle of friends, who will then show like a close fraternity held by some masonic tie. But we are impatient of the tedious introductions of Destiny, and a little faithless, and would venture something to accelerate them. One thing is plain, that discontent and the luxury of tears will bring nothing to pass. Regrets and Bohemian castles and æsthetic villages are not a very self-helping class of productions, but are the voices of debility. Especially to one importunate correspondent we must say that there is no chance for the æsthetic village. Every one of the villagers has committed his several blunder; his genius was good, his stars consenting, but he was a marplot. And though the recuperative force in every man may be relied on infinitely, it must be relied on before it will exert itself. As long as he sleeps in the shade of the present error, the after-nature does not betray its resources. Whilst he dwells in the old sin, he will pay the old fine.

More letters we have on the subject of the position of young men, which accord well enough with what we see and hear. There is an American disease, a paralysis of the active faculties, which falls on young men of this country as soon as they have finished their college education, which strips them of all manly aims and bereaves them of animal spirits; so that the noblest youths are in a few years converted into pale Caryatides to uphold the temple of conventions. They are in the state of the young Persians, when "that mighty Yezdam prophet" addressed them and said, "Behold the signs of evil days are come; there is now no longer any right course of action, nor any self-devotion left among the Iranis." As soon as they have arrived at this term, there are no employments to satisfy them, they are educated above the work of their times and country, and disdain it. Many of the more acute minds pass into a lofty criticism of these things, which only embitters their sensibility to the evil and widens the feeling of hostility between them and the citizens at large. From this cause, companies of the best-educated young men in the Atlantic states every week take their departure for Europe; for no business that they have in that country, but simply because they shall so be hid from the reproachful eyes of their countrymen and agreeably entertained for one or two years, with some lurking hope, no doubt, that something may turn up to give them a decided direction. It is easy to see that this is only a postponement of their proper work, with the additional disadvantage of a two years' vacation. Add that this class is rapidly increasing by the infatuation of the active class, who, whilst they regard these young Athenians with suspicion and dislike, educate their own children in the same courses, and use all possible endeavors to secure to them the same result.

Certainly we are not insensible to this calamity, as described by the observers or witnessed by ourselves. It is not quite new and peculiar; though we should not know where to find in literature any record of so much unbalanced intellectuality, such undeniable apprehension without talent, so much power without equal applicability, as our young men pretend to. Yet in Theodore Mundt's account of Frederic Hölderlin's Hyperion, we were not a little struck with the following Jeremiad of the despair of Germany, whose tone is still so familiar that we were somewhat mortified to find that it was written in 1799. "Then came I to the Germans. I cannot conceive of a people more disjoined than the Germans. Mechanics you shall see, but no man. Is it not like some battle-field, where hands and arms and all members lie scattered about, whilst the life-blood runs away into the sand? Let every man mind his own, you say, and I say the same. Only let him mind it with all his heart, and not with this cold study, — literally, hypocritically, to appear that which he passes for, — but in good earnest, and in all love, let him be that which he is; then there is a soul in his deed. And is he driven into a circumstance where the spirit must not live? Let him thrust it from him with scorn, and learn to dig and plough. There is nothing holy which is not desecrated, which is not degraded to a mean end among this people. It is heartrending to see your poet, your artist, and all who still revere genius, who love and foster the Beautiful. The Good! They live in the world as strangers in their own house; they are like the patient Ulysses whilst he sat in the guise of a beggar at his own door, whilst shameless rioters shouted in the hall and asked, Who brought the ragamuffin here? Full of love, talent and hope spring up the darlings of the muse among the Germans; some seven years later, and they flit about like ghosts, cold and silent; they are like a soil which an enemy has sown with poison, that it will not bear a blade of grass. On earth all is imperfect! is the old proverb of the German. Aye, but if one should say to these God-forsaken, that with them all is imperfect only because they leave nothing pure which they do not pollute, nothing holy which they do not defile with their fumbling hands; that with them nothing prospers because the godlike nature which is the root of all prosperity they do not revere; that with them, truly, life is shallow and anxious and full of discord, because they despise genius, which brings power and nobleness into manly action, cheerfulness into endurance, and love and brotherhood into towns and houses. Where a people honors genius in its artists, there breathes like an atmosphere a universal soul, to which the shy sensibility opens, which melts self-conceit, — all hearts become pious and great, and it adds fire to heroes. The home of all men is with such a people, and there will the stranger gladly abide. But where the divine nature and the artist is crushed, the sweetness of life is gone, and every other planet is better than the earth. Men deteriorate, folly increases, and a gross mind with it; drunkenness comes with a disaster; with the wantonness of the tongue and with the anxiety for a livelihood the blessing of every year becomes a curse, and all the gods depart."

The steep antagonism between the money-getting and the academic class must be freely admitted, and perhaps is the more violent that whilst our work is imposed by the soil and the sea, our culture is the tradition of Europe. But we cannot share the desperation of our contemporaries; least of all should we think a preternatural enlargement of the intellect a calamity. A new perception, the smallest new activity given to the perceptive power, is a victory won to the living universe from Chaos and old Night, and cheaply bought by any amounts of hard fare and false social position. The balance of mind and body will redress itself fast enough. Superficialness is the real distemper. In all the cases we have ever seen where people were supposed to suffer from too much wit, or, as men said, from a blade too sharp for the scabbard, it turned out that they had not wit enough. It may easily happen that we are grown very idle, and must go to work, and that the times must be worse before they are better. It is very certain that speculation is no succedaneum for life. What we would know, we must do. As if any taste or imagination could take the place of fidelity! The old Duty is the old God. And we may come to this by the rudest teaching. A friend of ours went five years ago to Illinois to buy a farm for his son. Though there were crowds of emigrants in the roads, the country was open on both sides, and long intervals between hamlets and houses. Now after five years he has just been to visit the young farmer and see how he prospered, and reports that a miracle had been wrought. From Massachusetts to Illinois the land is fenced in and builded over, almost like New England itself, and the proofs of thrifty cultivation abound; — a result not so much owing to the natural increase of population as to the hard times, which, driving men out of cities and trade, forced them to take off their coats and go to work on the land; which has rewarded them not only with wheat but with habits of labor. Perhaps the adversities of our commerce have not yet been pushed to the wholesomest degree of severity. Apathies and total want of work, and reflection on the imaginative character of American life, etc., etc., are like seasickness, and never will obtain any sympathy if there is a wood-pile in the yard, or an unweeded patch in the garden; not to mention the graver absurdity of a youth of noble aims who can find no field for his energies, whilst the colossal wrongs of the Indian, of the Negro, of the emigrant, remain unmitigated, and the religious, civil and judicial forms of the country are confessedly effete and offensive. We must refer our clients back to themselves, believing that every man knows in his heart the cure for the disease he so ostentatiously bewails.

As far as our correspondents have entangled their private griefs with the cause of American Literature, we counsel them to disengage themselves as fast as possible. In Cambridge orations and elsewhere there is much inquiry for that great absentee American Literature. What can have become of it? The least said is best. A literature is no man's private concern, but a secular and generic result, and is the affair of a power which works by a prodigality of life and force very dismaying to behold, — every trait of beauty purchased by hecatombs of private tragedy. The pruning in the wild gardens of Nature is never forborne. Many of the best must die of consumption, many of despair, and many be stupid and insane, before the one great and fortunate life which they each predicted can shoot up into a thrifty and beneficent existence.[1]

VIII

THE TRAGIC

HE has seen but half the universe who never has been shown the house of Pain. As the salt sea covers more than two thirds of the surface of the globe, so sorrow encroaches in man on felicity. The conversation of men is a mixture of regrets and apprehensions. I do not know but the prevalent hue of things to the eye of leisure is melancholy. In the dark hours, our existence seems to be a defensive war, a struggle against the encroaching All, which threatens surely to engulf us soon, and is impatient of our short reprieve. How slender the possession that yet remains to us; how faint the animation! how the spirit seems already to contract its domain, retiring within narrower walls by the loss of memory, leaving its planted fields to erasure and annihilation. Already our thoughts and words have an alien sound. There is a simultaneous diminution of memory and hope. Projects that once we laughed and leapt to execute find us now sleepy and preparing to lie down in the snow. And in the serene hours we have no courage to spare. We cannot afford to let go any advantages. The riches of body or of mind which we do not need to-day are the reserved fund against the calamity that may arrive to-morrow. It is usually agreed that some nations have a more sombre temperament, and one would say that history gave no record of any society in which despondency came so readily to heart as we see it and feel it in ours. Melancholy cleaves to the English mind in both hemispheres as closely as to the strings of an Æolian harp. Men and women at thirty years, and even earlier, have lost all spring and vivacity, and if they fail in their first enterprises, they throw up the game. But whether we and those who are next to us are more or less vulnerable, no theory of life can have any right which leaves out of account the values of vice, pain, disease, poverty, insecurity, disunion, fear and death.

What are the conspicuous tragic elements in human nature? The bitterest tragic element in life to be derived from an intellectual source is the belief in a brute Fate or Destiny; the belief that the order of Nature and events is controlled by a law not adapted to man, nor man to that, but which holds on its way to the end, serving him if his wishes chance to lie in the same course, crushing him if his wishes lie contrary to it, and heedless whether it serves or crushes him. This is the terrible meaning that lies at the foundation of the old Greek tragedy, and makes the Œdipus and Antigone and Orestes objects of such hopeless commiseration. They must perish, and there is no overgod to stop or to mollify this hideous enginery that grinds or thunders, and snatches them up into its terrific system. The same idea makes the paralyzing terror with which the East Indian mythology haunts the imagination. The same thought is the predestination of the Turk. And universally, in uneducated and unreflecting persons on whom too the religious sentiment exerts little force, we discover traits of the same superstition: "If you balk water you will be drowned the next time;" "if you count ten stars you will fall down dead;" "if you spill the salt;" "if your fork sticks upright in the floor;" "if you say the Lord's prayer backwards;" — and so on, a several penalty, nowise grounded in the nature of the thing, but on an arbitrary will. But this terror of contravening an unascertained and unascertainable will cannot co-exist with reflection: it disappears with civilization, and can no more be reproduced than the fear of ghosts after childhood. It is discriminated from the doctrine of Philosophical Necessity herein: that the last is an Optimism, and therefore the suffering individual finds his good consulted in the good of all, of which he is a part. But in destiny, it is not the good of the whole or the *best will* that is enacted, but only *one particular will.* Destiny properly is not a will at all, but an immense whim; and this the only ground of terror and despair in the rational mind, and of tragedy in literature. Hence the antique tragedy, which was founded on this faith, can never be reproduced.[1]

After reason and faith have introduced a better public and private tradition, the tragic element is somewhat circumscribed. There must always remain, however, the hindrance of our private satisfaction by the laws of the world. The law which establishes nature and the human race, continually thwarts the will of ignorant individuals, and this in the particulars of disease, want, insecurity and disunion.

But the essence of tragedy does not seem to me to lie in any list of particular evils. After we have enumerated famine, fever, inaptitude, mutilation, rack, madness and loss of friends, we have not yet included the proper tragic element, which is Terror, and which does not respect definite evils but indefinite; an ominous spirit which haunts the afternoon and the night, idleness and solitude.

A low, haggard sprite sits by our side, "casting the fashion of uncertain evils" — a sinister presentiment, a power of the imagination to dislocate things orderly and cheerful and show them in startling array. Hark! what sounds on the night wind, the cry of Murder in that friendly house; see these marks of stamping feet, of hidden riot. The whisper overheard, the detected glance, the glare of malignity, ungrounded fears, suspicions, half-knowledge and mistakes, darken the brow and chill the heart of men. And accordingly it is natures not clear, not of quick and steady perceptions, but imperfect characters from which somewhat is hidden that all others see, who suffer most from these causes. In those persons who move the profoundest pity, tragedy seems to consist in temperament, not in events. There are people who have an appetite for grief, pleasure is not strong enough and they crave pain, mithridatic stomachs which must be fed on poisoned bread, natures so doomed that no prosperity can soothe their ragged and dishevelled desolation. They mis-hear and mis-behold, they suspect and dread. They handle every nettle and ivy in the hedge, and tread on every snake in the meadow.

> "Come bad chance,
> And we add it to our strength,
> And we teach it art and length,
> Itself o'er us to advance."[1]

Frankly, then, it is necessary to say that all sorrow dwells in a low region. It is superficial; for the most part fantastic, or in the appearance and not in things. Tragedy is in the eye of the observer, and not in the heart of the sufferer. It looks like an insupportable load under which earth moans aloud. But analyze it; it is not I, it is not you, it is always another person who is tormented. If a man says, Lo! I suffer — it is apparent that he suffers not, for grief is dumb. It is so distributed as not to destroy. That which would rend you falls on tougher textures. That which seems intolerable reproach or bereavement does not take from the accused or bereaved man or woman appetite or sleep. Some men are above grief, and some below it. Few are capable of love. In phlegmatic natures calamity is unaffecting, in shallow natures it is rhetorical. Tragedy must be somewhat which I can respect. A querulous habit is not tragedy.

A panic such as frequently in ancient or savage nations put a troop or an army to flight without an enemy; a fear of ghosts; a terror of freezing to death that seizes a man in a winter midnight on the moors; a fright at uncertain sounds heard by a family at night in the cellar or on the stairs,—are terrors that make the knees knock and the teeth clatter, but are no tragedy, any more than seasickness, which may also destroy life. It is full of illusion. As it comes, it has its support. The most exposed classes, soldiers, sailors, paupers, are nowise destitute of animal spirits. The spirit is true to itself, and finds its own support in any condition, learns to live in what is called calamity as easily as in what is called felicity; as the frailest glass bell will support a weight of a thousand pounds of water at the bottom of a river or sea, if filled with the same.

A man should not commit his tranquillity to things, but should keep as much as possible the reins in his own hands, rarely giving way to extreme emotion of joy or grief. It is observed that the earliest works of the art of sculpture are countenances of sublime tranquillity. The Egyptian sphinxes, which sit to-day as they sat when the Greek came and saw them and departed, and when the Roman came and saw them and departed, and as they will still sit when the Turk, the Frenchman and the Englishman, who visit them now, shall have passed by,—"with their stony eyes fixed on the East and on the Nile," have countenances expressive of complacency and repose, an expression of health, deserving their longevity, and verifying the primeval sentence of history on the permanency of that people, "Their strength is to sit still."[1] To this architectural stability of the human form, the Greek genius added an ideal beauty, without disturbing the seals of serenity; permitting no violence of mirth, or wrath, or suffering. This was true to human nature. For in life, actions are few, opinions even few, prayers few; loves, hatreds, or any emissions of the soul. All that life demands of us through the greater part of the day is an equilibrium, a readiness, open eyes and ears, and free hands. Society asks this, and truth, and love, and the genius of our life. There is a fire in some men which demands an outlet in some rude action; they betray their impatience of quiet by an irregular Catilinarian gait; by irregular, faltering, disturbed speech, too emphatic for the occasion. They treat trifles with a tragic air. This is not beautiful. Could they not lay a rod or two of stone wall, and work off this superabundant irritability? When two strangers meet in the highway, what each demands of the other is that the aspect should show a firm mind, ready for any event of good or ill, prepared alike to give death or to give life, as the emergency of the next moment may require. We must walk as guests in Nature; not impassioned, but cool and disengaged. A man should try Time, and his face should wear the expression of a just judge, who has nowise made up his opinion, who fears nothing, and even hopes nothing, but who puts Nature and fortune on their merits: he will hear the case out, and then decide.[1] For all melancholy, as all passion, belongs to the exterior life. Whilst a man is not grounded in the divine life by his proper roots, he clings by some tendrils of affection to society — mayhap to what is best and greatest in it, and in calm times it will not appear that he is adrift and not moored; but let any shock take place in society, any revolution of custom, of law, of opinion, and at once his type of permanence is shaken. The disorder of his neighbors appears to him universal disorder; chaos is come again. But in truth he was already a driving wreck before the wind arose, which only revealed to him his vagabond state. If a man is centred, men and events appear to him a fair image or reflection of that which he knoweth beforehand in himself. If any perversity or profligacy break out in society, he will join with others to avert the mischief, but it will not arouse resentment or fear, because he discerns its impassable limits. He sees already in the ebullition of sin the simultaneous redress.[1]

Particular reliefs, also, fit themselves to human calamities; for the world will be in equilibrium, and hates all manner of exaggeration.

Time the consoler, Time the rich carrier of all changes, dries the freshest tears by obtruding new figures, new costumes, new roads, on our eye, new voices on our ear. As the west wind lifts up again the heads of the wheat which were bent down and lodged in the storm, and combs out the matted and dishevelled grass as it lay in night-locks on the ground, so we let in Time as a drying wind into the seed-field of thoughts which are dark and wet and low bent. Time restores to them temper and elasticity. How fast we forget the blow that threatened to cripple us. Nature will not sit still; the faculties will do somewhat; new hopes spring, new affections twine, and the broken is whole again.

Time consoles, but Temperament resists the impression of pain. Nature proportions her defence to the assault. Our human being is wonderfully plastic; if it cannot win this satisfaction here, it makes itself amends by running out there and winning that. It is like a stream of water, which, if dammed up on one bank, overruns the other, and flows equally at its own convenience over sand, or mud, or marble. Most suffering is only apparent. We fancy it is torture; the patient has his own compensations. A tender American girl doubts of Divine Providence whilst she reads the horrors of "the middle passage;" and they are bad enough at the mildest; but to such as she these crucifixions do not come; they come to the obtuse and barbarous, to whom they are not horrid, but only a little worse than the old sufferings. They exchange a cannibal war for the stench of the hold. They have gratifications which would be none to the civilized girl. The market-man never damned the lady because she had not paid her bill, but the stout Irishwoman has to take that once a month. She, however, never feels weakness in her back because of the slave-trade. This self-adapting strength is especially seen in disease. "It is my duty," says Sir Charles Bell, "to visit certain wards of the hospital where there is no patient admitted but with that complaint which most fills the imagination with the idea of insupportable pain and certain death. Yet these wards are not the least remarkable for the composure and cheerfulness of their inmates. The individual who suffers has a mysterious counterbalance to that condition, which, to us who look upon her, appears to be attended with no alleviating circumstance." Analogous supplies are made to those individuals whose character leads them to vast exertions of body and mind. Napoleon said to one of his friends at St. Helena, "Nature seems to have calculated that I should have great reverses to endure, for she has given me a temperament like a block of marble. Thunder cannot move it; the shaft merely glides along. The great events of my life have slipped over me without making any demand on my moral or physical nature." [1]

The intellect is a consoler, which delights in detaching or putting an interval between a man and his fortune, and so converts the sufferer into a spectator and his pain into poetry. It yields the joys of conversation, of letters and of science. Hence also the torments of life become tuneful tragedy, solemn and soft with music, and garnished with rich dark pictures. But higher still than the activities of art, the intellect in its purity and the moral sense in its purity are not distinguished from each other, and both ravish us into a region whereunto these passionate clouds of sorrow cannot rise.

NOTES

NOTES

NATURAL HISTORY OF INTELLECT

MR. CABOT, in his prefatory note to the volume named as above, the material for which he collected and edited in 1893, said of Mr. Emerson, "He had, from his early youth, cherished the project of a new method in metaphysics, proceeding by observation of the mental facts, without attempting an analysis and coördination of them, which must, from the nature of the case, be premature. With this view, he had, at intervals from 1848 to 1866, announced courses on the 'Natural History of Intellect,' 'The Natural Method of Mental Philosophy' and 'Philosophy for the People.' He would, he said, give anecdotes of the spirit, a calendar of mental moods, without any pretence of system.

"None of these attempts, however, disclosed any novelty of method, or indeed, after the opening statement of his intention, any marked difference from his ordinary lectures. He had always been writing anecdotes of the spirit, and those which he wrote under this heading were used by him in subsequently published essays so largely that I find very little left for present publication. The lecture which gives its name to the volume ["Natural History of Intellect"] was the first of the earliest course [at Harvard University], and it seems to me to include all that distinctly belongs to the particular subject."

In an old note-book, perhaps of 1835, is an endeavor by Mr. Emerson to write down some of the laws of "The First Philosophy, by which is meant the original laws of the mind." There is in *English Traits* (page 240) a passage from which one might infer that the reading of Bacon may have first suggested this plan.

While in England, he made a beginning of formulating these laws in lectures, and wrote to Miss Fuller: —

"I am working away in these mornings at some papers which, if I do not, as I suppose I shall not, get ready for lectures here, will serve me in a better capacity as a kind of book of metaphysics, to print at home. Does not James Walker [Professor of Moral Philosophy at Harvard College] want relief, and to let me be his lieutenant for one semester to his class in Locke?"

Soon after writing this, he gave a course in London called "Mind and Manners of the Nineteenth Century," of which the first three were on the Natural History of the Intellect, and were called respectively "Powers and Laws of Thought," "Relation of Intellect to Natural Science," and "Tendencies and Duties of Men of Thought." Mr. Cabot gives, in his *Memoir of Emerson* (vol. ii., pp. 558–560), in condensed form, the general import of these three lectures. Most of the matter reappears in different arrangement and with additions in the subsequent courses, namely, that of 1858, in Boston, on the Natural Method of Mental Philosophy, and that on the Philosophy of the People, in 1866.

When, in 1870, too late for the satisfactory performance of the duty, Mr. Emerson had the pleasure of being invited to give lectures on Philosophy in the university courses for advanced students at Cambridge, he made a serious effort to arrange and expand his previous notes. His strength was now failing, and the task of arrangement — always for him the most difficult part of his work — sorely burdened him, for he had to prepare two lectures a week for eight weeks. He used his old notes, with changes, and much that was later printed in the essays on Poetry and Imagination, Inspiration, and Memory. Mr. Cabot, as literary executor, has done what was possible in arrangement of the manuscript material, and in an Appendix to the Memoir has given an admirable chronological list of the addresses and lectures, often giving abstracts of unpublished lectures, from which Mr. Emerson had taken many passages to use elsewhere.

Mr. Cabot's opinion, as expressed in the quotation above given from his Prefatory Note, is entitled to high consideration in this matter, both because Mr. Emerson intrusted to his judgment the decision as to what should be published of his manuscripts, and as being himself a metaphysician of mind acute, yet broad. There was, however, in two lectures given in London and Boston, which followed that printed by Mr. Cabot in the former edition, much matter that was interesting, if "not distinctly belonging to the particular subject." Therefore in the notes to this lecture I have given many passages that belonged in it, in an earlier form, and to a second lecture, and have ventured to print a third lecture, with little pruning, in the text.

Although Mr. Cabot was not quite ready to agree with his friend in his expression, "Who has not looked into a metaphysical book? and what sensible man ever looked twice?" he gives in his Memoir a most friendly and interesting critique on the Cambridge course. Mr. Emerson admired his friend's character and the quality of his mind. The poet had great and increasing comfort in the metaphysician, whether or no he followed him exactly in his reasoning. In 1843 Mr. Emerson wrote to Miss Elizabeth Hoar: —

"Mr. Cabot came up here and comforted the dry land with a little philosophy. Is not philosophy the simular poetry of the understanding, the mirage of the Sahara? Tax me not with levity and the old aloofness. I truly revolve with humble docility and desire the world-old problems. I worship the real, I hate the critical, and athwart the whole sky-full of imperfections can keep some steady sight of the perfect, opening there a new horizon."

Mr. Emerson himself was disappointed and mortified as to his Cambridge courses, which proved too much for his strength and so became, as he called them to Carlyle, "a doleful ordeal." After the first course, he wrote to his friend: —

"Well, it is now ended, and has no shining side but this one, that materials are collected and a possibility shown me how a repetition of the course next year — which is appointed — will enable me, partly out of these materials, and partly by large rejection of these and by large addition to them, to construct a fair report of what I have read and thought on the subject. I doubt the experts in Philosophy will not praise my discourses; — but the topics give me room for my guesses, criticism, admirations and experiences with the accepted masters, and also the lessons I have learned from the hidden great. I have a fancy that a realist is the good corrector of formalism, no matter how incapable of syllogism or continuous linked statement. To great results of thought and morals the steps are not many, and it is not the masters who spin the ostentatious continuity."

He wrote even less happily of the second course, ending thus: —

"I have abundance of good readings and some honest writing on the leading topics, — but in haste and confusion they are misplaced and spoiled. I hope the ruin of no young man's soul will, here or hereafter, be charged to me as having wasted his time or confounded his reason."

Yet many persons have remembered these lectures with

pleasure. A hearer whom I think now it is proper to name — Mrs. Fields, wife of Mr. Emerson's friend, the publisher — wrote letters to a friend telling very pleasantly, from memory, what Mr. Emerson said, and after his death published this record in the *Atlantic Monthly*.[1] Mr. Emerson sometimes named his subject "The Natural History of Spirit."

Page 3, note 1. It seems a pity to omit the end of this sentence, — his words of honor for the student of science: —

"Sure too of their immense relations and of the grandeur of their tendency, and yet himself deriving an honest dignity from the nobility of his studies, they lend him a certain severe charm."

Writing to his wife from London, in 1848, Mr. Emerson said: "Mr. Owen, who is in England what Agassiz is in America, has given me a card to his lectures at the College of Surgeons, and shown me the Hunterian Museum [Owen was the curator]. His lecture gratified me the more, or entirely, I may say, because, like Agassiz, he is an idealist in physiology." Later Mr. Owen showed him the Museum. Dr. Forbes took him to the Royal Institution "to hear Faraday, who is reckoned the best lecturer in London." He met Lyell often, and went to the Geological Club and took great pleasure in the debate heard there; he also heard Dr. Carpenter lecture. That same year, though the Revolution was in progress in Paris, he "went to the Sorbonne and heard a lecture from Leverrier on mathematics. It consisted chiefly of algebraic formulas, which he worked out on the blackboard, — but I saw the man."

Page 4, note 1. Here followed in the original: —

"But what most delighted me, and deepened the silence in

[1] "Mr. Emerson in the Lecture Room," by A. F.; *Atlantic Monthly*, June, 1883.

the College of Surgeons, was, in every instance, the general statement, the statement of widest application. And I thought, could we only have a list or summary of these results! better still, could we have one collected from all the departments and presented in the same rigorous manner, without any effusion of eloquence!"

Page 4, note 2. "Faraday is an excellent writer, and a wise man, and whilst I read him, I think, that if natural philosophy is faithfully written, moral philosophy need not be, for it will find itself expressed in these theses to a perceptive soul. That is, we shall read off the commandments and Gospels in Chemistry without need of translation; as we read a Latin or a French book to scholars without translation."

Page 5, note 1.

Thou seek'st in globe and galaxy,
He hides in pure transparency.

"Woodnotes," II., *Poems.*

Page 6, note 1.

But thou, meek lover of the good!
Find me, and turn thy back on heaven.

"Brahma," *Poems.*

Page 7, note 1. An interesting abstract of passages in the original which preceded this paragraph is given in Mr. Cabot's Memoir, vol. ii., p. 558.

Page 8, note 1. It is evident that this and the two preceding paragraphs were written in England in 1848. See Mr. Cabot's Memoir, vol. ii., p. 559.

Page 9, note 1. This matter is treated more fully in the essay "Aristocracy," in *Lectures and Biographical Sketches.*

Page 10, note 1. Here followed, in the English lecture: —

"Blessed is the region of Thought,

"'Calm pleasures there abide, majestic pains.'

One would say whoever had tasted this beatitude would hold all other goods cheap. There is a certain medicinal value to the Intellect; 't is a fine ablution which chastens and encourages. Affairs make us stout and supple, but they engage us in low connections and compromises and hurt us. Palaces and luxury degrade and starve us as much as hard work and the society of the ignorant. Thoughts refresh and dignify us again and restore price to life. Thought, while it lasts, is the only thing of value, and appears of universal and eternal value.

"Whatever addresses itself to the intellect subordinates the senses. The Intellect absorbs so much vital power that it kills or suspends the senses. This is the meaning of the famous sentence that Vice loses half its evil by losing all its grossness. In vice it restores, in gloom and skepticism it replaces things.

"There is no day so dark but I know that the worst facts will presently appear to me in that high order which makes skepticism impossible. How can a man of any inwardness not feel the inwardness of the Universe? If he is capable of science and moral sentiment, the masses of nature undulate and flow; and in this hour of thought the world, the galaxy, is a scrap before the metaphysical power. In the words of the Koran, 'Verily worlds upon worlds can add nothing to it.'

"It is the interest of the whole human race. We announce, in contradiction to all doubt and all desperation, the tidings that the best is to be had: that the best is accessible and cheap. Every man cannot get land or jewels, but every man can get what land and money and rank are valued for, namely, substantial manhood, thoughts self-realizing and prophetic of the farthest future, thoughts of which poetry and music are the necessary expression."

Page 10, note 2. In reply to criticism of his friend Alcott, Mr. Emerson used to say that his commanding merit was his habit of looking at things with a larger angle of vision than his critics, whether he brought his lines to a focus or not.

Page 11, note 1. Here followed: "I claim the same irresponsibleness and security with the chemist and astronomer. The observer has no duties but fidelity. He simply sets down on tablets the height of the mercury, the variation of the needle, the declination of the star, quite assured that these cold records will be found, when a century, or their natural cycle is complete, more beautiful rhythm, a more lovely dance, than any invention could have combined. It ought not to be less true of the metaphysician."

Page 14, note 1. In *Representative Men*, Mr. Emerson wrote:—

"A philosopher must be more than a philosopher. Plato is clothed with the powers of a poet, stands upon the highest place of the poet, and (though I doubt he wanted the decisive gift of lyric expression), mainly is not a poet because he chose to use the poetic gift to an ulterior purpose."

Page 16, note 1. Compare in the *Poems* "The Two Rivers" and the last verse in "Peter's Field."

Mr. Emerson's pleasure in Cæsar's offer to renounce the empire, the army and Cleopatra, if he could be shown the fountains of the ancient Nile (the story told by Lucan), seems to have been for its symbolism.

Page 19, note 1.

> Melting matter into dreams,
> Panoramas which I saw

And whatever glows or seems
Into substance, into Law.
"Fragments on the Poet," *Poems*, Appendix.

Page 20, note 1. The philosophy of Xenophanes, "one in all," appears constantly in the essays. See a passage in "Plato," in *Representative Men:* "The Same, the Same: friend and foe are of one stuff; the ploughman, the plough and the furrow are of one stuff; and the stuff is such and so much that the variations of form are unimportant."

Page 21, note 1.

Love me then and only, when you know
Me for the channel of the rivers of God
From deep ideal fontal heavens that flow.
"Fragments on Life," *Poems*, Appendix.

A passage from the earlier lecture may here be introduced: "Show us what you will, and we are agitated with dim sentiments that we already know somewhat of this; somewhere, sometime, some eternity, we have played this game before, and have still retained some vague memory of the thing, which, though not sufficient to furnish us an account of it, yet enables us to understand it better, now that we are here."

Page 23, note 1. In Mr. Cabot's Memoir, and also in the biographical sketch of Mr. Emerson in the first volume of this edition, some account is given of his visit, in 1833, to the Jardin des Plantes in Paris and its remarkable influence on his thought.

This passage in the lecture about the visits to museums is thus continued by Mr. Emerson on the influence of the stars, always felt by him: —

"Neither can a tender soul stand [under] the starry heaven and explore the solar and stellar bodies and arrangements without the wish to mix with them by knowledge. If men are analogues of acids and alkalis, of beast and bird, so are they of geometric laws and of astronomic galaxies. . . . This knowledge and sympathy only needs augmentation and it becomes active or creative. The love of the stars becomes inventive and constructive. Descartes, Kepler, Newton, Swedenborg, Laplace, Schelling, wrestle with the problem of genesis, and occupy themselves with constructing cosmogonies. Nature is saturated with deity; the particle is saturated with the elixir of the Universe. Little men, just born, Copernicize: they cannot radiate as suns, or revolve as planets, and so they do it in effigy by building the orrery in their brain.

"Who can see the profuse wealth of Raphael's or Angelo's designs without feeling how near these were to the secret of structure; how little added power it needs to convert this rush of thoughts and forms into bodies.

"And we are very conscious that this identity reaches farther than we know, has no limits, or none that we can ascertain; as appears in the language that men use in regard to men of extraordinary genius. For the signal performances of great men seem an extension of the same art that built animal bodies applied to toys or miniatures. Thus in Laplace and Napoleon is the old planetary arithmetic now walking in a man, in the builder of Egyptian or in the designer of Gothic piles, a reduction of Nature's great aspects in caverns or forests, to a scale of human convenience; and there is a conviction in the mind that some such impulse is constant.

"Something like this is the root of all the great arts, of picture, music, sculpture, architecture, poetry, and the history of the highest genius will warrant the conclusion that, as a man's life comes into union with Nature, his thoughts run parallel with the highest law. . . .

"Intellect agrees with Nature. Thought is a finer chemistry, a finer vegetation, a finer animal action. It agrees also with the moral code of the universe. There is nothing anomalous or antinomian in its higher properties, but a complete normality or allegiance to general laws, as shown by the moss, or the egg.

"The same laws which are kept in the lower parts, in the mines and workshops of Nature, are kept in the palaces and council-chambers. One police is good for the grub and for the seraphim. Nature is a shop of one price — *prix fixé*. Great advantages are bought at great cost. It is good to see the stern terms on which all these high prizes of fortune are obtained, and which parallel in their selectness the rigor of material laws.

"Knowledge is the straight line. Wisdom is the power of the straight line, or the *square*. Virtue is the power of the square, or the *solid*. A man reads in the *Cultivator* the method of planting and hoeing potatoes, and follows a farmer hoeing along the row of potato-hills. That is knowledge. At last he seizes the hoe, and at first with care and heed pulls up every root of sorrel and witch-grass. The day grows hot; the row is long; he says to himself, 'This is wisdom; but one hill is like another; I have mastered the art. It is trifling to do many times over the same thing:' and he desists. But the last lesson was still unlearned: the moral power lay in the continuance in fortitude, in working against pleasure to the excellent end and conquering all opposition. He has knowledge, he has wisdom, but he has missed virtue, which he only acquires who endures routine and sweat and postponement of ease to the achievement of a worthy end.

"The whole history of man is a series of conspiracies to win from Nature some advantage without paying for it: especially the history of arts and of education. . . . It is curious to see what grand powers we have a hint of and are mad to get hold of, yet how slow Heaven is to trust us with edged tools. . . . The condition of participation in any man's thought is entering the gate of that life. No man can be intellectually apprehended as long as you see only with your eyes. You do not see him. You must be committed before you shall be intrusted with the secrets of any party.

"Besides, really and truly there were no short cuts. Every perception costs houses and lands. Every word of Genius apprises me how much he has turned his back upon. Every image, every truth, cost him a great neglect, the loss of an estate, the loss of a brilliant career opened to him; of friend, wife, child; the flat negation of a duty.

"Ah! the whole must come by his own proper growth, and not by addition; by education, not by inducation. If it could be pumped into him, what prices would not be paid; money, diamonds, houses, counties for that costly power that commands and creates all these: but no, the art of arts, the power of thought, Genius, cannot be taught."

Page 24, note 1. The original ending of the sentence about the grass should be given: —

"An identity long ago observed, or, I may say, never not observed, as if the gardener among his vines is in the presence of his ancestors, or shall I say, the orchardist is a pear raised to the highest power."

And the poor grass will plot and plan
What it will do when it is man.

"Bacchus," *Poems.*

Page 26, note 1. The paragraph originally ended as follows, passing from remote history to the wood-walk of the day: —

"And in the conduct of the mind the blending of two tendencies or streams of thought, the union of two brains is a happy result. And usually every mind of a remarkable efficiency owes it to some new combination of traits not observed to have met before. All that delight which the eye owes to complemental colors, which the ear owes to the complemental sounds, the beautiful surprises of music, delights us still more in the combination of human life, and gives rise to love and joy. (For example, in Nature, those two harmonies of color which our winter scenery so frequently offers us, the contrast of snow lying under green pine-trees, and the snow under the dead oak-leaves; each of which contrasts gives the eye a lively pleasure.)"

Page 28, note 1. "As with events, so is it with thoughts. When I watch that flowing river, which, out of regions I see not, pours for a season its streams into me, I see that I am a pensioner; not a cause, but a surprised spectator of this ethereal water; that I desire and look up and put myself in the attitude of reception, but from some alien energy the visions come." — "Over-Soul," *Essays, First Series.*

Page 29, note 1.

Day by day for her darlings to her much she added more;
In her hundred-gated Thebes every chamber was a door,
A door to something grander, — loftier walls, and vaster
floor.

"Fragments on Nature," *Poems*, Appendix.

Page 30, note 1. Mr. Emerson used to warn against doing things consciously for example's sake, and said, "Act always from the simplest motive."

Page 34, note 1. In the lecture "School," in the course on Human Culture given in 1838–39, Mr. Emerson said: —

"*Instinct*, in the high sense, is so much our teacher as

almost to exclude all other teaching, but its means and weapons are the secondary instincts, the wants and faculties that belong to our organization."

Page 35, note 1. In the essay on "Self-Reliance" the question is raised, "What is the aboriginal Self on which a universal reliance may be grounded?" and answered: "The inquiry leads us to that source, at once the essence of genius, of virtue, and of life, which we call Spontaneity or Instinct. We denote this primary wisdom as Intuition, whilst all later teachings are tuitions."

This shows that reliance is urged, not on the little self, but the Universal self of the Over-Soul.

Page 36, note 1. This passage is metrically rendered by Mr. Emerson in the first of the "Fragments on Nature," in the *Poems.*

Page 39, note 1. In "Art," in the first series of *Essays,* the importance of detachment in that field is considered (p. 354).

Page 41, note 1. Compare with the concluding lines of the poem "Freedom."

Page 43, note 1. This demand is made in the poem "Culture."

Page 44, note 1. Here followed in the lecture: —

"There is a story in the Nursery-books, which always seemed to me a covert satire directed at the Universities, of Velent, who had a sword so wonderfully sharp that its entrance into the body was hardly to be perceived. 'I feel thy sword,' cried Æmilius, 'like cold water, gliding through my body.' 'Shake thyself,' said Velent. He did so, and fell down dead in two pieces." [Mr. Emerson, writing this in a slightly different form, spoke of this sword as "not named Excalibur, but Thought."]

After this story followed some further remarks on detachment: —

"In speaking of identity, I said, All things grow; in a living mind the thoughts live and grow, and what happens in the vegetable happens to them. There are always individuals under generals; not stagnant, not childless, but everything alive reproduces, and each has its progeny which fast emerge into light; or what seemed one truth presently multiplies itself into many.

"Of course this detachment the intellect contemplates. The intellect forever watches, foresees this detachment. 'T is an infinite series. Every detachment prepares a new detachment. Of course the prophecy becomes habitual and reaches to all things. Having seen one thing that once was firmament enter into the kingdom of growth and change, the conclusion is irresistible, there is no fixture in the universe. Everything was moved, did spin, and will spin again. This changes once for all his view of things. Things appear as seeds of an immense future. Whilst the dull man always [lives] in a finished world, the thinker always finds himself in the early ages; the world lies to him in heaps."

Here follows the paragraph in the text: "The intellect that sees the interval partakes of it," etc.

Page 45, note 1. The coldness of Intellect is somewhat grimly pictured in the verses called "Philosopher," in the Appendix to the *Poems*. The above paragraph in the text was originally thus continued: —

"You may see it in any obscure family in which the boy of genius is born; it makes him strange among his housemates. He can take what interest he will in their interests and pursuits, he cannot be mixed with them; he holds a Gyges ring in his hand, and can disappear from them at will. . . .

"This inevitable interval is one of the remarkable facts in the natural history of man, a fact fraught with good and evil. It is only those who have this detachment who interest us. If we go to any nation, who are they whom we seek? The men of thought. If we go to any society, though of seraphim, he only would interest us who comprehended and could interpret the thought and theory, and that act does instantly detach him from them. That thought is the unfolding of wings on his shoulders. The poet, in celebrating his hero, celebrates to the wise ear his superiority to his hero, and announces to the intelligent the lowness of that he magnifies. Shall I say that it is an exquisite luxury, for so I feel it, the speech of those who speak of things by the genius of the things, and not by the facts themselves? What is vulgar but the laying the emphasis on persons and facts, and not on the quality of the fact?"

Page 45, note 2. Here followed in one lecture: —

"The correction for this insubordination is here, that religion runs in true and parallel lines through the Intellect, as through Morals. All the powers and rewards of Faith which we find in the Good hold equally in the region of the True. Integrity is really the fountain of power in one as in the other. Seek first the kingdom of Heaven and all shall be added. It is the office of the poet to justify the moral sentiment and establish its eternal independence of demoniac agencies."

Page 45, note 3. "Emerson's method was to let the inspirations of the spirit lead the way, instead of inflicting one's hypotheses and presuppositions on the spirit. He wanted to know what life was for the spirit, not what it could be made for a certain philosophic demand." — *Man and the Divine Order*, by Horatio W. Dresser.

Page 46, note 1. Two thoughts in this paragraph are to

be found in the collection of fragmentary verses in the Appendix to the *Poems*: —

> That book is good
> Which puts me in a working mood.
> Unless to Thought is added Will,
> Apollo is an imbecile; —

and

> Hold of the Maker, not the Made;
> Sit with the Cause, or grim or glad.

Page 49, note 1. "The intellect constructive, which we popularly designate by the word Genius," is discussed in "Intellect," in the first series of Essays. It is there spoken of as "the generation of the mind, the marriage of thought with Nature."

Page 50, note 1. Compare the "Song of Nature," in the *Poems*.

A passage on this subject from a lecture may here be inserted: —

"A small acceleration of the intellectual processes without loss of tenacity (continuance) would of course add indefinite ages to human life; a small increase of perception would be equivalent to any increase of power. Observe the effect upon one mind of being comprehended by another mind and forced to take a leap forward, the first hint perhaps of a larger dialectic. He who has seen one proof, ever so slight, of the terrific powers of this organ, will remember it all the days of his life. The most venerable proser will be surprised into silence. It is like the first hint that the earth moves, or that iron is a conductor of fluids, or that granite is a gas. The solids, the centres, rest itself, fly and skip. Rest is a relation, and not rest any longer. And here is revealed to me some neighboring activity, a mere intellection, some new condition of ideal order, which seems to have dropped wings to solid earth and solid houses and real estates, which, like so many nimble mosquitoes, do exceedingly leap and fly. How many times? — once at least in every man's experience has repeated itself the question of Callicles, 'If you are in earnest, Socrates, and these things which you say are true, is not our human life subverted, and are not all our actions (as it seems) contrary to what they ought to be?'"

Page 51, note 1. In his journal in the autumn of 1838, Mr. Emerson records the visit to him of Jones Very, then in a state of strange exaltation of mind in which his host found food for thought. He writes: "Entertain every thought, every character that goes by with the hospitality of your soul. . . . Especially if one of these monotones (whereof, as my friends think, I have a savage society like a menagerie of monsters) come to you, receive him. For the partial action of his mind in one direction is a telescope for the objects on which it is pointed."

Page 52, note 1. The paragraph suggests the complaint of Alphonso of Castile, in the *Poems*.

Page 53, note 1. Mr. Emerson's method of listening for the thought and recording it in its purity, and his fear of the "ambitious interference which we miscall Art," as he once expressed himself, naturally resulted in the sentence — or paragraph — being, for him, the natural limit of expression, as his biographer has said. He himself complained to Carlyle of these "infinitely repellant particles" which he was striving to unite into a whole. Matthew Arnold and others have complained of his style's lacking "the requisite wholeness of good tissue." Yet his best work stands as he would have it. He meant, like Plotinus, not to "hastily disclose to every one the syllogistic necessities of his discourse." He allowed intervals for the electric spark to pass and thrill the reader. As he told a young friend, "Try and leave a little thinking for him; that will be better for both. The trouble of most writers is that they spread too thin. The reader is as quick as they, has got there before, and is ready and waiting. . . . If you can see how the harness fits, he can. But be sure that you see it."[1]

There are many readers who would not wish the method changed. Herman Grimm wrote: —

"What he has written is like life itself — the unbroken thread ever lengthened through the addition of the small events which make up each day's experience. . . . His sentences are series of thoughts. He begins as if continuing a discourse whose opening we had not heard, and ends as if only pausing to take breath before going on.

"We feel that Emerson never wished to say more than just what at the moment presented itself to his soul. He never sets up a system, never defended himself. He speaks as if he had never been assailed; as if all men were his friends, and held the same opinions as himself."

Page 56, note 1. This teaching is found in "Literary Ethics," in the volume *Nature, Addresses and Lectures*, and in "The Scholar," in *Lectures and Biographical Sketches*.

Page 58, note 1. These paragraphs follow in one of the lectures: —

"The brain and hands are hardly contemporaries. The brain is the ancestor of the man. The intellectual is the watchman, the angel in the sun, and announces the far-off age. All its laws it can read before yet the happy men arrive who enter into power; but the rest of the man must follow his

[1] *Talks with Ralph Waldo Emerson*, by Charles J. Woodbury. New York: The Baker and Taylor Co., 1890.

head, and if I can see the eyes, I will trust that he will soon be able to disengage his hands.

"Every truth tends to become a power; every idea from the moment of its emergence begins to gather material forces, and, after a little while, makes itself known in the spheres of politics and commerce. It works first on thoughts, then on things, and makes feet and afterwards shoes; first hands and then gloves; makes the men, and so the age and its material soon after."

Page 59, note 1.

The heavens that now draw him
With sweetness untold,
Once found, — for new heavens
He spurneth the old.

"The Sphinx," *Poems.*

Page 61, note 1. In the essay on Character (*Lectures and Biographical Sketches*) Mr. Emerson says the Moral Sentiment "helps us, not by adding, but by putting us in place," and speaks of Truth, Power, Goodness and Beauty as convertible terms; and in "Greatness" (*Letters and Social Aims*) says that "the Intellect and Moral Sentiment cannot be separated." See also "Worship," in *Conduct of Life.*

Page 62, note 1. He counselled young writers, "Omit all negative propositions; it will save ninety-nine one hundredths of your labor and increase the value of your work in the same measure."

See also his poem "Music."

Page 62, note 2. This last Ego is the self of "Self-Reliance."

Page 64, note 1. The conclusion brings to mind the last lines in the poem "Wealth."

These sheets from the early lecture may be added: —

"Every truth is universally applicable, thousand-sided. Every drop of blood has great talent; the original cellule seems identical in all animals, and only varied in its growth by the varying circumstance which opens now this kind of cell and now that, causing in the remote effect now horns, now wings, now scales, now hair; and the same numerical atom, it would seem, was equally ready to be a particle of the eye or brain of man, or of the claw of a tiger. In the body of a man, all those terrific agencies which belong to it, the capability of being developed into a saurus or a mammoth, a baboon that would twist off heads, or a grampus that tears a square foot of flesh from a whale, are held in check and subordinated to human genius and destiny, but it is ready at any time to pass into other circles and take its part in poorer or in better forms. Nay, it seems that the animal and vegetable texture at last are alike. Well, as thus the drop of blood has many talents lurking in it, so every truth is much more rich.

"Every law detected in any part of Nature holds in every other part. The law of music is law of anatomy, of algebra and astronomy, of human life and social order. . . . It is certain that the laws are all versions of each other. The symmetry and coördination of things is such that from any creature, well and inly known, the law of any other might be legitimately deduced. Palmistry, phrenology, astrology, rest on a real basis. 'T is certain that there is a relation between the stars and your wedding-day, between the lines of your hand and the works done by it, between the activity of your brain and its outward figure, — there is a relation, — though you may easily fail to find it.

"The world, the universe, may be reeled off from any idea like a ball of yarn. Just see how the chemist, how the Christian, how the negro, disposes of it with the greatest ease after his own peculiar habit, and finds all the facts fit and confirm his view. And each science and law is, in like manner, prospective and fruitful. Astronomy is not yet astronomy while it only counts the stars in the sky. It must come nearer and be related to men and their life, and interpret the moral laws. In learning one thing you learn all. Egg and stratum go together. . . .

"The ground of hope is in the infinity of the world which reappears in every particle. The man truly conversant with life knows, against all appearances, that there is a remedy for every wrong, and that every wall is a gate."

These two passages from the journals should be also given:

1843. "That the Intellect grows by moral obedience seems to me the Judgment Day. Let that fact once obtain credence and all wrongs are righted; sorrow and pity are no more, nor fear, nor hatred; but a justice as shining and palpable as the best we know of kings and caliphs and ordeals, and what we call 'poetical justice,' that is, thorough justice, justice to the eye and justice to the mind — takes place."

1865. "Our thoughts have a life of their own, independent of our will."

INSTINCT AND INSPIRATION

This lecture is not presented in its completeness. Many passages in the one preceding it were at one time portions of this, as were also some of the most important parts of the essays on Worship and Immortality. Some of the matter came from the lecture called "Tendencies and Duties of Men of Thought," given by Mr. Emerson in London in 1848, as is shown by the reports of those lectures in Douglas Jerrold's newspaper. The lecture as here printed is exactly as I found it (its sheets sewed together for delivery), with the exception of the passages printed elsewhere, most of which are indicated in the notes. The heading "Instinct and Inspiration" is found on many of the sheets.

Page 67, note 1. Here followed the paragraph in "Worship" (*Conduct of Life*, p. 230), "Why should I hasten to solve every riddle which life offers me?" etc.

Page 68, note 1. In the Address at Tufts College in July, 1862, called "Celebration of Intellect," printed in this volume, Instinct as an oracle is spoken of.

Page 70, note 1. Here was a short passage on the need of heat, animal spirits, to cold, arid natures, printed in the essay "Society and Solitude."

Page 70, note 2. This suggests one of the last stanzas in "The Poet," beginning, —

"Suns and stars their courses keep."

Page 70, note 3. A paragraph follows, now found in the preceding lecture, on the limited interest we take in the personality of people, beginning, "There is a conflict between a man's private dexterity."

Page 72, note 1. A page now printed in "Poetry and Imagination" (*Letters and Social Aims*, p. 40) was taken from this lecture concerning the writer and artist, as to the astonishing results that may come through him when he is "at the top of his condition."

Page 76, note 1. Here followed a few sentences, now printed in "Illusions" (*Conduct of Life*, p. 321), as to the rare moments when the capital questions of human life are revealed to our eyes.

Page 77, note 1. A passage comparing wisdom to electricity, — a transient state of which some men are capable, — originally here, is now in the concluding paragraph of "Clubs" (*Society and Solitude*).

Page 78, note 1. See *Essays, Second Series*, p. 69.

Page 79, note 1. See "Immortality," in *Letters and Social Aims*, p. 346.

Page 85, note 1. Here follows the passage beginning, "He must be armed, not necessarily with musket and pike," etc., now in "Worship" (*Conduct of Life*, p. 224).

Page 86, note 1. The two following pages in the manuscript are now printed respectively in "Inspiration" (*Letters and Social Aims*, p. 275), "What is a man good for without enthusiasm?" etc., and in the preceding lecture on Natural History of Intellect, apropos of "monotones" in the value of concentration.

Page 87, note 1. Here follows the passage, now in "Immortality," beginning, "Ignorant people confound reverence," and ending, "and these by man's suffering are enlarged and enthroned."

Page 87, note 2. Several following pages of the lecture which treated of immortality were printed in "Worship" (*Conduct of Life*), and so are here omitted.

Page 88, note 1. Here followed the last paragraph but one in "Worship."

Page 88, note 2. The concluding paragraph of "Worship" came here.

MEMORY

Few men would write of Memory until past

> The middle of the mount
> Up which the incarnate soul must climb;

and it was not until 1857 that we know of Mr. Emerson's having written a lecture on that subject. He read it to his neighbors at the Concord Lyceum. The next year it appears as the fifth lecture in the course on the Natural Method of Mental Philosophy read by him at the Freeman Place Chapel in Boston. Essentially the same lecture, no doubt with additions, held the same place in the course then called "The Natural History of Intellect," in the University lectures for students and outsiders given at Cambridge in 1870 and 1871.

Page 92, note 1. Critics complain that Mr. Emerson makes so little of sin. Mr. Cabot said: "Sin and he had nothing to do with one another," and found the early poem "Grace" (printed in the *Dial* first and now included in the Appendix to the *Poems)* the more surprising.

Page 94, note 1. "The difference between the actual and the ideal force of man is happily figured by the Schoolmen, in saying that the knowledge of man is an evening knowledge, *vespertina cognitio*, but that of God is a morning knowledge, *matutina cognitio*" (*Nature, Addresses and Lectures*, p. 73; see note there).

Page 99, note 1. Mrs. Ednah D. Cheney tells the following story: —

"After hearing the lecture on Memory, a smart young lawyer approached a lady the next evening, who was talking of it to a friend. 'O, it was all very pretty and pleasant,' he said, 'but no real thought in it! I can't remember anything he said; can you?' 'Yes,' replied the lady, 'he said "Shallow brains have short memories."'"

Some one who heard this lecture at the University course, when Mr. Emerson's memory had failed with his strength, told with much amusement that he spoke of the value, in keeping dates, of some old-fashioned mnemonic verses, which he repeated and then tried to explain, but failed, because the key had slipped from his memory. The hearer did not remember Ecclesiasticus's word that "Even some of us wax old."

Page 102, note 1. Mr. Emerson tells of the "great days" and their demands in "Friendship," in the first series of *Essays*.

Page 104, note 1. In an early journal Mr. Emerson wrote of the comfort the high collar of his cloak gave him when the preaching was bad. He alluded to it in the Divinity School Address.

Page 104, note 2. I am unable to find this line.

Page 104, note 3.

> And I shall hear my bluebirds' note
> And dream the dream of Auburn dell.
>
> "May-Day," *Poems.*

Page 108, note 1.

> This passing moment is an edifice
> Which the omnipotent cannot rebuild.
>
> "Fragments on Life," *Poems*, Appendix.

THE CELEBRATION OF INTELLECT

This Address, as its opening passage shows, was made in the early days of the Civil War, before the forces of North and South had met in the disastrous battle of Bull Run. The task before the Government, the vast proportions and issues of the four years' struggle, were not then appreciated, and as yet the colleges had not been called on to furnish their splendid quota to save the country, — in Lowell's words, —

"To stand beside her
When craven churls deride her
To front a lie in arms, and not to yield;"

nor had Holmes made his terrible appeal in "Never or Now!" Yet later, in the dark days when Emerson wrote

Peril around, all else appalling,
Cannon in front and leaden rain,
Him Duty through the clarion calling
To the van, called not in vain, —

he would, none the less, have urged the higher function of the scholar, after he had shown his manhood by repelling the foe at the gate, in making Peace lasting, and the Country worth saving, by his standards and counsels.

This address is incomplete, as many passages were taken from it for the Essays on the same general theme, "The Man of Letters," "The Scholar" (*Lectures and Biographical Sketches*).

Page 118, note 1. Here followed the passage later printed in "The Man of Letters" (*Lectures and Biographical Sketches*, p. 256) on the absurdity of talking of the classic studies of statesmen who confound the first principles of right and wrong in their public words and action.

Page 120, note 1. Here on the manuscript sheet are notes: "Luther; Kossuth; Quincy Adams in his magnificent defence on the floor of Congress."

Page 121, note 1. Passages now found in "The Man of Letters" (*Lectures and Biographical Sketches*, pp. 252–3) were taken from this part of the discourse, commending to students their profession as thinkers as the real secret of power, the Art of Command, and as to the superiority of intellect to material force.

Page 122, note 1. Here followed a short passage now in "The Scholar" (*Lectures and Biographical Sketches*, p. 264) as to the perverse affectation of scholars to be men of the world. And after this the remarkable paragraph on pages 282 and 283 in the same essay, as to a need of a revival of the human mind, and upon Instinct.

Page 123, note 1. Here follows a passage now found on pages 279, 280, in "The Scholar," on the disappointment the youth feels in the existing order of things, followed by that on page 263 of the same essay, on the "beatitude of the intellect flowing into the faculties."

Page 125, note 1. This was the case both with Emerson and Thoreau, who both knew how to find their own food in the College Library, which they eagerly used, but incurred some academic censure for neglect of the curriculum.

Page 126, note 1. These strictures on Harvard College at that period were bracketed in the manuscript, as if Mr. Emerson questioned whether or no to read them.

Page 126, note 2. First written "decrepit bostonians" (*sic*).

Page 130, note 1. Here followed a passage like one in

"Education:" "Talk of Columbus and Newton! The babe born in the hovel yonder is the beginning of a revolution as great as theirs. Why try to be somewhat else?"

Page 131, note 1. Here follow the questions, as in "The Scholar" (p. 284): —

"And the questions they put are, *Who are you? What do you? What is your talent, your contribution to the common weal? Can you obtain your wish? Is there method in your consciousness? Can you see tendency in your life? Can you help any soul? What is it you existed to say?*"

This is followed by a passage on the need to the scholar of courage to admit ignorance and ask questions, and on the great lessons of momentary defeat (see "Social Aims," pp. 95, 96, in *Letters and Social Aims*).

COUNTRY LIFE

"Country Life" was the opening lecture of a course given by Mr. Emerson in the Freeman Place Chapel in Boston, in March, 1858. It was followed by "Works and Days" (printed in *Society and Solitude*), "Powers of the Mind," "Natural Method of Mental Philosophy," "Memory" (the matter of these three mostly now found in "Natural History of Intellect") and "Self-Possession."

Page 136, note 1. Mr. Emerson, in the lecture, made a version of Chaucer's lines more intelligible to modern hearers, thus: —

"Then long the folk to go on pilgrymages
And palmers for to seeken stranger strands,
To serve the saints beknown in sondry lands."

Page 147, note 1. Here follows in the manuscript the passage about trees, now printed in the Address at Sleepy Hollow Cemetery (see *Miscellanies*).

Page 148, note 1. These were Mr. Lane and Mr. Wright, the companions of Mr. Alcott in the unsuccessful Fruitlands community at Harvard. Cows were dispensed with there on the ground that it was wrong to enslave them, rob the calf of its food or the animal of its life; also that animal manure defiled the ground.

Page 151, note 1. These pictures of the advance from winter to spring may be found in "May-Day," in the *Poems.*

Page 153, note 1. The original prose form of the poem "Seashore" is here omitted. It may be found in the Notes to the *Poems.*

Page 155, note 1. From Linnæus's *Flora Laplandica* (Pulteney).

Page 156, note 1. See some fragmentary verses, "October," in the Appendix to the *Poems.*

Page 163, note 1. Here is omitted the passage in praise of the farmer with which the essay "Farming" ends (*Society and Solitude*).

CONCORD WALKS

This lecture was evidently given by Mr. Emerson as his contribution to the village Lyceum, probably in 1867. Its shortness seems to show that it was the more domestic and local part of the larger lecture on Country Life which here precedes it. Both manuscripts bear that name, and some sheets that occur in both are preserved, in this volume, only in the lecture into which they fit best.

Page 171, note 1. The charm of a river trip with Thoreau is celebrated in the essay "Nature" (*Essays, Second Series*, p. 173).

Page 172, note 1. The young girls and the boys who passed the house daily on their way to the Grammar or High School had little thought of the interest and pleasure with which the older scholar looked at them from his study window. Mr. Emerson was for many years on the School Committee. He much enjoyed the public examinations (they would be called "exhibitions" now, but they are obsolete), trying to the teacher and the more sensitive pupils, but highly interesting to the elders. Yet there, as elsewhere, he sat as a learner, and came home to praise the declamation or recitation of the girls and boys, and the Napoleonic *aplomb* of the schoolmistress, daughter of one of his farmer neighbors.

Page 173, note 1. The Belgian pomologist, whose results with coarse wild stock in a "state of variation" (by endless resowing of the better products obtaining fine fruit), are often alluded to in the Essays, and his "Theory of Amelioration" was carried by Emerson into higher fields. (See note 2 to page 49 in *English Traits*.)

Page 174, note 1. The delight in the wood-walks is set forth in the poem "Waldeinsamkeit."

Mr. Emerson wrote to Carlyle, in May, 1846:—

"I, too, have a new plaything, the best I ever had,—a wood-lot. Last fall I bought a piece of more than forty acres, on the border of . . . Walden Pond,—a place to which my feet have for years been accustomed to bring me once or twice a week at all seasons. . . . In these May days, when maples, poplars, oaks, birches, walnut and pine are in their spring glory, I go thither every afternoon."

Page 174, note 2. The Upas tree of the tropics was reputed fatal to those who sat beneath it. The Soma was used in sacrifices in ancient India. *Asclepias Viminalis*, a remarkable plant of the milkweed family. The Mandrake root, because of its resemblance to a human body, was viewed with superstition; it was said to shriek when torn up by night. Mr. Emerson saw the Papyrus reed, which gave the ancients paper, growing in Sicily. Dittany, supposed to be named from Mount Dicte, in Crete, where it grew. Asphodel, associated with legends of Greece and Sicily. Nepenthe, a plant which brought calm and forgetfulness, mentioned in the *Odyssey* (book IV.) where Helen gives it to Telemachus. Hæmony, a Thessalian magic herb, mentioned in Milton's *Comus*. The herb Moly, with black root and white flower, was given by Hermes to Odysseus to overcome the charms of Circe (*Odyssey*, book X.). Amomum, a tropical plant allied to ginger and cardamon.

Page 176, note 1. These friends Mr. Emerson had. His walks were usually alone, for, as he said, Nature's rule is *One to one, my dear*; but in the earlier years of his Concord life he went as a pupil to be shown the sights and learn the lore of each season, now with Henry Thoreau, the naturalist who knew the facts, but read also the higher meaning, and now with Ellery Channing, the poet with an artist's eye and speech.

Page 177, note 1. Dr. Jeffries Wyman of Cambridge, the comparative anatomist, as remarkable for his modesty as his attainments, is here alluded to. He was one of the company celebrated in "The Adirondacs" (*Poems*). Dr. Charles T. Jackson (the brother of Mrs. Emerson) and Professor J.

Hall of Albany, separately, made the first geological surveys of several States.

Page 179, note 1.

> But the meanings cleave to the lake,
> Cannot be carried in book or urn;
> Go thy ways now, come later back,
> On waves and hedges still they burn.
>
> "My Garden," *Poems.*

BOSTON

It must be remembered that Emerson was Boston born and schooled. His birthplace was on the ground now occupied by Hovey's great store; he played in the pleasant gardens on Summer and Chauncy streets whence the blue Bay could then be seen, and he drove his mother's cow to pasture along Beacon Street. Boston was his home until he left college. Mrs. Cheney tells that an earnest young woman of that favored city put this question to another native of the place, "Which could you have least spared out of your life, — the Common or Emerson?"

This lecture was the closing one in the course on Life and Literature given in Boston in the spring of 1861. It was first printed in the *Atlantic Monthly* for January, 1892.

Page 183, note 1.

> Ever the Rock of Ages melts
> Into the mineral air,
> To be the quarry whence to build
> Thought and its mansions fair.
>
> "Fragments on Life," *Poems*, Appendix.

Page 185, note 1. The following is from a sheet of "Aristocracy," as delivered in Boston: —

"But I consider this city of New England an exceptional community; that here the extraordinary abundant means, provided by private bounty and public law, have enabled every poor man to secure to any talent in his child a good culture, and to the great multitudes (of the middle classes) a finished education, — what with libraries, high schools, Latin schools, college scholarships and other foundations; schools of design; and the great sympathy of the community with any superior talent, and the great opportunity and career opened to it, — I consider this city to lie in sunlight, and citizenship in it to be a sort of nobility. And the poet Saxe seems to believe that all of us share this good will for our city,

"'And born in Boston needs no second birth.'"

Page 197, note 1. He might well have added the name of Carlyle, but for his own part in introducing his works here.

Page 198, note 1.

"Come dal fuoco il caldo, esser diviso
Non puo 'l bel dall' eterno."
Michael Angelo.

(As from fire the heat cannot be separated, — neither can beauty from the eternal.)

Page 200, note 1. Mr. Emerson first used this phrase in vain endeavor to get his friend Carlyle to come to see America in 1854. In the letter it followed the remark, "John Bull interests you at home, and is all your subject."

Page 203, note 1. "New England, on each new political event, resolves itself into a debating society, and is the Germany of the States." — Lecture on New England.

Page 206, note 1. Some members of the Society of Friends have been troubled that Mr. Emerson should have quoted this amusing if harsh expression of an old author. The late Mr. Richard P. Hallowell, in his work, *The Quaker Invasion of Massachusetts*, has produced evidence rebutting much of the received history of the disturbances by the Quakers, which seems to have been exaggerated. Mr. Emerson merely incidentally alludes to one of these as reported. His feeling towards the Friends was always one of respect and much sympathy. He once told his cousin, the Rev. D. G. Haskins, "I believe I am more of a Quaker than anything else; I believe in the 'still, small voice.'"

Page 209, note 1. Mr. Emerson puts this playfully in his Boston poem: —

> What care though rival cities soar
> Along the stormy coast,
> Penn's town, New York and Baltimore,
> If Boston knew the most!

Page 211, note 1. The editor would be glad to know the source of these lines, which neither he nor his friends have been able to find.

MICHAEL ANGELO

I find the following entry in Mr. Emerson's diary during his short visit to Italy in his younger days: —

FLORENCE, 28th April, 1833.

I have been this day to Santa Croce, which is to Florence what Westminster Abbey is to England. I passed with consideration the tomb of Nicholas Macchiavelli, but stopped long before that of Galilias Galileo, for I love and honor that man, — except in the recantation, — with my whole heart.

But when I came to Michael Angelo Buonarotti my flesh crept as I read the inscription. I had strange emotion; I suppose because Italy is so full of his fame. I have lately continually heard of his name and works and opinions. I see his face in every shop window, and now I stood over his dust.

In 1835, soon after his return, he gave before the Society for the Diffusion of Useful Knowledge, in Boston, six lectures on Biography. The first of these was on the tests of Great Men, — very possibly in part the chapter on the Uses of Great Men with which *Representative Men* opens, — and then he treated of the lives of five, beginning with Michael Angelo the artist, followed by the reformer Luther, the preacher George Fox, the poet Milton, and the statesman and orator, Edmund Burke. Dr. Holmes says, —

"Why Emerson selected Michael Angelo as the subject of one of his earliest lectures is shown clearly enough by the last sentence as printed in the Essay: 'He was not a citizen of any country; he belonged to the human race; he was a brother and a friend to all who acknowledged the beauty that beams in universal Nature, and who seek by labor and self-denial to approach its source in perfect goodness.'"

Greatly as Mr. Emerson admired his work, — a copy of "The Fates" always hung over his study mantel, and engravings of the Sibyls from the Sistine Chapel hung on the walls, — the character and recorded utterance of the man interested him even more. In 1868 he wrote, "I told W—— that I prize Michael Angelo so much, that, whilst I look at his figures, I come to believe the grandiose is grand. Thomas Gray, in poetry, has relations to Michael Angelo, and the like question between the grandiose and grand is suggested in reading his odes."

The lecture was published in the *North American Review* in June, 1837; the present essay is a reprint of that article.

Page 216, note 1. From Andrew Marvell's "Horatian Ode, on the Return of Cromwell:"

"He nothing common did, or mean,
Upon that memorable scene,
. . . . .
Nor called the Gods in vulgar spite
To vindicate his helpless right," etc.

Page 232, note 1. Michael Angelo, however, seems to have doubted the inherent stability in the construction of the dome, and girded it with great chains, which in later years have been reinforced.

Page 233, note 1. I believe this portrait is lost, but that it is alluded to by Michael Angelo in a sonnet.

Page 243, note 1. This was undoubtedly the noble statue of St. George by Donatello, until lately in a niche outside of one of the churches, now in the National Museum of Fine Arts at Florence.

Page 244, note 1. Mr. Emerson was fond of repeating, in looking at an engraving of Michael Angelo which hung in his house, the lines of Tennyson in *In Memoriam*:—

"And over those ethereal eyes
The bar of Michael Angelo."

Page 244, note 2. In the journal for 1864 Mr. Emerson quotes Niebuhr thus: "Michael Angelo was the man to be first King of Italy," and adds, "And I should say of Michael that the power of his pictures and works is not so much correct art as it is great humanity. I accept easily all the criticism I hear on his style. It does not lessen him."

MILTON

From his early student days, Emerson honored and loved Milton. He often praised the majesty and courageous rectitude of his prose, but he took delight in *Comus* and *Lycidas*. He used to tell how, in his youth, confined to his berth in a small schooner on a stormy voyage to Florida, he, little by little, recollected all of *Lycidas* but three lines. He had not known that it lay there in his memory ready for his solace.

As has been said in the notes to the foregoing essay, Milton's was one of the five lives which Mr. Emerson chose to celebrate in his first course of Boston lectures. In speaking of these, Bancroft, in an article in the *North American Review*, written two years after Mr. Emerson's death, says: —

"Emerson, in the choice of the next hero over whom he was to shed the lustre of his praise, was equally guided by his own nature. In spite of all his gracefulness and reserve and love of the unbroken tranquillity of serene thought, he was by the right of heredity a belligerent for the cause of freedom, of which John Milton, among all the great English poets, was the foremost champion. From the inmost core of his character Milton was the herald of rightful liberty, and its ever-ready warrior where it fell into danger. He wrote in sublime and impassioned prose for liberty of mind, of man, and of the state. He has furnished to the English-speaking world the best epic, the best ode, the best elegies, in the mood of joyousness and in the mood of meditation; sonnets full of high thought expressed in the strongest and noblest words, and the most delightful mask for representation in the social circle. In advanced life, when all his hopes for the political reform of England had been wrecked, he writes the best tragedy that has ever been written in modern times according to the rules of the Greek drama, and in it paints in perfection the comeliness and the reviving power of men 'armed with celestial vigor and heroic magnitude of mind;' and then, mindful of the sorrows that had fallen on himself and his associates, is driven for consolation to remember that

> "'Patience is more oft the exercise
> Of saints, the trial of their fortitude.'

Such a hero had a right to find a resting-place on Emerson's breast."

Dr. Holmes, in his Life of Emerson, thus showed the necessary bond between the writer and his subject: —

"Consciously or unconsciously men describe themselves in the characters they draw. One must have the mordant in his own personality or he will not take the color of his subject. He may force himself to picture that which he dislikes or even detests; but when he loves the character he delineates, it is his own, in some measure, at least, or one of which he feels that its possibilities and tendencies belong to himself. Let us try Emerson by this test in his Essay on Milton. . . .

"'It is the prerogative of this great man to stand at this hour foremost of all men in literary history, and so (shall we not say?) of all men, in the power to inspire. Virtue goes out of him into others. . . . He is identified in the mind with all select and holy images, with the supreme interests of the human race. . . . Better than any other he has discharged the office of every great man, namely, to raise the idea of Man in the minds of his contemporaries and of posterity, — to draw after Nature a life of man, exhibiting such a composition of grace, of strength, and of virtue as poet had not described nor hero lived. Human nature in these ages is indebted to him for its best portrait. Many philosophers in England, France, and Germany have formally dedicated their study to this problem; and we think it impossible to recall one in those countries who communicates the same vibration of hope, of self-reverence, of piety, of delight in beauty, which the name of Milton awakes.'

"Emerson had the same lofty aim as Milton, 'To raise the idea of man;' he had 'the power *to inspire*' in a preëminent degree. If ever a man communicated those *vibrations* he speaks of as characteristic of Milton, it was Emerson. In elevation, purity, nobility of nature, he is worthy to stand with the great poet and patriot, who began, like him, as a schoolmaster, and ended as the teacher in a school-house which had for its walls the horizons of every region where English is spoken."

The "Milton" was published in the *North American Review* for July, 1838.

Page 248, note 1. In the early verses on The Poet, given in the Appendix to the *Poems*, Mr. Emerson said: —

> Yet every scroll, whereon he wrote
> In latent fire his secret thought,
> Fell unregarded to the ground,
> Unseen by such as stood around.
> The pious wind took it away.

Page 250, note 1. Saumaise, by his pamphlet *Défense de Charles I.*, drew out Milton's *Defense of the English People.* A French writer said of him: "Aujourd'hui on ne connait plus Claude de Saumaise que de certaines discussions beaucoup trop retentissantes qu'il eut avec plusieurs de ses contemporains;" and adds, regarding the *Défense de Charles I.*, "Saumaise y défendit fort mal une fort bonne cause, et le poëte eut raison du critique."

Page 253, note 1. Journal, 1841. "I think that Milton wrote his verse to his own ear, well knowing that England did not hold, and might not for a century, another ear that could hear their rhythm. That is the magnanimity of a poet, that he writes for the Gods — as those Egyptian obelisks which Goethe saw raised from the ground at Rome, were carved with the utmost finish on the upper surface, which faced the heaven and which man was never to see."

Page 256, note 1. Master Samuel Hartlib, apparently a scholar from the continent, a friend of Milton, who speaks of him as "sent hither from a far country," seems to have studied with peculiar diligence the science of education. Milton's letter to him is "On Education."

Page 260, note 1. Journal, 1845. "The language is made, — who has not helped to make it? Then come Milton, Shakspeare, and find it all made to their hand, and use it as if there never had been language before."

Page 260, note 2. From an early college poem of Milton, "Anno Ætatis XIX." "At a Vacation Exercise at the College, part Latin, part English, the Latin speeches ended, the English thus began, 'Hail, native language!'" etc.

Page 261, note 1. From "L' Allegro."

Page 263, note 1. As is evident throughout this essay, Mr. Emerson was drawn to Milton by the likeness of their characters and tastes, as well as their ideals. He himself loved temperance "for its elegancy, not for its austerity," as he says of the Hero (*Essays, First Series*, p. 254). His temperance was of the unconscious kind, a part of his refined taste.

Page 265, note 1. The young Emerson, as his letters to his brothers during his college course show, was sometimes writing his thoughts and attempts at verse, at his high desk, before winter daylight had fully come.

Page 267, note 1. From Wordsworth's sonnet beginning, "Milton, thou should'st be living at this hour."

Page 268, note 1. Journal, 1836. "With what satisfaction I read last night with G. P. B[radford] some lines from Milton! In Samson Agonistes and elsewhere with what dignity he felt the office of the bard, the solemn office borne by the great and grave of every age for the behoof of all men; a call which never was heard in the frivolous brains of the Moores and Hugos and Bérangers of the day."

Page 269, note 1. Compare with this a remarkable passage in "Aristocracy" (*Lectures and Biographical Sketches*, p. 63).

Page 273, note 1. It was Mr. Emerson's religious feeling that kept him away from the preachings and prayers of his day.

Page 274, note 1. *Paradise Lost*, book iv., 301.

Page 277, note 1. *Paradise Lost*, book iv., 361.

ART AND CRITICISM

The manuscript of the lecture has on it the name "Art and Criticism," but it is incomplete, and nearly the first quarter is missing. This was presumably upon Art (to judge by some few notes which remain), and very likely the essay "Art," in *Society and Solitude*, contains much of the matter.

"Art and Criticism" was the fourth lecture in a course given in the spring of 1859, at the Freeman Place Chapel in Boston.

Page 283, note 1. The *Néant*, the Negative aspect of the Universe.

Page 284, note 1. Mr. Cabot was told that the congregation to which Mr. Emerson preached in the Second Church of Boston was composed mainly of middle-class people. His hearers at the church in East Lexington were simple people, but, in confessing this, they said that they could understand Mr. Emerson. Most of his lectures for forty years thereafter were "tried on," as he said, on audiences from farm and shop in the lyceums of New England towns or on enterprising but uncultivated settlers of "the West." He would not "talk down," but made it his business to try to give them his best thought in vigorous, simple words, with homely illustration or classic anecdote.

Page 288, note 1. The street as a school for the orator is treated of in "Eloquence" (*Letters and Social Aims*, pp. 124, 125).

Page 288, note 2. Vathek, the hero of an Eastern romance published by Beckford in 1787.

Page 289, note 1. Mr. Emerson took much pleasure in Burns's poem "To the Deil."

Page 289, note 2. Here follows a passage on the necessity of shade to balance sun, etc., printed in "Considerations by the Way" (*Conduct of Life*, p. 255).

Page 290, note 1. Mr. Emerson well understood the force of the pause. After an important passage, delivered forcibly or searchingly, he made a marked pause to allow the thought to strike in; then with great flexibility of voice would begin the next paragraph in a quiet conversational tone. In preparing a lecture for publication as an essay it was unsparingly pruned, not merely of passages but of words.

Page 292, note 1. For "development" Mr. Emerson

often used the more pleasing and picturesque "unfolding." As for the "family of *fero*" and its participle *latum*, he would rather say "choice" than "preference," "give way" than "defer," "gather" than "infer," "bring together" than "collate," "render" than "translate," with a poet's preference for simple rather than pedantic words.

Page 293, note 1. He objected to the Germanic "*stand-point*, for the English *point of view*, recently corrupted into view-point."

Page 293, note 2. It is the cheap use of these words that is blamed. "Flamboyant" is advisedly used by Mr. Emerson a few paragraphs earlier in this lecture.

Page 294, note 1. A writer in a recent New York newspaper, who remembered this lecture, said of this characteristic illustration drawn from New England country life, "This searching criticism, enforced by a metaphor borrowed from the universal experience of the rude New England climate, is of the essence of the man. The more he is studied, the more — again in Yankee phrase — we summer and winter with him, the more we get from him. The foundations of his fun and earnest are also below the frost."

I cannot deny myself the pleasure of here introducing another reminiscence by the same writer illustrating Mr. Emerson's humor: —

"The present writer recalls a lecture in the middle sixties, in which Mr. Emerson surprised his audience into laughter with the closing of what seemed about to be an especially lofty appeal: 'If we could only make up our minds always to tell the truth, the whole truth, and nothing but the truth,' he said, in his musical and curiously impersonal voice, and added — 'to what embarrassing situations it would give rise.'"

Page 296, note 1. Of course in commending "writing

down" Mr. Emerson meant simple subject and style, not deliberate lowering of thought to the supposed standard of others.

Page 302, note 1. Mr. Emerson is here telling of the humors of his friend William Ellery Channing, as they walked in Concord Woods. In the essay on Concord Walks, his company is extolled. Mr. Emerson had love of wild nature, Mr. Channing opened his eyes to what was artistic, and helped him to perception of color and composition.

Page 305, note 1. Hence the denier and the pessimist were offensive to him: "Nothing good that way, everything good the other way." See in "Demonology" (*Lectures and Biographical Sketches*, p. 24) the application of "the infallible test, the state of mind in which much notice of them [alleged spiritualistic revelations, necromancy, etc.] leaves us."

THOUGHTS ON MODERN LITERATURE

This paper was the leading article in the second number of the *Dial* (October, 1840), of which Mr. Emerson was then editor.

The original opening pages, omitted by Mr. Cabot, are given below, excepting a few sentences.

"There is no better illustration of the laws by which the world is governed than Literature. There is no luck in it. It proceeds by Fate. Every scripture is given by the inspiration of God. Every composition proceeds out of a greater or less depth of thought, and this is the measure of its effect. The highest class of books are those which express the moral element; the next, works of imagination; and the next, works of science; — all dealing in realities, — what ought to be, what is, and what appears. These, in proportion to the truth and beauty they involve, remain; the rest perish. They proceed out of the silent, living mind to be heard again by the living mind. Of the best books it is hardest to write the history. Those books which are for all time are written indifferently at any time. For high genius is a day without night, a Caspian Ocean which hath no tides. And yet is literature in some sort a creature of time. Always the oracular soul is the source of thought, but always the occasion is administered by the low mediation of circumstances. Religion, Love, Ambition, War, some fierce antagonism, or it may be some petty annoyance, must break the round of perfect circulation, or no spark, no joy, no event can be. The poet, rambling through the fields or the forest, absorbed in contemplation to that degree that his walk is but a petty dream, would never awake to precise thought, if the scream of an eagle, the cries of a crow or curlew near his head did not break the sweet continuity. Nay, the finest lyrics of the poet come of this unequal parentage; the imps of matter beget such child on the soul, fair daughter of God. Nature mixes facts with thoughts to yield a power. But the gift of immortality is of the mother's side. In the spirit in which they are written is the date of their duration, and never in the magnitude of the facts. Everything lasts in proportion to its beauty. In proportion as it was not polluted by the wilfulness of the writer, but flowed from his mind after the divine order of cause and effect, it was not his, but Nature's, and shared the sublimity of the sea and sky. That which is truly told, Nature herself takes in charge against the whims and injustice of men. For ages Herodotus was reckoned a credulous gossip in his descriptions of Africa, and now the sublime, silent desert testifies through the mouths of Bruce, Lyon, Caillaud, Burckhardt, Belzoni, to the truth of the calumniated historian.

"And yet men imagine that books are dice and have no merit in their fortune; that the trade and favor of a few critics can speed one book into circulation and kill another; and that in the production of these things the author has chosen and may devise to do thus and so. Society also wishes to assign subjects and methods to its writers. But neither reader nor author may intermeddle. You cannot reason at will in this and that other vein, but only as you must. You cannot make quaint combinations and bring to the crucible and alembic of truth things far-fetched or fantastic or popular, but your method and your subject are foreordained in your nature and in all nature or ever the earth was, or it has no worth. All that gives currency still to any book, advertised in the morning's newspaper in London or Boston, is the remains of faith in the breasts of men that, not adroit book-makers, but the inextinguishable soul of the universe, reports of itself in articulate discourse to-day as of old. The ancients strongly expressed their sense of the unmanageableness of these words of the spirit by saying that the God made his priest insane, took him hither and thither, as leaves are whirled by the tempest. But we sing as we are bid. Our inspirations are manageable and tame. Death and sin have whispered in the ear of the wild horse of Heaven, and he has become a dray and a hack. And step by step with the entrance of this era of ease and convenience, the belief in the proper Inspiration of man has departed. . . ."

Here followed a passage on the Bible and the Scriptures of the nations, and the secondary quality of Shakspeare compared to these, much of which, quoted from the journal of

1839, is given in a note to the essay on Shakspeare. (*Representative Men*, p. 357.)

"All just criticism will not only behold in literature the action of necessary laws, but must also oversee literature itself. The erect mind disparageth all books. What are books? it saith: they can have no permanent value. How obviously initial they are to their authors. The books of the nations, the universal books, are long ago forgotten by those who wrote them, and one day we shall forget this primer learning. Literature is made up of a few ideas and a few fables. It is a heap of nouns and verbs enclosing an intuition or two. We must learn to judge books by absolute standards. When we are aroused to a life in ourselves, these traditional splendors of letters grow very pale and cold. Men seem to forget that all literature is ephemeral, and unwillingly entertain the supposition of its utter disappearance. They deem not only letters in general, but the best books in particular, parts of a preëstablished harmony, fatal, unalterable, and do not go behind Virgil and Dante, much less behind Moses, Ezekiel and Saint John. But no man can be a good critic of any book who does not read it in a wisdom which transcends the instructions of any book, and treats the whole extant product of the human intellect as only one age revisible and reversible by him."

Page 312, note 1. Here follows a paragraph, telling with what eagerness the new generation studies the history of freedom in civil, religious and philosophic matters, and also the rude poetry of antiquity; then how it "celebrates its wants, achievements and hopes." "The time is marked by the multitude of writers. Soldiers, sailors, servants, nobles, princes, women, write books. The progress of trade and the facilities for locomotion have made the world nomadic again. . . . All facts are exposed. Let there be no ghost-stories more. . . . Let us have charts true and gazetteers correct. We will know where Babylon stood, and settle the topography of the Roman Forum. We will know whatever is to be known of Australasia, of Japan, of Persia, of Egypt, of Timbuctoo, of Palestine. . . .

"Christendom has become a great reading-room. . . . The age is well-bred, knows the world, has no nonsense, and herein is well distinguished from the learned ages that preceded ours. [He alludes to the superstitions that filled the heads of the English and European scholars for the half-millennium that preceded the eighteenth century.] The best heads of this time build or occupy such card-house theories of religion, politics and natural science as a clever boy now would blow away. What stuff in Kepler, in Cardan, in Lord Bacon. Montaigne with all his French wit and downright sense is little better; a sophomore would wind him round his finger. Some of the Medical Remains of Lord Bacon in the book for his own use, 'Of the Prolongation of Life,' will move a smile in the unpoetical practitioners of the Medical College. [He then gives amusing citations from Bacon and Cardan and odd anecdotes from Burton's *Anatomy of Melancholy*.]

"All this sky-full of cobwebs is now forever swept clean away. Another race is born. Humboldt and Herschel, Davy and Arago, Malthus and Benham have arrived. If Robert Burton should be quoted to represent the army of scholars who have furnished a contribution to his moody pages, Horace Walpole, whose letters circulate in the libraries, might be taken with some fitness to represent the spirit of much recent literature. He has taste, common sense, love of facts, impatience of humbug, love of history, love of splendor, love of justice, and the sentiment of honor among gentlemen: but no life whatever of the higher faculties, no faith, no hope, no aspiration, no question concerning the secret of Nature.

"The favorable side of this research and love of facts is the bold and systematic criticism which has appeared in every department of literature. From Wolff's attack upon the authenticity of the Homeric Poems dates a new impulse on learning. . . . Niebuhr has sifted Roman history by the like methods. Heeren has made good essays towards ascertaining the necessary facts in the Grecian, Persian, Assyrian, Egyptian, Ethiopic, Carthaginian nations. English history has been analyzed by Turner, Hallam, Brodie, Lingard, Palgrave. Goethe has made the circuit of human knowledge, as Lord Bacon did before him, writing True or False on every article. Bentham has attempted the same scrutiny in reference to Civil Law. Pestalozzi, out of a deep love, undertook the reform of education. The ambition of Coleridge in England embraced the whole problem of Philosophy; to find, that is, a foundation in thought for everything that existed in fact. The German philosophers Schelling, Kant, Fichte, Hegel, have applied their analysis to Nature and thought with an antique boldness. There can be no honest inquiry which is not better than acquiescence. . . .

"This skeptical activity, at first directed on circumstances and historical views deemed of great importance, soon penetrated deeper than Rome or Egypt, than history or institutions or the vocabulary of metaphysics, namely, into the thinker himself and into every function he exercises."

From this point on, the paper in the *Dial* is like that here printed, except that Mr. Emerson's corrections, pencilled on the margin, have been adopted here in the text, as well as in the omitted passages given above.

Page 314, note 1. Mr. Emerson's use of his own life in his journals, and hence in his works, was of this sort. Incidents are generalized and personality merged in a type. In the poetry, often intimate personal experiences are used, but purified and adorned. Dr. Holmes treats of this matter with charming wit in his chapter on Emerson as a Poet.

Page 319, note 1. In a lecture in a course on English Literature in 1835, Mr. Emerson said of Byron: "He has a marvellous power of language, but, from pride and selfishness, which made him an incurious observer, it lacked food. One's interest dies from famine of meaning. Cursing will soon be sufficient in the most skilful variety of diction. Of Scott it would be ungrateful to speak but with cheerful respect, and we owe to him some passages of genuine pathos. But in general, what he contributes is not brought from the deep places of the mind, and of course cannot reach thither." In a lecture in 1861, he said, "Byron had declamation, he had delicious music, but he knew not the mania which gives creative power."

Page 321, note 1. In a lecture, "Books," in 1864, Mr. Emerson said: "I read lately with delight a casual notice of Wordsworth in a London journal, in which with perfect aplomb his highest merits were affirmed, and his unquestionable superiority to all English poets since Milton. I thought how long I travelled and talked in England, and found no person, or only one (Clough), in sympathy with him and admiring him aright, in face of Tennyson's culminating talent and genius in melodious verse. This rugged countryman walks and sits alone for years, assured of his sanity and inspiration, sneered at and disparaged, yet no more doubting the fine oracles that visited him than if Apollo had visibly descended to him on Helvellyn. Now, so few years after, it is lawful in that obese England to affirm unresisted the superiority of his genius."

Page 322, note 1. In the last lecture in a course on New England, read in New York in 1843, Mr. Emerson said: "The influence of Wordsworth, Coleridge and Carlyle found readier reception here than at home. It is remarkable that we have our intellectual culture from one country and our duties from another. . . . But there is an ethical element in the mind of our people that will never let them long rest without finding exercise for the deeper thoughts. It very soon found both Wordsworth and Carlyle insufficient."

Page 323, note 1. In the journal for 1838 occurs this passage: —

"Goethe hates dissection, hates the sundering a thing from the universal connection of Nature, and you shall see that love of synthesis working in all his rhetoric. As when he apostrophizes Erwin of Steinbach and his Minster, he sees all the Netherlands and all the year."

Page 332, note 1. This suggests the passage in "Aristocracy" (*Lectures and Biographical Sketches*, pp. 63, 64) on the selfish man of learning who is not faithful to his duties to humble humanity around him.

Page 334, note 1. I am unable to find the sources of the lines quoted on this and on the following page.

WALTER SAVAGE LANDOR

This paper appeared in the *Dial* for October, 1841. It was eight years since Mr. Emerson had had the pleasure of visiting Landor at his Villa Gherardesca at Fiesole, by his invitation. The opportunity of seeing Landor, Coleridge, Carlyle and Wordsworth reconciled him to travel, always a matter of indifference to him, at that sad time. In the first pages of *English Traits*, an account of this visit and Landor's conversation and opinions is given, which called out from Landor an "Open Letter" some years later. The account of this letter, with extracts from it, may be found in the notes to *English Traits*.

Page 342, note 1. From Tennyson's "Lotus Eaters."

Page 342, note 2. Compare a similar passage in the "Lecture on the Times" (*Nature, Addresses and Lectures*, p. 280).

Page 348, note 1. In these sentences on Landor, Mr. Emerson also states his own theory and practice.

Page 349, note 1. The article in the *Dial* is followed by a few pages of selections made by Mr. Emerson from Landor's writings.

PRAYERS

This paper was printed in the *Dial* for July, 1842.

The remarkable prayer in verse, "Great God, I ask thee for no meaner pelf," etc., was Henry Thoreau's. It is thought by a friend of the Thoreau family that the prayers preceding and following it were written by his loved brother John, who had died a few months before the publication of this paper. Nothing is known of the "deaf and dumb boy."

Page 350, note 1. From *Measure for Measure*, Act II., Scene 2.

AGRICULTURE OF MASSACHUSETTS

This paper, reprinted exactly from the *Dial* of July, 1842, is Mr. Emerson's rendering — much affected by the medium through which it passed — of the sensible criticism on the Report of the State Commissioner of Agriculture, made by his friend and neighbor, Mr. Edmund Hosmer. Mr. Hosmer was a farmer of the old New England type, versed in agricultural and domestic economics, and was the oracle constantly consulted by Mr. Emerson, and the ally called in, in dealing with the interesting but to him puzzling management of his increasing acres. Mr. Hosmer and his oxen are the Hassan and the camels of the third stanza in the "Fragments on the Poet," in the *Poems*. He used to attend and join in the conversations of the philosophers at Mr. Emerson's house.

EUROPE AND EUROPEAN BOOKS

This paper, as printed, is that published in the *Dial* for April, 1843, with the exception of the opening pages, most of which are here given, omitting, however, the first paragraph, on the temporary dominations of European books, and prophesying a new world literature. The review thus continues: —

"But at present we have our culture from Europe and Europeans. Let us be content and thankful for these good gifts for a while yet. The collections of art, at Dresden, Paris, Rome, and the British Museum and libraries offer their splendid hospitalities to the American. And beyond this, amid the dense population of that continent, lifts itself ever and anon some eminent head, a prophet to his own people, and their interpreter to the people of other countries. The attraction of these individuals is not to be resisted by theoretic statements.

"It is true there is always something deceptive, self-deceptive in our travel. We go to France, to Germany, to see men, and find but what we carry. A man is a man, one as good as another, many doors to one open court, and that open court as entirely accessible from our private door, or through John or Peter, as through Humboldt and Laplace. But we cannot speak to ourselves.

"We brood on our riches, but remain dumb; that makes us unhappy; and we take ship and go man-hunting in order, by putting ourselves *en rapport*, according to laws of personal magnetism, to acquire speech or expression. Seeing Herschel or Schelling, or Swede or Dane, satisfies the conditions, and we can express ourselves happily.

"But Europe has lost weight lately. Our young men go thither in every ship, but not as in the golden days, when the same tour would show the traveller the noble heads of Scott, of Mackintosh, Coleridge, Wordsworth, Goethe, Cuvier, and Humboldt. We remember, when arriving in Paris, we crossed the river on a brilliant morning, and at the book-shop of Papinot, in the Rue de Sorbonne, at the gates of the University, purchased for two sous a Programme, which announced that every Monday we might attend the lecture of Dumas on Chemistry at noon; at a half hour later either Villemain or Ampère on French Literature; at other hours, Guizot on Modern History; Cousin on the Philosophy of Ancient History; Fauriel on Foreign Literature; Prévost on Geology; Lacroix on the Differential Calculus; Jouffroy on the History of Modern Philosophy; Lacretelle on Ancient History; Desfontaines or Mirbel on Botany.

"Hard by, at the Place du Panthéon, Dégérando, Royer Collard, and their colleagues were giving courses on Law, on the law of nations, the Pandects and commercial equity. For two magical sous more, we bought the Programme of the Collége Royal de France, on which we still read with admiring memory, that every Monday, Silvestre de Sacy lectures on the Persian Language; at other hours, Lacroix on the Integral Mathematics; Jouffroy on Greek Philosophy; Biot on Physics; Lerminier on the History of Legislation; Élie de Beaumont on Natural History; Magendie on Medicine; Thénard on Chemistry; Binet on Astronomy; and so on, to the end of the week. On the same wonderful ticket, as if royal munificence had not yet sufficed, we learned that at the Museum of Natural History, at the Garden of Plants, three days in the week, Brongniart would teach Vegetable Physiology, and Gay-Lussac, Chemistry, and Flourent, Anatomy. With joy we read these splendid news in the Café Procope, and straightway joined the troop of students of all nations, kindreds and tongues, whom this great institution drew together to listen to the first *Savans* of the world without fee or reward. The professors are changed, but the liberal doors still stand open at this hour. This royal liberality, which seems to atone for so many possible abuses of power, could not exist without important consequences to the student on his return home.

"The University of Göttingen has sunk from its high place by the loss of its brightest stars. The last was Heeren, whose learning was really useful and who has made ingenious attempts at the solution of ancient historical problems. Ethiopia, Assyria, Carthage and the Theban Desert are still revealing secrets, latent for three millenniums, under the powerful night-glass of the Teutonic Scholars, who make astronomy, geology, chemistry, trade, statistics, medals, tributary to their Inquisitions.

"In the last year also died Sismondi, who by his History of the Italian Republics reminded mankind of the prodigious wealth of life and event, which Time, devouring his children as fast as they are born, is giving to oblivion in Italy, the piazza and forum of History, and for a time made Italian subjects of the middle ages popular for poets and romancers, and by his kindling chronicles of Milan and Lombardy perhaps awoke the great genius of Manzoni. That history is full of events, yet, as Ottilie writes in Goethe's novel, that she never can bring away from history anything but a few anecdotes, so the *Italian Republics* lies in the memory like a confused *mêlée*, a confused noise of slaughter and rapine, and garments rolled in blood. The method, if method there be, is so slight and artificial, that it is quite overlaid and lost in the unvaried details of treachery and violence. Hallam's sketches of the same history were greatly more luminous and memorable, partly from the advantage of his design, which compelled him to draw outlines, and not bury the grand lines of destiny in municipal details.

"Italy furnished in that age no man of genius to its political arena, though many of talent, and this want degrades the history. We still remember, with great pleasure, Mr. Hallam's fine sketch of the external history of the rise and establishment of the Papacy, which Mr. Ranke's voluminous researches, though they have great value for their individual portraits, have not superseded."

Page 366, note 1. Mr. Emerson's impatience of Wordsworth's foibles was at first great. In the journal for 1832 he wrote: —

"I never read Wordsworth without chagrin. A man of such great powers and ambition, so near to the *Dii majores*, to fail so meanly in every attempt. A genius that hath epilepsy, a deranged archangel."

Page 367, note 1. Mr. Emerson gave an account of his visits to Wordsworth in 1833, and again in 1848, in *English Traits* (pp. 19 ff. and 294.)

Page 370, note 1. Soon after Tennyson's poems appeared, Mr. Emerson wrote to a friend: —

"I think Tennyson got his inspiration in gardens, and that in this country, where there are no gardens, his musky verses could not be written. The Villa d' Este is a memorable poem in my life."

Page 372, note 1. Mr. Alexander Ireland of Manchester, England, the friend who made arrangements for Mr. Emerson's coming to England to lecture in 1828, gives in his Memoir[1] an account of Mr. Emerson's visit to Leigh Hunt.

Page 372, note 2. Mr. Emerson prized Tennyson more highly as years went on.

Journal, 1853. "When I see the waves of Lake Michigan toss in the bleak snowstorm, I see how small and inadequate the common poet is. But Tennyson with his eagle over the sea has shown his sufficiency."

In the summer of 1868, he wrote at some length in his journal in high praise of the quality and elevation of the poem "The Holy Grail," and, looking over the journal two years later, added more to the same effect. Below these notes he wrote in October, 1871: "The only limit to the praise of Tennyson as a lyric poet is that he is alive. Were he an ancient, there would be none."

Page 374, note 1. In *English Traits* Mr. Emerson wrote: —

[1] *Ralph Waldo Emerson, His Life, Genius, and Writings.* London: Simpkin, Marshall & Co.

"Bulwer, an industrious writer, with occasional ability, is distinguished for his reverence of intellect as a temporality, and appeals to the worldly ambition of the student. His romances tend to fan these low flames."

Page 377, note 1. In his chapter on Goethe, *Wilhelm Meister* is criticised. (*Representative Men*, pp. 277, 278.)

Page 377, note 2. Disraeli's novel is alluded to in the pages in *Representative Men* just referred to.

PAST AND PRESENT

Page 381, note 1. This celebration of his friend's work was published by Mr. Emerson in the *Dial* for July, 1843.

Page 382, note 1.

For Genius made his cabin wide,
And Love led Gods therein to bide.

"Fragments on the Poet," *Poems*, Appendix.

Page 386, note 1. Now and then Mr. Emerson grew weary of his friend's personality in his work, as when he exclaimed: —

"O Carlyle, the merit of glass is not to be seen, but to be seen through; whereas every lamina and spicule of the Carlyle glass is visible!"

Page 387, note 1. Mr. Charles J. Woodbury, comparing Carlyle and Emerson, says: —

"Neither could tolerate insincerity, which they destroyed, one with lightning, and the other with light."[1]

In his journal of 1863, Mr. Emerson said of Carlyle's style: —

"It is like the new Parrott guns. There were always

[1] *Talks with Emerson.* Baker and Taylor Co., New York, 1890.

guns and powder. But here to-day are latest experiments and a success which exceeds all previous performance in throwing far, and in crushing effect. Much is sacrificed for this, but this is done — so with Carlyle's projectile style."

Page 389, note 1. In his English note-book, Mr. Emerson called Carlyle "a bacchanal in the strong waters of vituperation."

Page 391, note 1. In sending this book to Emerson, Carlyle wrote: "I have finished a book, . . . one solid volume; . . . it is a somewhat fiery and questionable 'Tract for the Times,' *not* by a Puseyite, which the terrible aspect of things here has forced from me." Mr. Emerson in his reply praised "the deep, steady tide taking in, either by hope or by fear, all the great classes of society, — and the philosophic minority also, by the powerful lights which are shed on the phenomenon. It is true contemporary history, which other books are not, and you have fairly set solid London city aloft, afloat, in bright mirage of the air. I quarrel only with the popular assumption, which is perhaps a condition of the Humor itself, that the state of society is a new state, and was not the same thing in the days of Rabelais and Aristophanes as of Carlyle. Orators always allow something to masses, out of love to their own art, whilst austere philosophy will only know the particles. This were of no importance if the historian did not so come to mix himself in some manner with his erring and grieving nations, and so saddens the picture; for health is always private and original, and its essence is in its unmixableness."

Five months later, October 31, 1843, Carlyle wrote: —

"In this last number of the *Dial*, . . . I found one little essay, a criticism on myself, — which, if it should do me mischief, may the Gods forgive you for! It is considerably the most dangerous thing I have read for some years. A decided likeness of myself recognizable in it, as in the celestial mirror of a friend's heart; but so enlarged, exaggerated, all *transfigured*, — the most delicious, the most dangerous thing! Well, I suppose I must try to assimilate it also, to turn it also to good, if I be able. Eulogies, dyslogies, in which one finds no features of one's own natural face, are easily dealt with, . . . but here is another sort of matter! . . . May the gods forgive you! — I have purchased a copy for three shillings and sent it to my Mother, one of the indubitablest benefits I could think of in regard to it."

A LETTER

The position of Editor of the *Dial* must have been trying to one like Mr. Emerson, who joined to sympathy with young idealists and wish to foster "divine discontent," a high standard of thought and expression, a dislike for the negative, and a New England common sense.

So he wrote to disappointed contributors, or those restless seekers who asked for counsel, this wholesome circular letter, which ended by referring each to the oracle within which he or she neglected in seeking help abroad.

The "Letter" was published in the *Dial* for October, 1843.

Page 404, note 1. In the *Dial* the letter ends by referring to a correspondent who had sent in a generous and just tribute to Bettine von Arnim, and giving a translation from the *Deutsche Schellpost* "of a sketch, though plainly from no very friendly hand, of the new work of that eminent lady, who, in the silence of Tieck and Schelling, seems to hold a monopoly of genius in Germany."

THE TRAGIC

This lecture, under the name "Tragedy," was the seventh in a course on Human Life given by Mr. Emerson in Boston in the winter of 1838–39. The eighth lecture was "Comedy," included among the lectures which Mr. Cabot gathered for him into the volume *Letters and Social Aims*, when Mr. Emerson's failing strength required such aid. "The Tragic," for so the name was altered, was printed by Mr. Emerson in the last number of the *Dial*, April, 1844.

It was a subject quite foreign to Mr. Emerson's habit of mind, but one which his serene faith could dispose of and bring, as he would have said, "within the sphere."

Page 408, note 1. The subject of Fate is treated at length in the Essay of that name in *Conduct of Life*. In the poem "Worship," the motto to the Essay on that theme, Fate, miscalled, is represented as beneficent, living Law.

Page 410, note 1. From a song by Donne, beginning: —

"Sweetest love, I doe not goe."

Page 412, note 1. Isaiah, xxx., 7.

Page 413, note 1. The serenity and composure of Mr. Emerson's venerable friend Samuel Hoar were such that Mr. Emerson wrote of him in his journal: —

"I know a man who tries time."

Page 414, note 1. The doctrine of the "Compensation," in the first series of *Essays*.

Page 416, note 1. As modesty is the cardinal virtue of woman, so Mr. Emerson held that

"Composure
Is the pudency of man."
"The Poet," *Poems*, Appendix.

GENERAL INDEX

The following list gives the titles of the volumes to which the Roman numerals in this Index refer: —

GENERAL INDEX

[Titles of Essays and Poems are printed in SMALL CAPITALS.]

The Riverside Press
CAMBRIDGE . MASSACHUSETTS
U · S · A